Communications
in Computer and Information Science

2160

Rationale

The CCIS series is devoted to the publication of proceedings of computer science conferences. Its aim is to efficiently disseminate original research results in informatics in printed and electronic form. While the focus is on publication of peer-reviewed full papers presenting mature work, inclusion of reviewed short papers reporting on work in progress is welcome, too. Besides globally relevant meetings with internationally representative program committees guaranteeing a strict peer-reviewing and paper selection process, conferences run by societies or of high regional or national relevance are also considered for publication.

Topics

The topical scope of CCIS spans the entire spectrum of informatics ranging from foundational topics in the theory of computing to information and communications science and technology and a broad variety of interdisciplinary application fields.

Information for Volume Editors and Authors

Publication in CCIS is free of charge. No royalties are paid, however, we offer registered conference participants temporary free access to the online version of the conference proceedings on SpringerLink (http://link.springer.com) by means of an http referrer from the conference website and/or a number of complimentary printed copies, as specified in the official acceptance email of the event.

CCIS proceedings can be published in time for distribution at conferences or as post-proceedings, and delivered in the form of printed books and/or electronically as USBs and/or e-content licenses for accessing proceedings at SpringerLink. Furthermore, CCIS proceedings are included in the CCIS electronic book series hosted in the SpringerLink digital library at http://link.springer.com/bookseries/7899. Conferences publishing in CCIS are allowed to use Online Conference Service (OCS) for managing the whole proceedings lifecycle (from submission and reviewing to preparing for publication) free of charge.

Publication process

The language of publication is exclusively English. Authors publishing in CCIS have to sign the Springer CCIS copyright transfer form, however, they are free to use their material published in CCIS for substantially changed, more elaborate subsequent publications elsewhere. For the preparation of the camera-ready papers/files, authors have to strictly adhere to the Springer CCIS Authors' Instructions and are strongly encouraged to use the CCIS LaTeX style files or templates.

Abstracting/Indexing

CCIS is abstracted/indexed in DBLP, Google Scholar, EI-Compendex, Mathematical Reviews, SCImago, Scopus. CCIS volumes are also submitted for the inclusion in ISI Proceedings.

How to start

To start the evaluation of your proposal for inclusion in the CCIS series, please send an e-mail to ccis@springer.com.

Jinyang Guo · Yuqing Ma · Yifu Ding ·
Ruihao Gong · Xingyu Zheng · Changyi He ·
Yantao Lu · Xianglong Liu
Editors

Generalizing from Limited Resources in the Open World

Second International Workshop, GLOW 2024
Held in Conjunction with IJCAI 2024
Jeju, South Korea, August 3, 2024
Proceedings

 Springer

Editors
Jinyang Guo
Beihang University
Beijing, China

Yuqing Ma
Beihang University
Beijing, China

Yifu Ding
Beihang University
Beijing, China

Ruihao Gong
SenseTime Research
Beijing, China

Xingyu Zheng
Beihang University
Beijing, China

Changyi He
Beihang University
Beijing, China

Yantao Lu
Northwestern Polytechnical University
Xi'an, China

Xianglong Liu
Beihang University
Beijing, China

ISSN 1865-0929   ISSN 1865-0937 (electronic)
Communications in Computer and Information Science
ISBN 978-981-97-6124-1   ISBN 978-981-97-6125-8 (eBook)
https://doi.org/10.1007/978-981-97-6125-8

Preface

This book collected the accepted articles in the 2nd International Workshop on Generalizing from Limited Resources in the Open World, dubbed GLOW. This workshop was held at the International Joint Conference on Artificial Intelligence (IJCAI) 2024 at Jeju Island, which is South Korea's largest island.

After months of soliciting, we received twenty-two papers in total encompassing a variety of topics around the theme of our workshop. We invited expert scholars from various institutions in this field to serve as reviewers. They carefully appraised these manuscripts based on their novelty, preciseness, objectivity and reproducibility, and graded them on OpenReview with the "double-blind" review policy. On average, each manuscript was reviewed by three reviewers, with each reviewer handling 2.4 manuscripts. We thank all the reviewers for their selfless support.

Considering the quality and the relevance to the theme of GLOW, we ultimately accepted fifteen papers, including eleven full papers and four short papers. These papers focus on the academic exploration of efficient methodologies within the realm of artificial intelligence (AI) models. We concentrated on both data-efficient strategies, such as zero/few-shot learning and domain adaptation, as well as model-efficient approaches like model sparsification and compact model design. Considering the recent significant success of the large model, this year, we included more generalization approaches in the open world for generative AI models.

We categorized all articles into four chapters. The first two chapters revolve around efficient methodologies. The first chapter includes four studies conducted under the resource constraint of edge devices, such as the compression of point cloud data, spiking neural networks, circuit fault detectors and autonomous tracking on unmanned aerial vehicles. These tasks operate on edge hardware with low computational resources and energy, necessitating efficient inference for low latency and energy consumption. The studies in the second chapter focus on efficient data utilization, specifically parameter fine-tuning with limited samples. Since training a large model from scratch requires substantial time and electric power, model fine-tuning with a small calibration dataset is an efficient approach to mitigate resource demands. It effectively generalizes large models to new fields and facilitates applications in various real-world scenarios.

The third and fourth chapters focus on AI in new scenarios and complex tasks in the real world. The third chapter showcases multi-modal systems in diverse scenarios, including medical applications like Alzheimer's disease prediction, language gaps in medical terminologies, as well as spatiotemporal forecasting and navigation systems. These applications present a significant challenge in aligning semantic features across different modalities. The research in the fourth chapter illustrates a more realistic view of the world. Human beings can comprehend new things by relating unknowns to knowns. However, one of the major challenges for AI trained within known classes is handling the uncertainty of real-world unknowns. Therefore, enabling AI to recognize and interpret the unknowns in the open world can enhance the robustness of AI in real applications.

We would like to extend our deepest gratitude to all the friends who dedicated their valuable time and effort to drive the forum forward and afterward compiled this book. We also express our admiration for all contributing authors. Their brilliant inspiration and ideas fuel the vibrant development of new AI technologies. Without them, the world would be far less exciting.

Holding this forum and compiling the book has been a deeply rewarding experience. By convening researchers specializing in these areas, we collected excellent research findings and creative ideas spanning a range of topics. We published this book to facilitate the sharing of recent technology advancements and engage in discussions about the future trajectories of AI model generalization. Efficient methodologies and open-world challenges have garnered substantial attention from the research community due to their direct implications for practical applications. Through this book, we aimed to facilitate intellectual exchange, providing an avenue for novel insights in addressing the challenges of AI generalization, thereby contributing to the practical applications of real-world AI.

June 2024

Jinyang Guo
Ruihao Gong
Ning Liu
Yuqing Ma

Organization

General Chair

Jinyang Guo   Beihang University, China

Program Committee Chairs

Ruihao Gong   SenseTime Research, China
Ning Liu   Midea Group, China
Yuqing Ma   Beihang University, China

Steering Committee

Rogerio Schmidt Feris   MIT-IBM Watson AI Lab, USA
Xianglong Liu   Beihang University, China

Program Committee

Yifu Ding   Beihang University, China
Changyi He   Beihang University, China
Olivera Kotevska   Oak Ridge National Laboratory, USA
Pengfei Liu   Shanghai Jiao Tong University, China
Ge Yang   Beihang University, China
Shanghang Zhang   Peking University, China
Xingyu Zheng   Beihang University, China

Additional Reviewers

Mao Anyu   Peiyao Li
Han Chen   Tengfei Liang
Yutong Gao   Yu Liang
Erjian Guo   Jiangfan Liu
Yue He   Kai Lv
Shenghao Jin   Xudong Ma

Jiankun Shi
Shiqi Sun
Lu Wang
Zicheng Wang
Zining Wang
Hui Xie

Xu Yang
Huizi Yu
Yue Zhang
Ruowen Zhao
Xiaotong Zhu

Contents

Recognition and Reasoning in the Open World

Efficient Methods for Low-resource Hardware

Towards Point Cloud Compression for Machine Perception: A Simple and Strong Baseline by Learning the Octree Depth Level Predictor

Lei Liu[1(✉)], Zhihao Hu[1], and Zhenghao Chen[2]

[1] School of Computer Science and Engineering, Beihang University, Beijing, China
liulei95@buaa.edu.cn
[2] School of Electrical and Information Engineering, The University of Sydney, Sydney, Australia

Abstract. Point cloud compression has garnered significant interest in computer vision. However, existing algorithms primarily cater to human vision, while most point cloud data is utilized for machine vision tasks. To address this, we propose a point cloud compression framework that simultaneously handles both human and machine vision tasks. Our framework learns a scalable bit-stream, using only subsets for different machine vision tasks to save bit-rate, while employing the entire bit-stream for human vision tasks. Building on mainstream octree-based frameworks like VoxelContext-Net, OctAttention, and G-PCC, we introduce a new octree depth-level predictor. This predictor adaptively determines the optimal depth level for each octree constructed from a point cloud, controlling the bit-rate for machine vision tasks. For simpler tasks (*e.g.*, classification) or objects/scenarios, we use fewer depth levels with fewer bits, saving bit-rate. Conversely, for more complex tasks (*e.g.*, segmentation) or objects/scenarios, we use deeper depth levels with more bits to enhance performance. Experimental results on various datasets (*e.g.*, ModelNet10, ModelNet40, ShapeNet, ScanNet, and KITTI) show that our point cloud compression approach improves performance for machine vision tasks without compromising human vision quality.

Keywords: Point Cloud Compression · Scalable Coding for Machine

1 Introduction

With the advancement of 3D data-capturing devices such as RGB-D cameras and LiDAR sensors, there is growing research interest in developing new approaches for point cloud-related machine vision tasks, including classification, segmentation, and detection. However, most of these tasks require raw point cloud data as input, leading to high bandwidth requirements for transmitting large volumes of point cloud data.

Recently, many neural compression frameworks [1–13] were proposed to meet the bandwidth/storage requirement for better point cloud data transmission/

J. Guo et al. (Eds.): IJCAI 2024, CCIS 2160, pp. 3–17, 2024.
https://doi.org/10.1007/978-981-97-6125-8_1

storage. However, those point cloud compression frameworks are only designed for the human vision task without considering the performance for the machine vision tasks. While some recent image coding for machines works [14–21] have tried to optimize the network by introducing additional loss functions for the machine vision tasks, we cannot simply adopt the similar strategy (*i.e.*, through adding similar loss functions) to improve the point cloud compression performance for the machine vision tasks. A possible explanation is that the mainstream point cloud compression algorithms like VoxelContext-Net [1], OctAttention [5], Geometry Point Cloud Compression (G-PCC) [22], and others [2,11,23] need to compress the pre-constructed octrees from different point clouds and the octree construction procedure is indifferentiable. In addition, while most coding for machines methods [14–18,24,25] improve the effectiveness of various machine vision tasks, the human vision performance is still degraded. Therefore, it is desirable to design a new point cloud compression framework for machine perception, which can improve the performance for the machine vision tasks without degrading the human vision performance.

In this work, we propose a point cloud compression method that simultaneously addresses human vision and multiple machine vision tasks. Our method adheres to the scalable coding paradigm [19–21], where the entire bit-stream is used for human vision tasks, and only subsets are used for various machine vision tasks. We demonstrate the generalizability of our approach using three mainstream point cloud compression methods: VoxelContext-Net [1], OctAttention [5], and G-PCC [22]. In our method, octrees pre-constructed from different point clouds are compressed into bit-streams, effectively balancing the needs of both human and machine vision tasks.

For machine vision tasks, we introduce a bit-stream partition method that transmits only part of the bit-stream to reconstruct the initial octree depth levels, thereby saving bit-rate. Additionally, we propose an octree depth level predictor to adaptively determine the optimal octree depth level for different machine vision tasks. Consequently, for simpler tasks (*e.g.*, classification) and straightforward objects/scenarios, fewer octree depth levels are used to save bit-rate. In contrast, for more complex tasks (*e.g.*, segmentation) and intricate objects/scenarios, deeper octree depth levels are utilized to enhance visual recognition performance. Experimental results show that our method delivers promising outcomes across various machine vision tasks. The main contributions of this work are summarized as follows: 1). We propose combining an octree depth level predictor with a bit-stream partition method to adaptively select the optimal octree depth level and split the bit-stream for various machine vision tasks. Our method serves as a simple yet strong baseline, facilitating further research in point cloud compression for both machine and human vision. 2). Our newly proposed compression methods can be seamlessly integrated into mainstream octree-based point cloud compression frameworks, including both deep learning methods (*e.g.*, VoxelContext-Net and OctAttention) and handcraft methods (*e.g.*, G-PCC), extending these methods for machine perception. 3). Comprehensive experiments show that our new baseline method, PCCMP-Net, delivers promising classification, detection, and segmentation results without compromising human vision performance.

2   Related Work

2.1   Point Cloud Compression

In the past few years, many hand-crafted and learning-based point cloud compression methods [1,2,5,11,22,23,26–28] have been proposed by transforming the point cloud data into octree representations for better compression, in which G-PCC (geometry based point cloud compression) [22] proposed by the MPEG is the most popular one.

In recent years, some learning-based point cloud compression methods [1–5,11,23,26,28–32] have achieved the state-of-the-art performance. Huang *et al.* [11] and Wang *et al.* [26] followed the learned image compression framework [33] to compress the voxelized point clouds. To reduce the bit-rate, Biswas *et al.* [23] exploited the spatio-temporal relationships across multiple LiDAR sweeps by developing a new conditional entropy model. Based on [26], Wang *et al.* [30] used the lossless compressed octree and the lossy compressed point feature to further improve the coding performance. To further improve point cloud compression performance, Que *et al.* [1] extended this framework by exploiting the context information among neighboring nodes and refining the 3D coordinate at the decoder side. Fu *et al.* [5] used masked context attention, while Chen *et al.* [2] used sibling context and surface priors to improve the compression performance.

While the above-mentioned works can be readily used for downstream visual recognition tasks, these existing methods aim to compress the point cloud data only for human perception without considering the machine vision tasks. To the best of our knowledge, there is no existing point cloud compression method for both machine vision and human vision.

2.2   Coding for Machines

Choi *et al.* [19] and Wang *et al.* [20] performed scalable image compression by dividing the bit-streams into different parts and transmitting parts of the bit-streams for both machine or human vision tasks, while Liu *et al.* [21] proposed a scalable image compression method for classification. Meanwhile, Bai *et al.* [18] redesigned the Vision Transformer model to improve the performance for both the image coding and the classification tasks. Yang *et al.* [14] designed the image encoder by using the edge extraction algorithm, and the reconstructed images from the decoder can achieve promising image coding for machine performance. Le *et al.* [15] directly added the additional machine vision task related losses to the compression loss functions to improve the reconstructed image quality for the machine vision tasks. Song *et al.* [16] compressed the source image through a corresponding quality map produced from different machine vision tasks. Torfason *et al.* [17] combined the image compression network with the detection network, and directly extracted the detection related information from bit-streams without using an image decoder. Liu *et al.* [24] designed a two branches compression method namely PCHM-Net, which is the first point cloud compression method

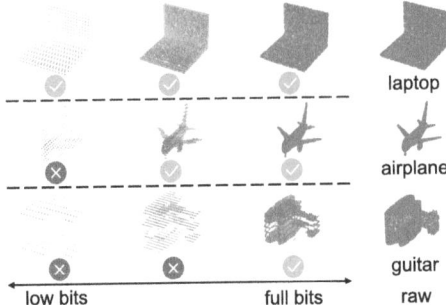

Fig. 1. The classification results of a pre-trained PointNet++ [34] model for recognizing the point clouds reconstructed from different octree depth levels. "raw" means the raw/original point cloud. The truly or falsely predicted results from the classification task are shown under the point clouds.

for both machine vision and human vision. However, PCHM-Net improved the machine vision performance while drop the human vision.

In contrast to those coding for machine approachs, we propose a simple and strong baseline method to improve point cloud coding for machine perception performance. Our new method PCCMP-Net achieves promising results for machine vision tasks without sacrificing human vision performance, which cannot be achieved by the above-mentioned methods.

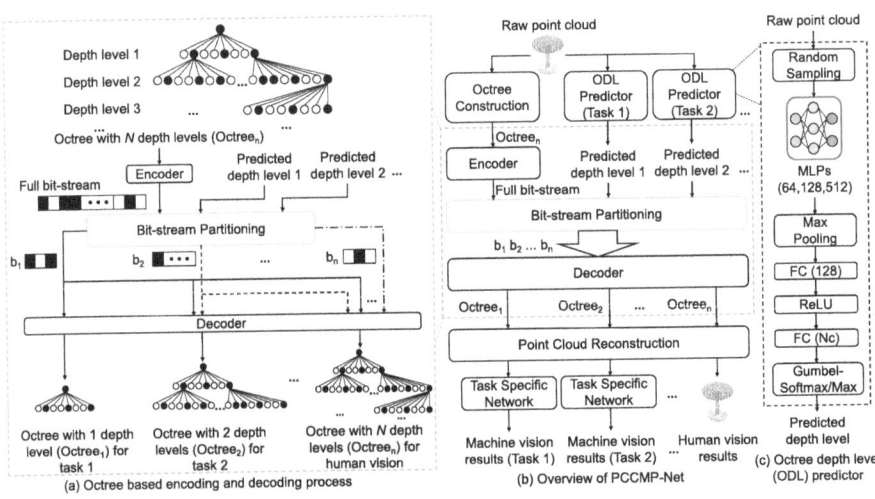

Fig. 2. (a) The octree-based encoding and decoding process. The bit-stream b_1 is used for the first machine vision task, while the bit-stream $b_1 \cup b_2$ will be used for the second machine vision task. And the bit-stream $b_1 \cup b_2 \cup ... \cup b_n$ denotes the full bit-stream for human vision. (b) The overall network architecture of our PCCMP-Net. (c) Details of our proposed octree depth level (ODL) predictor.

3   Methodology

3.1   Motivation

The mainstream octree-based point cloud compression methods [1,2,5,11] only use the entire bit-stream encoding information from all octree levels for the human vision task. These approaches are not optimal for machine perception. As shown in Fig. 1, it is unnecessary to use the entire bit-stream to recognize some objects (like laptop and airplane). Therefore, transferring the entire bit-stream for machine perception would waste the bandwidth. In order to save the bit-rate cost, it is desirable to propose a point cloud compression method for both human vision and machine vision.

3.2   Our New Framework

The overall network structure of our point cloud compression method is shown in Fig. 2(b). In this section, we will first introduce the overall pipeline of our baseline method, which can well handle the human vision task and multiple machine vision tasks as shown in our experiments. And then, each module in our baseline method will be introduced.

Overall Pipeline. Considering that the point cloud data is commonly used for various machine vision tasks, our approach is primarily used for the machine vision tasks (*e.g.,* detection of abnormal events like collision between pedestrians and vehicles) by only using subsets of bit-stream. If the human vision task must also be involved (*e.g.,* when our baseline method detects abnormal events), our baseline method can additionally reconstruct a high quality point cloud with the entire bit-stream to human for further analysis. Like the scalable coding methods, when reconstructing the point clouds for the human vision task, our method will reuse the subsets of the generated bit-stream for different machine vision tasks. In this way, our point cloud compression method can improve the performance for multiple machine vision tasks without degrading the human vision performance.

Octree Construction, Encoder, Decoder, and Point Cloud Reconstruction. The octree construction module constructs the octree for each input point cloud. Octree is a tree-like data structure used to describe three-dimensional space. An octree can be constructed from any 3D point cloud by first partitioning the 3D space into 8 cubes with the same size, and then recursively partitioning each non-empty cube in the same way until the maximum depth level is reached. Each node is represented by the 3D coordinate of the cube center. Each octree is encoded as the corresponding bit-stream by using the encoder. The decoder reconstructs the octree-based on the received bit-stream. The point cloud reconstruction module then restores the point cloud from the octree. In this work, we take VoxelContext-Net [1], OctAttention [5] and G-PCC [22] as the examples to introduce our method.

Bit-Stream Partitioning. Our bit-stream partitioning module can split the full bit-stream to multi-parts bit-stream for multiple machine vision tasks and human vision task. The details are shown in Sect. 3.3.

Octree Depth Level Predictor. Each of our octree depth level predictor is used to choose the optimal octree depth levels for one machine vision task, which can also guide how to split the entire bit-steam. The details of this module will be described in Sect. 3.4.

Task Specific Network. To handle different point cloud based machine vision tasks, this module will use different networks. For the classification task and the segmentation task, PointNet++ [34] will be used in this module. For the detection task, VoteNet [35] and PointRCNN [36] is adopted in this work.

3.3 Bit-Stream Partitioning

Although we can often achieve promising performance for the human vision task by using the full bit-stream to reconstruct point clouds, it has plenty of redundant information for the machine vision tasks and thus it is less effective in terms of the bit-rate cost. Therefore, we propose a simple bit-stream partitioning method to split the bit-stream for both human and machine vision tasks.

Before introducing how to divide the bit-stream, we first introduce how to generate the point cloud bit-stream. Figure 2(a) shows the encoding and decoding process of the octree. During the encoding process, the octree is encoded from the lower depth level to the higher depth level. Therefore, the final full bit-stream can be expressed as $\mathbf{B} = (b_1, b_2, ..., b_n)$, where n is the maximum octree depth level and b_i represents the bit-stream from the ith depth level. At the decoder side, each octree will be reconstructed from the lower depth level to the higher depth level. Particularly, the $(i + 1)$th depth level of the octree can be reconstructed with the previously reconstructed octree at the i depth level and the extra bits b_{i+1}. For example, with $b_1 \cup b_2$, we can reconstruct the octree with the first two depth levels, and we can readily reconstruct the octree with the first three depth levels with $b_1 \cup b_2 \cup b_3$.

As the example shown in Fig. 2, based on the above octree encoding and decoding process, we can split the full bit-stream $\mathbf{B}$ into multiple subsets of bit-streams $b_1, b_2, ..., b_n$ according to the predicted octree depth levels. Particularly, the first subset of bit-stream b_1 can be used to reconstruct the octree with the first depth level, which can be used for the machine vision task 1. By additionally using bit-stream b_2, $b_1 \cup b_2$ can be used to reconstruct the octree with the first two depth levels for the machine vision task 2. We can reconstruct the N depth levels of the octree by using the entire bit-stream $b_1 \cup b_2 \cup ... \cup b_n$, which will be used for the human vision task. And the optimal splitting depth levels are determined by the octree depth level predictors which will be discussed below.

3.4 Octree Depth Level Predictor

Our approach learns the octree depth level predictor to decide the optimal depth level of the octree for different machine vision tasks, which cannot only achieve the reasonable performance for various machine vision tasks but also reduce the bit-rate cost. It is worth mentioning that the encoder side (*e.g.*, the LiDAR sensors) always do not have enough computing power and cannot support the complex networks. Therefore, the networks (*e.g.*, PointNet++ [34], VoteNet [35] and PointRCNN [36]) for handling the complex machine vision tasks are placed behind the decoder instead of the encoder side. As shown in Fig. 2(c), our octree depth level predictor is designed by using the simple three layers MLP together with two fully connected layers.

Our octree depth level predictor can determine the optimal octree depth level for the machine vision tasks from the global feature extracted from the raw point cloud. According to different difficulty levels of the machine vision tasks, our octree depth predictor can generate n probabilities $\mathbf{p} = \{p_1, p_2, ..., p_n\}$ for n octree depth levels, and then choose the optimal octree depth level with the highest probability.

However, the process of choosing the octree depth level with the highest probability is non-differentiable, which makes it infeasible to train the octree depth level predictor. Therefore, we adopt the Gumbel-Softmax strategy [37] to address this issue. First, we generate the confidence score set $\hat{\mathbf{p}}$ from the probability set $\mathbf{p}$ with Gumbel noise as follows:

$$\hat{p}_i = p_i + G_i, i \in \{0, 1, ..., n\} \tag{1}$$

where $G_i = -\log(-\log \epsilon)$ is the standard Gumbel noise, and ϵ is randomly sampled from a uniform distribution between 0 and 1. Therefore, we can generate the one-hot vector $\hat{\mathbf{h}} = [\hat{h}_0, \hat{h}_1, ..., \hat{h}_n]$, where $\hat{h}_i = 1$ if $i = \arg\max_j \hat{p}_j, j \in \{0, 1, ..., n\}$. Otherwise $\hat{h}_i = 0$. $\hat{\mathbf{h}}$ is the one-hot vector from the depth level selection process. However, the argmax operation when generating the one-hot vector makes the whole network non-differentiable. Therefore, during the backward propagation process, we apply the Gumbel-Softmax strategy and relax the one-hot vector $\hat{\mathbf{h}}$ to $\tilde{\mathbf{h}} = [\tilde{h}_0, \tilde{h}_1, ..., \tilde{h}_n]$ as follows:

$$\tilde{h}_i = \frac{\exp(\hat{p}_i/\tau))}{\sum_{j=0}^{n} \exp(\hat{p}_j/\tau)}, i \in \{0, 1, ..., n\} \tag{2}$$

where τ is the temperature parameter and is set from 3 to 0.001 during the whole training process. Using the Gumbel-softmax strategy [37], we can select the optimal depth-level of each octree for the machine vision tasks based on the argmax function during forward propagation process and approximate the gradient of the argmax function by using Eq. (2) in the back propagation process. During the inference stage, we directly select the optimal octree depth level with the maximum probability in $\mathbf{p}$.

Our approach uses multiple octree depth level predictors to simultaneously handle multiple machine vision tasks. In fact, the amount of bit-stream requested for different machine vision tasks varies. And the human vision task often requires the entire bit-stream. So we can readily use multiple octree depth level predictors for multiple machine vision tasks by splitting the entire bit-stream as multiple subsets of bit-streams, which is shown in Fig. 2. In addition, only one decoder is requested for all subsets of bit-streams instead of one specific decoder for each subset of bit-stream, which is the strategy commonly used in image coding for machines works [19–21].

3.5 Training Strategy

For the encoder and decoder, we directly use the pre-trained compression codecs from VoxelContext-Net [1] and OctAttention [5]) or hand-crafted codecs from G-PCC. For the task specific network, we directly use the pre-trained network from PointNet++ [34], VoteNet [35], and PointRCNN [36]. When training the octree depth level predictor, we fix the parameters in the compression module and the task specific network module. The octree depth level predictors for different tasks are trained separately. To better compare the losses from the octrees with different depth levels from the machine vision tasks, we calculate the bits per point (bpp) and the task specific loss for each octree during the training process. But in the inference process, only the octree with the selected depth level will be transmitted and used for the machine vision tasks. And the loss function used for training our octree depth level predictor is shown below,

$$loss = \sum((\lambda \times \mathbf{bpp} + \mathbf{L}) \times \tilde{\mathbf{h}}) \tag{3}$$

Our method selects the optimal depth level from n candidate depth levels. $\mathbf{bpp} = (\text{bpp}_1, \text{bpp}_2, ..., \text{bpp}_n)$, and bpp means bits per point. $\text{bpp}_i (i \in \{0, 1, ..., n\})$ represents the bpp for constructing the octree at the ith depth levels, which can be calculated from the encoder. $\mathbf{L} = (L_1, L_2, ..., L_n)$, and L_i are defined as follows,

$$L_i = D(f(\hat{x}_i), y_{gt}), i \in \{0, 1, ..., n\} \tag{4}$$

where f is the machine vision task specific network (*i.e.*, PointNet++ for the classification and segmentation tasks or VoteNet and PointRCNN for the detection task). $\hat{x}_i$ is the reconstructed point cloud from the octree with i depth levels. y_{gt} is the ground-truth for the machine vision task. And the function D can calculate the loss between $f(\hat{x}_i)$ and y_{gt}. $\tilde{\mathbf{h}} = [\tilde{h}_0, \tilde{h}_1, ..., \tilde{h}_n]$, and $\tilde{h}_i$ is defined in Eq.(2). λ in Eq.(3) is a hyper-parameter, which is used to balance the trade off between $\mathbf{bpp}$ and $\mathbf{L}$.

4 Experiments

4.1 Experimental Details

Baseline Methods. Follow the [24], we directly use the encoder and the decoder from VoxelContext-Net [1], OctAttention [5] or G-PCC [22] as our baseline methods. We also use the same encoder and decoder for point cloud compression in our proposed framework for a fair comparison with the baseline methods.

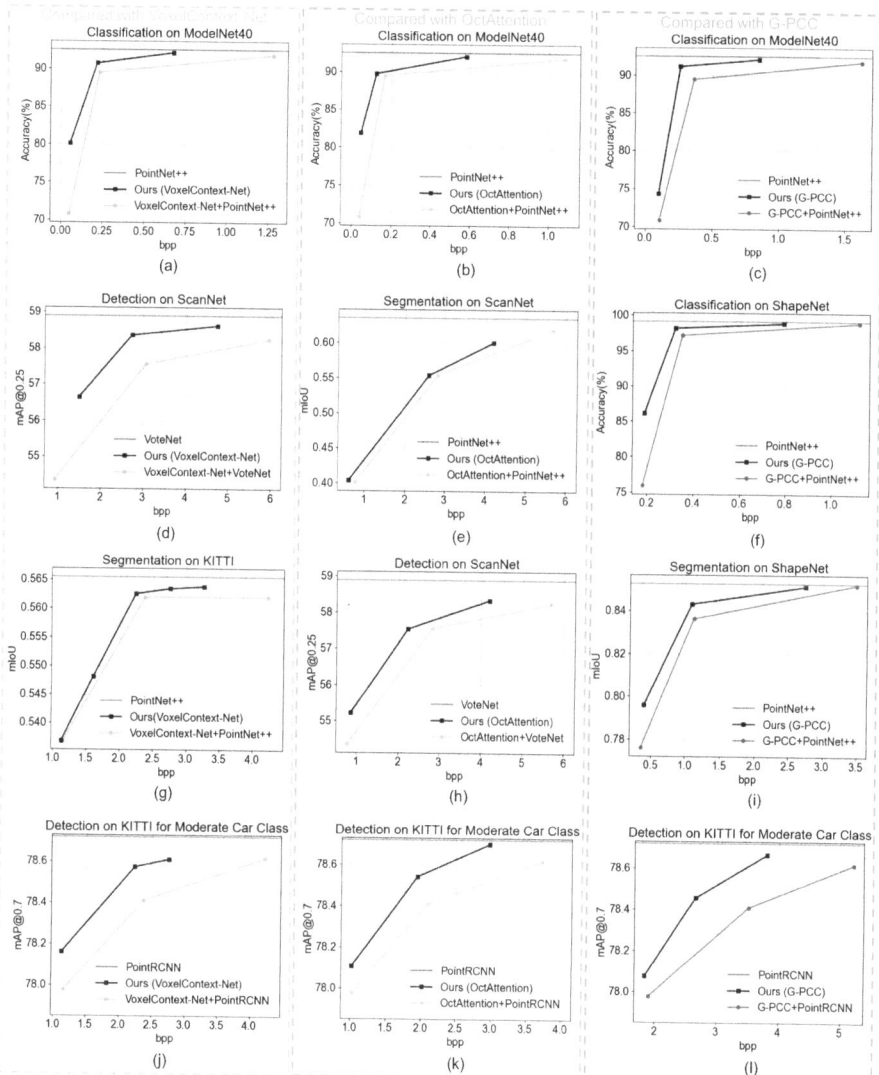

Fig. 3. Results in (a–c) are only for one single machine vision task (*i.e.*, the classification task) on the ModelNet10 and ModelNet40 datasets. The multi-task results in (f), (i) are for both classification and segmentation tasks on the ShapeNet dataset. The multi-task results in (d), (e), (g), (h), (j–l) are for both segmentation and detection tasks on the ScanNet and KITTI datasets. "Ours (VoxelContext-Net)"/"Ours (OctAttention)"/"Ours (G-PCC)" means VoxelContext-Net, OctAttention and G-PCC are used as the encoder and the decoder in our PCCMP-Net, respectively. The results of PointNet++, VoteNet, and PointRCNN are obtained by using the raw/uncompressed point cloud as the input.

For the baseline methods for the machine vision tasks, we directly use the reconstructed point clouds from VoxelContext-Net [1], OctAttention [5] or G-PCC [22] as the input of the networks for the machine vision tasks. Point-Net++ [34] is used for the classification task and the segmentation task. VoteNet [35] and PointRCNN [36] is adopted for the detection task. Note the baseline methods are referred to as the format "compression method + task specific network" (e.g., "VoxelContext-Net+PointNet++" means using the reconstructed point clouds from VoxelContext-Net as the input to PointNet++). As suggested in VoxelContext-Net [1], we train the machine vision task networks with the raw point clouds and evaluate the classification/segmentation/detection results based on the reconstructed point clouds.

Evaluation Metric. We use bits per point (bpp) to denote the bit cost in the compression procedure. For the machine vision tasks, accuracy, mean intersection-over-union (mIoU) and mean average precision (mAP) are used to measure the performance for the classification, segmentation and detection tasks, respectively. For the human vision, we use the standard metric D1 PSNR (Point-to-Point PSNR) to measure the reconstructed point cloud quality.

Implementation Details. The whole network is implemented in Pytorch with CUDA support. At the second training stage, we set the batch size as 48. We use the Adam optimizer [38] with the learning rates of 1e$-$3 for the first 40 epochs and 1e-4 for the next 10 epochs.

4.2   Experiment All Results

Results on ModelNet for Single Machine Vision Task. As the ModelNet dataset is only designed for the classification task, our PCCMP-Net can only be used for single machine vision task on this dataset. The classification results on the ModelNet10 and ModelNet40 datasets are shown in Fig. 3(a–c). When compared with the baseline method VoxelContext-Net+PointNet++, our method achieves about 10% accuracy improvement at 0.056 bpp and saves about 45% bpp at 91.8% accuracy on the ModelNet40 dataset shown in Fig. 3(a). In Fig. 3(b) and (c), our PCCMP-Net can also achieve better performance when compared with OctAttention+PointNet++ and G-PCC+PointNet++. The experimental results demonstrate that our PCCMP-Net can improve the performance when the input point cloud is compressed for the single classification task.

Results on ShapeNet for Multiple Machine Vision Tasks. The experiments for multiple machine vision tasks on the ShapeNet dataset are shown in Fig. 3(f) and (i), in which we use the ShapeNet dataset for both the classification task and the segmentation task. When compared with G-PCC+PointNet++ for the classification task, our PCCMP-Net achieves about 9% accuracy improvement at the 0.2 bpp and saves about 25% bpp at 98.9% accuracy, as shown in Fig. 3(f). For the segmentation task, our PCCMP-Net achieves 2% mIoU improvement at lowest bpp and saves more than 20% bpp at 0.85 mIoU, as shown in Fig. 3(i). Therefore, our PCCMP-Net achieves better performance than the baseline method when simultaneously handling multiple machine vision tasks (*i.e.*,the classification task and the segmentation task).

Results on ScanNet and KITTI for Multiple Machine Vision Tasks. The multi-tasks experiments on the ScanNet and KITTI dataset are shown in Fig. 3(d, e, g, h, j, k), in which we use the ScanNet and KITTI datasets for both segmentation task and the detection task. For the segmentation task, when compared with OctAttention+PointNet++, our PCCMP-Net saves about 10% bpp at the 0.40 mIoU, as shown in Fig. 3(e). For the detection task shown in Fig. 3(h), our PCCMP-Net saves above 25% bpp at the 0.583 mAP@0.25 when compared with OctAttention+VoteNet. In Fig. 3(j), our PCCMP-Net can also achieve better performance when compared with VoxelContext-Net+PointRCNN for the KITTI dataset. These experimental results demonstrate that our PCCMP-Net can simultaneously improve the performance for multiple machine vision tasks (*i.e.*,the segmentation task and the detection task).

Human Vision Results. Note that the encoder, the decoder, and the full bit-stream in our method are the same as our baseline methods VoxelContext-Net [1], OctAttention [5] and G-PCC [22] in human vision. So our PCCMP-Net achieves the same human vision performance when compared with the baseline methods. It is worth mentioning that in most coding for machines methods [14, 17–19,21,24], compression performance for human vision always drops in order to achieve better performance for the machine vision tasks. Therefore, the results indicate the advantage of our PCCMP-Net can improve the performance for the machine vision tasks without sacrificing the compression results for human vision.

4.3   Model Analysis

In order to balance the bit-rate cost and the performance of the machine vision tasks in different scenarios, our proposed octree depth level predictor can adaptively select the optimal depth levels for each point cloud. For different tasks at different bpp values, the selection percentages at different octree depth levels are shown in Fig. 5. We observe that when bpp value is smaller our method tends to select lower octree depth levels for more percentage of point clouds. With the increasing of the bpp values, our octree depth level predictor will select higher octree depth levels for more percentage of point clouds. The selection percentage in Fig. 5 demonstrates that our PCCMP-Net can adaptively select the optimal octree depth level for each point cloud at different bpp values for different machine vision tasks.

The visualization results of the segmentation task and the detection task are shown in Fig. 4. Figure 4(a) shows that it is easy to segment the table with only 2 regular parts, so our octree depth level predictor tends to select the lower depth level to save bits. It is harder to segment the airplane shown in Fig. 4(b) with 4 grotesque parts, therefore our octree depth level predictor prefers the higher depth level to achieve better segmentation performance (*e.g.*,mIoU). Figure 4(c) shows that the scene with sparse and regularly placed objects is relatively easier

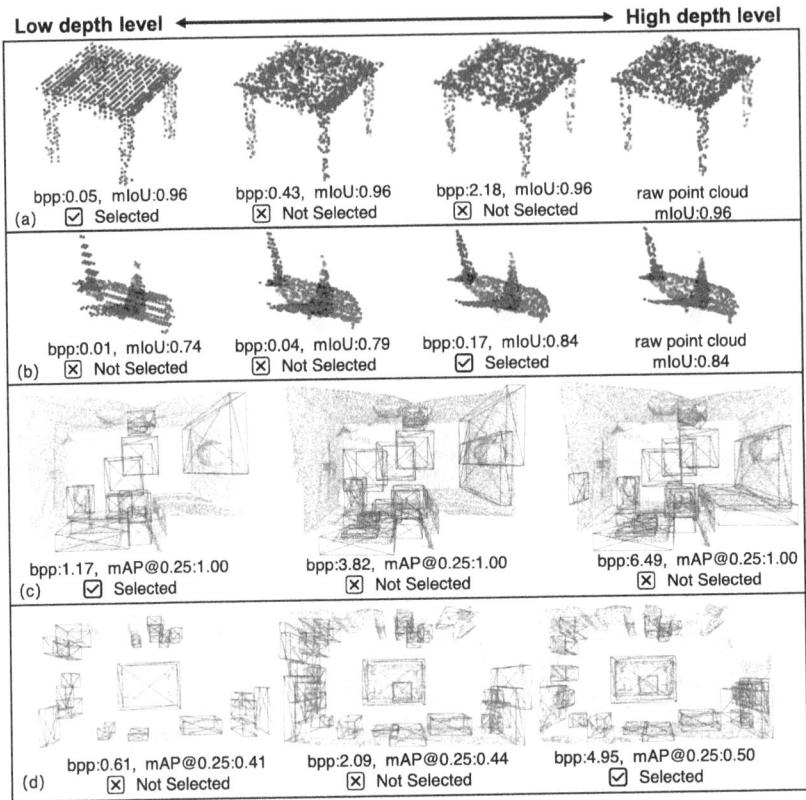

Fig. 4. Different qualitative results for the segmentation task on the ShapeNet dataset (a) and (b). Different qualitative results for the detection task on the ScanNet dataset (c) and (d).

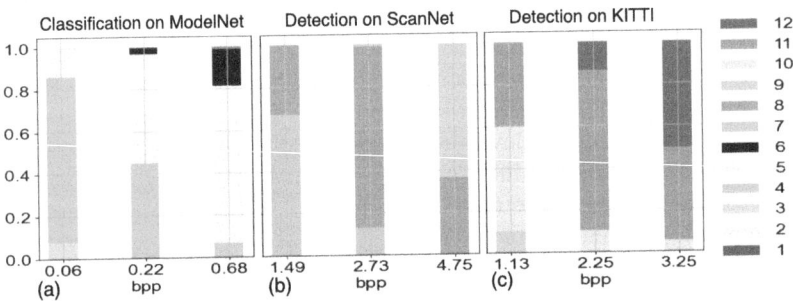

Fig. 5. The selection percentage of different octree depth levels at different bpp values for the classification task on the ModelNet40 dataset (a), and the detection task on the ScanNet dataset (b) and the KITTI dataset (c). Different colors represent different depth levels.

for the object detector, so our octree depth predictor selects the lower depth level for saving bits. On the other hand, the scene in Fig. 4(d) with crowded and stacked objects may be challenging for the object detector, hence our octree depth level predictor tends to choose the higher depth level for better detection performance (*e.g.*, mAP@0.25). It is observed that our proposed octree depth level predictor can select the optimal octree depth levels for different cases, which demonstrate the effectiveness of our proposed approach for different machine vision tasks.

5   Conclusion

In this work, we have proposed a new point cloud compression method for machine perception, which is referred to as PCCMP-Net. Particularly, observing that the octree-based approaches have become the main-stream point cloud compression methods, we propose to learn a set of octree depth level predictors for multiple machine vision tasks, which can be readily incorporated into both hand-crafted methods (*e.g.*, G-PCC [22]) and the recent learning-based methods (*e.g.*, VoxelContext-Net [1] and OctAttention [5]) and extend these methods towards point cloud compression for both human vision and machine vision. Comprehensive experiments on five benchmark datasets demonstrate that our newly proposed approach PCCMP-Net achieves promising results for multiple machine vision tasks (*i.e.*, classification, segmentation, detection) without sacrificing the performance of the human vision task. We believe our newly proposed approach PCCMP-Net can be used as a simple and strong baseline method to facilitate the subsequent works along the emerging research area of point cloud compression for machine perception.

References

1. Que, Z., Lu, G., Xu, D.: Voxelcontext-net: an octree based framework for point cloud compression. In: Proceedings of the IEEE/CVF Conference on Computer Vision and Pattern Recognition, pp. 6042–6051 (2021)
2. Chen, Z., Qian, Z., Wang, S., Chen, Q.: Point cloud compression with sibling context and surface priors. In: Avidan, S., Brostow, G., Cissé, M., Farinella, G.M., Hassner, T. (eds.) ECCV 2022, Part XXXVIII. LNCS, vol. 13698, pp. 744–759. Springer, Cham (2022). https://doi.org/10.1007/978-3-031-19839-7_43
3. Zhou, X., Qi, C.R., Zhou, Y., Anguelov, D.: RIDDLE: Lidar data compression with range image deep delta encoding. In: Proceedings of the IEEE/CVF Conference on Computer Vision and Pattern Recognition, pp. 17212–17221 (2022)
4. He, Y., Ren, X., Tang, D., Zhang, Y., Xue, X., Fu, Y.: Density-preserving deep point cloud compression. In: Proceedings of the IEEE/CVF Conference on Computer Vision and Pattern Recognition, pp. 2333–2342 (2022)
5. Chunyang, F., Li, G., Song, R., Gao, W., Liu, S.: OctAttention: octree-based large-scale contexts model for point cloud compression. In: Proceedings of the AAAI Conference on Artificial Intelligence, vol. 36, no. 1, pp. 625–633 (2022)

6. Hu, Z., Chen, Z., Xu, D., Lu, G., Ouyang, W., Gu, S.: Improving deep video compression by resolution-adaptive flow coding. In: Vedaldi, A., Bischof, H., Brox, T., Frahm, J.-M. (eds.) ECCV 2020, Part II. LNCS, vol. 12347, pp. 193–209. Springer, Cham (2020). https://doi.org/10.1007/978-3-030-58536-5_12

7. Chen, Z., Shuhang, G., Guo, L., Dong, X.: Exploiting intra-slice and inter-slice redundancy for learning-based lossless volumetric image compression. IEEE Trans. Image Process. **31**, 1697–1707 (2022)

8. Chen, Z., Lu, G., Hu, Z., Liu, S., Jiang, W., Xu, D.: LSVC: a learning-based stereo video compression framework. In: Proceedings of the IEEE/CVF Conference on Computer Vision and Pattern Recognition, pp. 6073–6082 (2022)

9. Chen, Z., Gu, S., Zhu, F., Xu, J., Zhao, R.: Improving facial attribute recognition by group and graph learning. In: 2021 IEEE International Conference on Multimedia and Expo (ICME), pp. 1–6. IEEE (2021)

10. Chen, Z., et al.: Neural video compression with spatio-temporal cross-covariance transformers. In: Proceedings of the 31st ACM International Conference on Multimedia, pp. 8543–8551 (2023)

11. Huang, L., Wang, S., Wong, K., Liu, J., Urtasun, R.: OctSqueeze: octree-structured entropy model for lidar compression. In: Proceedings of the IEEE/CVF Conference on Computer Vision and Pattern Recognition, pp. 1313–1323 (2020)

12. Chen, Z., Zhou, L., Hu, Z., Xu, D.: Group-aware parameter-efficient updating for content-adaptive neural video compression. arXiv preprint arXiv:2405.04274 (2024)

13. Han, T., Chen, Z., Guo, S., Xu, W., Bai, L., et al.: CRA5: extreme compression of ERA5 for portable global climate and weather research via an efficient variational transformer. arXiv preprint arXiv:2405.03376 (2024)

14. Yang, S., Hu, Y., Yang, W., Duan, L.-Y., Liu, J.: Towards coding for human and machine vision: scalable face image coding. IEEE Trans. Multimed. 1 (2021)

15. Le, N., Zhang, H., Cricri, F., Ghaznavi-Youvalari, R., Rahtu, E.: Image coding for machines: an end-to-end learned approach. In: ICASSP 2021 - 2021 IEEE International Conference on Acoustics, Speech and Signal Processing (ICASSP), pp. 1590–1594 (2021)

16. Song, M., Choi, J., Han, B.: Variable-rate deep image compression through spatially-adaptive feature transform. In: Proceedings of the IEEE/CVF International Conference on Computer Vision, pp. 2380–2389 (2021)

17. Torfason, R., Mentzer, F., Agustsson, E., Tschannen, M., Timofte, R., Van Gool, L.: Towards image understanding from deep compression without decoding. In: OpenReniew. net-ICLR 2018 (2018)

18. Bai, Y., et al.: Towards end-to-end image compression and analysis with transformers. In: Proceedings of the AAAI Conference on Artificial Intelligence, vol. 36, pp. 104–112 (2022)

19. Choi, H., Bajić, I.V.: Scalable image coding for humans and machines. IEEE Trans. Image Process. **31**, 2739–2754 (2022)

20. Wang, S., et al.: Towards analysis-friendly face representation with scalable feature and texture compression. IEEE Trans. Multimed. (2021)

21. Liu, K., Liu, D., Li, L., Yan, N., Li, H.: Semantics-to-signal scalable image compression with learned revertible representations. Int. J. Comput. Vision **129**(9), 2605–2621 (2021)

22. MPEG. MPEG G-PCC TMC13 (2021). https://github.com/MPEGGroup/mpeg-pcc-tmc13. Accessed 2022

23. Biswas, S., Liu, J., Wong, K., Wang, S., Urtasun, R.: MuSCLE: multi sweep compression of lidar using deep entropy models. Adv. Neural. Inf. Process. Syst. **33**, 22170–22181 (2020)

24. Liu, L., Hu, Z., Zhang, J.: PCHM-Net: a new point cloud compression framework for both human vision and machine vision. In: IEEE International Conference on Multimedia and Expo (2023)
25. Liu, L., Hu, Z., Chen, Z., Xu, D.: ICMH-Net: neural image compression towards both machine vision and human vision. In: Proceedings of the 31st ACM International Conference on Multimedia, pp. 8047–8056 (2023)
26. Wang, J., Zhu, H., Liu, H., Ma, Z.: Lossy point cloud geometry compression via end-to-end learning. IEEE Trans. Circ. Syst. Video Technol. (2021)
27. Chen, Z., Zhou, J., Wang, X., Swanson, J., Chen, F., Feng, D.: Neural net-based and safety-oriented visual analytics for time-spatial data. In: 2017 International Joint Conference on Neural Networks (IJCNN), pp. 1133–1140. IEEE (2017)
28. Zhu, W., Ma, Z., Xu, Y., Li, L., Li, Z.: View-dependent dynamic point cloud compression. IEEE Trans. Circuits Syst. Video Technol. **31**(2), 765–781 (2020)
29. Huang, T., Liu, Y.: 3D point cloud geometry compression on deep learning. In: Proceedings of the 27th ACM International Conference on Multimedia, pp. 890–898 (2019)
30. Wang, J., Ding, D., Li, Z., Ma, Z.: Multiscale point cloud geometry compression. In: 2021 Data Compression Conference (DCC), pp. 73–82. IEEE (2021)
31. Wang, Z., Huo, X., Chen, Z., Zhang, J., Sheng, L., Xu, D.: Improving RGB-D point cloud registration by learning multi-scale local linear transformation. In: Avidan, S., Brostow, G., Cissé, M., Farinella, G.M., Hassner, T. (eds.) ECCV 2022. LNCS, vol. 13692, pp. 175–191. Springer, Cham (2022). https://doi.org/10.1007/978-3-031-19824-3_11
32. Yang, X., Lin, G., Chen, Z., Zhou, L.: Neural vector fields: generalizing distance vector fields by codebooks and zero-curl regularization. arXiv preprint arXiv:2309.01512 (2023)
33. Ballé, J., Laparra, V., Simoncelli, E.P.: End-to-end optimized image compression. In: 5th International Conference on Learning Representations, ICLR 2017 (2017)
34. Qi, C.R., Yi, L., Su, H., Guibas, L.J.: PointNet++: deep hierarchical feature learning on point sets in a metric space. Adv. Neural Inf. Process. Syst. **30** (2017)
35. Qi, C.R., Litany, O., He, K., Guibas, L.J.: Deep hough voting for 3D object detection in point clouds. In: Proceedings of the IEEE/CVF International Conference on Computer Vision, pp. 9277–9286 (2019)
36. Shi, S., Wang, X., Li, H.: PointRCNN: 3D object proposal generation and detection from point cloud. In: The IEEE Conference on Computer Vision and Pattern Recognition (CVPR) (2019)
37. Jang, E., Gu, S., Poole, B.: Categorical reparametrization with gumble-softmax. In: International Conference on Learning Representations (ICLR 2017). OpenReview.net (2017)
38. Kingma, D.P., Ba, J.: Adam: a method for stochastic optimization. In: ICLR (Poster) (2015)

Toward Efficient Deep Spiking Neuron Networks: A Survey on Compression

Hui Xie, Ge Yang$^{(\boxtimes)}$, and Wenjuan Gao

Beihang University, Beijing, China
{xiehui,20231102,wjgao}@buaa.edu.cn

Abstract. With the rapid development of deep learning, Deep Spiking Neural Networks (DSNNs) have emerged as promising due to their unique spike event processing and asynchronous computation. When deployed on neuromorphic chips, DSNNs offer significant power advantages over Deep Artificial Neural Networks (DANNs) and eliminate time and energy consuming multiplications due to the binary nature of spikes (0 or 1). Additionally, DSNNs excel in processing temporal information, making them potentially superior for handling temporal data compared to DANNs. However, their deep network structure and numerous parameters result in high computational costs and energy consumption, limiting real-life deployment. To enhance DSNNs efficiency, researchers have adapted methods from DANNs, such as pruning, quantization, and knowledge distillation, and developed specific techniques like reducing spike firing and pruning time steps. While previous surveys have covered DSNNs algorithms, hardware deployment, and general overviews, focused research on DSNNs compression and efficiency has been lacking. This survey addresses this gap by concentrating on efficient DSNNs and their compression methods. It begins with an exploration of DSNNs' biological background and computational units, highlighting differences from DANNs. It then delves into various compression methods, including pruning, quantization, knowledge distillation, and reducing spike firing, and concludes with suggestions for future research directions.

Keywords: Deep Spiking Neuron Networks · Pruning · Quantization · Knowledge distillation · Reducing Spiking Firing · Compression

1 Introduction

As early as 1997, Maass [52] classified Spiking Neural Networks (SNNs) as third-generation neural networks based on their computational units, specifically spiking neurons or "integrate-and-fire neurons". In contrast, first-generation neural networks, developed around the 1950s and known as perceptrons, were based on McCulloch-Pitts neurons. These networks struggled with problems that were not linearly separable, such as the XOR operation. To address these limitations, second-generation neural networks, or Artificial Neural Networks (ANNs), were developed, utilizing activation functions that apply a continuous set of output values to a weighted sum (or polynomial) of the inputs.

© The Author(s), under exclusive license to Springer Nature Singapore Pte Ltd. 2024
J. Guo et al. (Eds.): IJCAI 2024, CCIS 2160, pp. 18–31, 2024.
https://doi.org/10.1007/978-981-97-6125-8_2

With the advancement of neuromorphic computing [61], SNNs have demonstrated significant potential due to their unique spike event processing and asynchronous computation capabilities. When deployed on neuromorphic chips, SNNs offer substantial power advantages over ANNs and avoid time and energy consuming multiplication operations due to the binary nature of spikes (0 or 1) [3]. Moreover, SNNs more closely mimic the complex workings of the biological brain [34], enhancing their potential to achieve genuine artificial intelligence. Their ability to process temporal information naturally makes them particularly suited for tasks involving temporal data [45], surpassing the capabilities of ANNs in this regard. SNNs are also uniquely suited for applications like event-based cameras [20], which are event-driven, asynchronous, and binary, making them ideal for processing with SNNs on neuromorphic chips.

In recent years, deep learning [40] has achieved tremendous success with DANNs [6,53,78,84] and, correspondingly, with DSNNs [36,49,83]. Numerous new architectures have been proposed to improve performance on various tasks in DANNs [29,33,37,68], with similar advancements seen in DSNNs, including Spiking VGG [41,64], Spiking ResNet [19,32], and Spiking Transformers [67,79,82].

However, the deep network structure and large number of parameters in these models lead to significant computational costs and energy consumption, limiting their practical deployment. To achieve efficient DSNNs, researchers have adapted methods from DANNs, such as pruning, quantization, and knowledge distillation. Additionally, unique methods specific to DSNNs, such as reducing spike firing and pruning time steps, have been developed.

Previous surveys on SNNs have primarily focused on algorithms [12,81], hardware deployment [4], and general overviews [60], without specifically addressing DSNNs compression and efficiency. Conversely, there is extensive research on compressing DANNs, including structured pruning [30], quantization [22], knowledge distillation [23]. Therefore, a focused survey on DSNNs compression is needed.

This survey addresses this gap by concentrating on efficient DSNNs and their compression methods. It begins with an exploration of the biological background and computational units of SNNs to understand how they differ from ANNs. It then analyzes various compression methods, including pruning, quantization, knowledge distillation, and reducing spike firing. Finally, it suggests directions for future research.

2   Background

The introduction of activation functions in neural networks is primarily driven by the need to introduce non-linear functions into a linear system, thereby increasing its complexity and enhancing its representative capabilities. In contrast, the computational units in SNNs, such as the Leaky Integrate-and-Fire (LIF) neuron or Integrate-and-Fire (IF) neuron, are designed to more closely mimic the properties of biological neurons. This distinction in computational units is a fundamental difference between SNNs and ANNs.

2.1   Biological Background

A typical neuron consists of three main parts: dendrites, soma, and axon. Dendrites collect input signals from other neurons and transmit them to the soma. The soma acts as a computational unit, generating an action potential when the accumulated incoming current causes the membrane potential to exceed a certain threshold. This action potential then travels along the axon and transmits the signal to the next neuron through synapses at the axon's terminal.

LIF Model. The Leaky Integrate-and-Fire (LIF) model, first proposed by Lapicque in 1907, describes the process of action potentials in neurons. Neurons fire impulses when the membrane potential reaches the threshold voltage $V_{threshold}$, after which the membrane potential resets to the resting potential V_{reset}. The LIF model focuses on the patterns of sub-threshold potential voltage variations. [14].

$$\tau_m \frac{dV}{dt} = V_{reset} - V + R_m I. \tag{1}$$

where τ_m represents the membrane time constant, V_{reset} is the resting potential, and R_m and I are the cell membrane's impedance and the input current, respectively.

The LIF neuron model provides a simplified representation of biological neurons, emphasizing essential features like membrane potential leakage, accumulation, and excitation. While its biological accuracy is limited, its simplicity makes it suitable for computational simulations.

Other Models. The Hodgkin-Huxley (H-H) model, proposed by Hodgkin and Huxley in 1952 [31], offers a highly precise approximation of the principles governing biological neuron action potentials, earning them the Nobel Prize in Physiology or Medicine in 1963. Although the H-H model has high biological fidelity, it is computationally intensive. Other models, such as the Adaptive Exponential Integrate-and-Fire (aEIF) model [5] and the Izhikevich model [35], strive to balance biological fidelity and computational simplicity.

2.2   Computational Unit of SNNs

In contemporary SNNs, neuron models predominantly rely on the LIF model. While the mathematical formulation of the LIF model involves a time-dependent differential equation, actual computer computations discretize this process for approximation.

$$H[t] = V[t-1] + \frac{1}{\tau}(X[t] - (V[t-1] - V_{reset})) \tag{2}$$

$$S[t] = \Theta(H[t] - V_{threshold}) \tag{3}$$

$$V[t] = H[t](1 - S[t]) + V_{reset}S[t] \tag{4}$$

$$\Theta(x) = \begin{cases} 0 & \text{if } x < 0 \\ 1 & \text{if } x \geq 0 \end{cases} \tag{5}$$

where τ represents the membrane time constant, V_{reset} is the resting potential, $V_{threshold}$ is the threshold voltage, and $X[t]$, $H[t]$, $V[t]$ represent the input current, the membrane potential before and after spiking firing at time step t, respectively. The specific implementation of LIF neurons can vary [18] (Fig. 1).

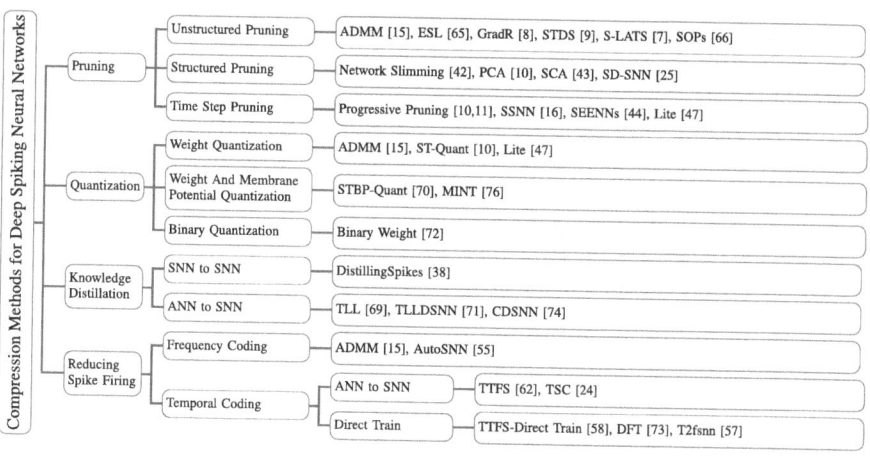

Fig. 1. Taxonomy of Model Compression methods for Deep Spiking Neural Networks.

3 Methods

DSNNs share many commonalities with DANNs, and some research has focused on these commonalities and proposed a unified pruning architecture [7]. Concepts like pruning, quantization, and knowledge distillation, initially developed for DANNs, can be adapted for DSNNs. However, the unique spiking and temporal characteristics of DSNNs often necessitate modifications to these techniques to ensure optimal performance. Additionally, DSNNs can be compressed in unique ways, such as leveraging spike sparsity, temporal coding, and pruning of time steps.

3.1 Pruning

DSNNs need to be deployed on neuromorphic hardware [77], which differs significantly from general-purpose computers in terms of operational logic. As a result, the value of pruning must be reassessed. Both unstructured and structured pruning are important for DSNNs, contrary to the inefficiency of unstructured pruning in DANNs [51], despite the scarcity of related work [46].

Unstructured Pruning. Unstructured pruning involves pruning weights or neurons.

ADMM-method [15] utilizes the Alternating Direction Method of Multipliers (ADMM) for connection pruning based on soft constraints, demonstrating effectiveness in reducing parameter memory space and baseline computational cost in DSNNs. It compresses connections, weight bit-widths, and spike frequencies simultaneously.

ESL [65] begins with a sparse network generated using the Erdős-Rényi random graph model, dynamically pruning weak connections and generating new ones according to structural plasticity rules. This approach, which updates the connection mask every $Titter$ iterations and employs various growth methods, outperforms the ADMM-method.

GradR [8], inspired by synapse formation and elimination in the nervous system, redefines synaptic parameters using $w = sReLU(\theta)$, where s is determined at initialization and remains unchanged. It employs different training strategies for active and inactive connections, enhancing network exploration and recovery of dead neurons.

STDS [9] improves on GradR by using nonlinear reparameterization with $w = sign(\theta) \cdot (|\theta| - d)_+, d \geq 0$. When the size of the connection w is below threshold d, it is considered a filopodium, and the equivalent weight is zero. In any state, the parameters have gradients, allowing transitions between positive and negative weights, exploring the network space more fully. Pruning speed is adjusted by regulating the change in d.

S-LATS [7], a theoretical framework that reformulates soft threshold pruning as an implicit optimization problem and solves it using the Iterative Shrinkage-Thresholding Algorithm (ISTA), which is a classic method in the fields of sparse recovery and compressed sensing. It is proven that in the underlying optimization problem, the L1 coefficient is jointly determined by the threshold and the learning rate, allowing any threshold tuning strategy to be interpreted as a scheme for adjusting the L1 penalty. Through in-depth research on threshold scheduling based on the framework, an optimal threshold scheduler is derived, which maintains a stable L1 regularization coefficient, thereby providing a time-invariant objective function from an optimization perspective. A new family of pruning algorithms is proposed, including pruning during training, early pruning, and pruning at initialization, and get the best result both in DANNs and DSNNs.

SOPs-method [66] introduces an synaptic operation (SOP) metric (this paper define SOP as the operations performed when a spike passes through a synapse) to quantify power consumption in SNNs and uses an energy penalty term for energy-constrained unstructured weight and neuron pruning, maximizing efficiency through sparsity. During training, a binary mask m is reparameterized by α as $m = H(\alpha)$ and approximated with a scaled sigmoid function as $\lim_{\beta \to \infty} \sigma(\alpha; \beta) = \frac{1}{1+e^{-\beta\alpha}}$. Gradual scheduling methods adjust the scale factor β, to achieve different compressing rate.

Structured Pruning. Structured Pruning focuses on channel pruning for deep convolutional spiking neural networks.

Just the migration from DANNs Networks Slimming [48], DSNNs Networks Slimming [42] penalizes the scaling factors of the Batch-Normal layers, pruning channels with smaller scaling factors. However, due to the thresholding nature of DSNNs, the pruning is not thorough enough, achieving only 60% channel pruning while maintaining accuracy without much loss.

Principal Component Analysis(PCA) based pruning [10] targets redundant filters, a method also used in ANNs [21], adapted for SNNs. The pruning method is modified by using the principal component analysis of neurons' average cumulative membrane potentials to determine significant spatial dimensions for structured pruning. This step results in a 10–14 fold reduction in model size.

The network pruning framework based on Spike Channel Activity(SCA) [43] is inspired by synaptic plasticity mechanisms. During training, channels with lower average spike firing frequency are pruned, and convolutional kernels are dynamically adjusted based on the gradients of the Batch-Normal layers scaling factors, regenerating those with larger gradients which is same to before work [17].

Adaptive structural development of SNN(SD-SNN) [25] is based on synaptic constraints inspired by dendritic spine plasticity. Synaptic constraints detect and remove significant redundancy in SNNs, and synapse regeneration effectively prevents and repairs excessive pruning. During the learning process, the neuron pruning rate and synapse regeneration rate are adaptively adjusted, leading to a stable SNN structure.

Time Step Pruning. Time step pruning is unique to SNNs due to their temporal dimension in data input.

In algorithms transfer DANNs to DSNNs, a high number of time steps is needed to accurately capture the values of the ReLU activation function, requiring 20–50 steps or more. This is unacceptable for SNNs in practical applications, as it introduces step times computational and memory burdens [3].

The main challenge of time step pruning is that when the number of time steps is too low, neurons in the latter parts of the model cannot fire, leading to vanishing gradients. This means back-propagation cannot occur, and the model cannot be trained.

A simple idea is progressive pruning [10, 11]. First, train the model with a long time step to ensure a high spike rate in the final layer. Then, prune the time steps while the model can still produce spikes in the final layer even with fewer time steps, allowing back-propagation to proceed normally. Gradually reduce the time steps until reaching an extremely low number, potentially achieving good results even with a single time step. The test dataset used for this approach is a standard image dataset.

Shrinking SNN (SSNN) [16] addresses the issue of disappearing spikes by modifying the model structure, enabling the model to derive loss from the spikes of intermediate neurons, back-propagate, and train normally. This method has shown good results but is currently limited to the DVS dataset, demonstrating its compression capabilities on datasets with temporal sequences. It may also be extendable to static datasets.

Spiking Early-Exit Neural Networks (SEENNs) [44] focus on balancing efficiency and accuracy. This method treats the time step as a variable and filters uncertain predictions through a confidence threshold. For uncertain predictions, reinforcement learning is used to determine the appropriate number of time steps, achieving automatic time step adjustment. On the CIFAR-10 dataset, this method achieved an average of nearly one time step while maintaining higher accuracy compared to other methods with longer time step.

Lite [47] thoroughly explores the optimal number of time steps for each layer through neural architecture search, characterizes the energy consumption through the metric of total synaptic operations, and achieves a good balance between energy efficiency and accuracy by controlling the pruning strength with a penalty factor.

3.2 Quantization

Quantization transforms large numerical data into a discrete set of values, aiming to minimize bit usage while maintaining computational precision. In DSNNs, quantization includes membrane potential quantization alongside weights, without activation quantization. This study categorizes quantization efforts into weight quantization and weight and membrane potential quantization, along with specialized binary quantization.

Weight Quantization. ADMM-Quant [15] employs the ADMM to enforce quantization constraints on weights, albeit with a limitation to weight-only uniform quantization.

ST-Quant [10] utilizes K-means clustering-based weight sharing quantization techniques to further compress the model, akin to the approach taken by [26] for weight quantization.

Lite [47] adopts Neural Architecture Search (NAS) to automatically discover suitable mixed-precision bit-widths, enabling different layers to adopt varying levels of quantization. This is integrated within a unified framework that concurrently searches for optimal bit-widths, time steps, and network architectures, guided by a penalty term incorporated into the loss function for joint training.

Weight and Membrane Potential Quantization. STBP-Quant [70] transforms high-precision floating-point computations in existing direct training algorithms to low-bitwidth integer operations, introducing Integer-STBP, an algorithm that facilitates training and inference of SNNs using solely integer arithmetic. This enables implementation on low-power edge devices for online learning and inference.

MINT [76], building upon STBP-Quant, eliminates the requirement for multipliers in conventional uniform quantization during inference by sharing scaling factors between weights and membrane potentials. Scaling factors are retained during training to ensure competitive accuracy, while their necessity is obviated during inference through shared scaling, thus removing 32-bit multipliers in hardware. By quantizing memory-intensive membrane potentials to extremely low precision (2-bits), significant reductions in memory usage are achieved.

Binary Quantization. A novel weight-threshold balancing transformation [72] is proposed, adjusting the threshold of spiking neurons to convert high-precision weights into binary values (-1 or 1), effectively yielding binary SNNs. This drastically reduces weight memory requirements, albeit accompanied by increased neuron threshold storage (originally all are same).

3.3 Knowledge Distillation

Knowledge distillation (KD) is a commonly used model compression method, which uses a large teacher model to guide the training of a small student model. Specifically, knowledge distillation takes the knowledge of the teacher model as a supervision signal during the training process, so that the student model not only learns from the data, but also receives guidance from the teacher model, thereby achieving better performance.

Knowledge Distillation from SNN to SNN. As the scale of SNNs continues to expand, its demand for storage and computing resources also gradually increases, hindering its application in real life. To address this issue, Kushawaha et al. [38] proposed the first knowledge distillation method specially designed for SNNs to minimize loss of accuracy. They use the spiking activation tensors of the teacher and student models to simultaneously calculate the full loss and the sliding window loss as new loss functions. Then they froze the weights of the teacher SNN and trained the student SNN. Moreover, they also introduced a multi-stage distillation procedure to further improve the performance of student SNN. Experiments on three standard image classification datasets show that their method improves the performance of student SNN.

Knowledge Distillation from ANN to SNN. Takuya et al. [69] proposed to use knowledge distillation of KL divergence to train low-latency SNN. They first utilized a large ANN as the teacher model to train a small ANN, and then converted the small ANN into a SNN. Finally, they distill knowledge from the large teacher ANN into the SNN and use approximate gradients to solve the problem of non-differentiable spikes. The experimental results on the CIFAR-100 dataset show that they achieved the lowest inference latency while maintaining accuracy.

Tran et al. [71] proposed a training technique to convert ANNs to SNNs which is able to learn more hidden information by using knowledge distillation. They combined knowledge distillation and batch normalization through time (BNTT) to improve the performance of converted SNNs and reduce its power consumption. Experiments on Tiny-ImageNet, CIFAR-10 and CIFAR-100 show that their method successfully improves accuracy and reduces inference latency.

Xu et al. [74] proposed a knowledge distillation training method combining ANN and SNN. They combined spike coding and joint loss function to solve the problem of non-differentiable SNN spikes. They proposed two knowledge distillation methods: response-based KD and feature-based KD, which extract knowledge from the last layer output of the teacher model and some intermediate layers of the teacher model respectively. Comprehensive experimental results demonstrate the effectiveness of their approach.

3.4 Reducing Firing Rate

In neuromorphic hardware, a common metric for characterizing the energy consumption is synaptic operations [13], and reducing the number of spikes can effectively decrease synaptic operations. Frequency coding is a commonly used encoding method, favored for its simplicity and efficiency, which is conducive to training; however, it typically requires a higher number of spikes to achieve satisfactory results under this encoding. Temporal coding, on the other hand, conveys the same information with fewer spikes, allowing at most a single spike per neuron in the neural network, effectively reducing the number of spikes during inference. The trade-off is longer time steps, which are typically used in the transition from ANN-SNN algorithms. Due to space constraints, we will only discuss the Temporal coding of ANN-SNN. Direct training temporal coding can be seen here [57,58,73].

Frequency Coding. ADMM-method [15] reduces spike firing frequency during training by imposing a penalty factor on the membrane potential. AutoSNN [55] is a direct training algorithm that adopts a one-shot weight-sharing approach based on an evolutionary algorithm to automatically search for and discover energy-efficient SNN architectures suitable for specific tasks. The article mentions that the global average pooling layer can reduce the energy efficiency of SNNs, so the maximum pooling layer is recommended.

Temporal Coding. Time-to-First-Spike (TTFS) coding [62] approximates the real-valued ReLU activation in DANNs to the delay of the first spike in the corresponding spike sequence in DSNNs, requiring at most one spike per activation. However, the cost is a longer time step, and the memory access and computational costs associated with long time steps remain high, as peak neurons need to track synapses and receive the first peak from synapses after each time step.

    Temporal-SwitchCoding (TSC), and the corresponding TSC spiking neuron model [24], is presented better then TTFS. Each pixel of the input image is presented through two spikes, with the time interval between the two spikes being proportional to the pixel intensity. Throughout the inference process, each synapse performs at most two memory accesses and two addition operations, significantly improving the energy efficiency of SNNs.

4   Future Directions

Efficient Neuron Model. There are models that increase accuracy with more parameters and complex structures [27,75], as well as models that precisely model biological neurons. However, there is limited research on developing more efficient neuron models specifically for deep learning [54]. Two potential paths exist: one involves modeling neurons more finely but with fewer neurons in shallow networks, and the other involves modeling neurons more coarsely with a larger number of neurons in deep networks. Precise modeling of biological neurons requires substantial computational resources but offers greater representational capacity. By accurately simulating biological neurons, we can achieve complex network functions with fewer neurons [1,39,80], which may present an energy efficiency advantage.

    Balancing biological fidelity with computational efficiency presents a trade-off. Exploring how to abstract better neuron characteristics for modeling is a key problem that warrants further investigation to realize efficient neural networks.

Unified Compression Architecture. DANNs and DSNNs share commonalities, and their similarities may represent the fundamental characteristics of neural networks. Methods applicable only to specific types of neural networks might not address the essence of neural networks. For instance, a unified framework for soft threshold pruning has been proposed, revealing the characteristics of neural network soft threshold pruning [7]. Similarly, the PCA method's analysis of convolutional kernel similarity followed by pruning demonstrates the effectiveness of pruning similar components in neural networks [10,21]. The difficulties encountered in regularization pruning of Batch-Normal layer parameters suggest that a unified solution is needed [42,48].

Key issues in DSNNs compression include: What are the differences between DANNs and DSNNs during compression? Which DANNs methods can be transferred to DSNNs? If there are differences, how should they be modified? Is there a unified method?

Efficient Specialization Program. Are there more efficient encoding schemes? Time encoding requires long time steps, and frequency encoding requires higher firing frequencies. Fully utilizing the time and frequency information of spikes is an important issue. Existing work combines time and frequency, but can we go further? Moreover, we may need more specialized model structures and further research on them, beyond just minor modifications to VGG and ResNet like VGGSNN and Sew-ResNet [28,39,50].

Co-design Compression with Hardware. The requirement for DSNNs to be deployed on neuromorphic hardware to gain advantages over DANNs affects the direction of DSNNs optimization. A variety of neuromorphic hardware platforms [2,13,56,59,63] may necessitate hardware-related collaborative compression work.

Disclosure of Interests. The authors have no competing interests to declare that are relevant to the content of this article.

References

1. Beniaguev, D., Segev, I., London, M.: Single cortical neurons as deep artificial neural networks. Neuron **109**(17), 2727–2739 (2021)
2. Benjamin, B.V., et al.: Neurogrid: a mixed-analog-digital multichip system for large-scale neural simulations. Proc. IEEE **102**(5), 699–716 (2014)
3. Bhattacharjee, A., Yin, R., Moitra, A., Panda, P.: Are SNNs truly energy-efficient? - a hardware perspective. ArXiv abs/2309.03388 (2023)
4. Bouvier, M., et al.: Spiking neural networks hardware implementations and challenges: a survey. ACM J. Emerg. Technol. Comput. Syst. (JETC) **15**(2), 1–35 (2019)
5. Brette, R., Gerstner, W.: Adaptive exponential integrate-and-fire model as an effective description of neuronal activity. J. Neurophysiol. **94**(5), 3637–3642 (2005)
6. Chen, L., Li, S., Bai, Q., Yang, J., Jiang, S., Miao, Y.: Review of image classification algorithms based on convolutional neural networks. Remote Sens. **13**(22), 4712 (2021)
7. Chen, Y., Ma, Z., Fang, W., Zheng, X., Yu, Z., Tian, Y.: A unified framework for soft threshold pruning. arXiv preprint arXiv:2302.13019 (2023)
8. Chen, Y., Yu, Z., Fang, W., Huang, T., Tian, Y.: Pruning of deep spiking neural networks through gradient rewiring. In: Zhou, Z.H. (ed.) Proceedings of the Thirtieth International Joint Conference on Artificial Intelligence, IJCAI-21, pp. 1713–1721. International Joint Conferences on Artificial Intelligence Organization (2021). https://doi.org/10.24963/ijcai.2021/236. Main Track
9. Chen, Y., Yu, Z., Fang, W., Ma, Z., Huang, T., Tian, Y.: State transition of dendritic spines improves learning of sparse spiking neural networks. In: International Conference on Machine Learning, pp. 3701–3715. PMLR (2022)

10. Chowdhury, S.S., Garg, I., Roy, K.: Spatio-temporal pruning and quantization for low-latency spiking neural networks. In: 2021 International Joint Conference on Neural Networks (IJCNN), pp. 1–9. IEEE (2021)
11. Chowdhury, S.S., Rathi, N., Roy, K.: Towards ultra low latency spiking neural networks for vision and sequential tasks using temporal pruning. In: Avidan, S., Brostow, G., Cissé, M., Farinella, G.M., Hassner, T. (eds.) ECCV 2022. LNCS, vol. 13671, pp. 709–726. Springer, Cham (2022). https://doi.org/10.1007/978-3-031-20083-0_42
12. Dampfhoffer, M., Mesquida, T., Valentian, A., Anghel, L.: Backpropagation-based learning techniques for deep spiking neural networks: a survey. IEEE Trans. Neural Netw. Learn. Syst. (2023)
13. Davies, M., et al.: Loihi: a neuromorphic manycore processor with on-chip learning. IEEE Micro **38**(1), 82–99 (2018)
14. Dayan, P., Abbott, L.F.: A mathematical model of spiking neurons. In: Theoretical Neuroscience: Computational and Mathematical Modeling of Neural Systems (2001)
15. Deng, L., et al.: Comprehensive SNN compression using ADMM optimization and activity regularization. IEEE Trans. Neural Netw. Learn. Syst. **34**(6), 2791–2805 (2021)
16. Ding, Y., Zuo, L., Jing, M., He, P., Xiao, Y.: Shrinking your timestep: towards low-latency neuromorphic object recognition with spiking neural network. In: Proceedings of the AAAI Conference on Artificial Intelligence (2024)
17. Evci, U., Gale, T., Menick, J., Castro, P.S., Elsen, E.: Rigging the lottery: making all tickets winners. In: International Conference on Machine Learning, pp. 2943–2952. PMLR (2020)
18. Fang, W., et al.: SpikingJelly: an open-source machine learning infrastructure platform for spike-based intelligence. Sci. Adv. **9**(40), eadi1480 (2023)
19. Fang, W., Yu, Z., Chen, Y., Huang, T., Masquelier, T., Tian, Y.: Deep residual learning in spiking neural networks. In: Neural Information Processing Systems (2021)
20. Gallego, G., et al.: Event-based vision: a survey. IEEE Trans. Pattern Anal. Mach. Intell. **44**, 154–180 (2019)
21. Garg, I., Panda, P., Roy, K.: A low effort approach to structured CNN design using PCA. IEEE Access **8**, 1347–1360 (2019)
22. Gholami, A., Kim, S., Dong, Z., Yao, Z., Mahoney, M.W., Keutzer, K.: A survey of quantization methods for efficient neural network inference. In: Low-Power Computer Vision, pp. 291–326. Chapman and Hall/CRC (2022)
23. Gou, J., Yu, B., Maybank, S.J., Tao, D.: Knowledge distillation: a survey. Int. J. Comput. Vision **129**(6), 1789–1819 (2021)
24. Han, B., Roy, K.: Deep spiking neural network: energy efficiency through time based coding. In: Vedaldi, A., Bischof, H., Brox, T., Frahm, J.-M. (eds.) ECCV 2020. LNCS, vol. 12355, pp. 388–404. Springer, Cham (2020). https://doi.org/10.1007/978-3-030-58607-2_23
25. Han, B., Zhao, F., Zeng, Y., Pan, W.: Adaptive sparse structure development with pruning and regeneration for spiking neural networks. arXiv preprint arXiv:2211.12219 (2022)
26. Han, S., Mao, H., Dally, W.J.: Deep compression: Compressing deep neural networks with pruning, trained quantization and Huffman coding. arXiv preprint arXiv:1510.00149 (2015)
27. Hao, Z., Shi, X., Huang, Z., Bu, T., Yu, Z., Huang, T.: A progressive training framework for spiking neural networks with learnable multi-hierarchical model. In: The Twelfth International Conference on Learning Representations (2023)
28. Hasani, R., Lechner, M., Amini, A., Rus, D., Grosu, R.: Liquid time-constant networks. In: Proceedings of the AAAI Conference on Artificial Intelligence, vol. 35, pp. 7657–7666 (2021)
29. He, K., Zhang, X., Ren, S., Sun, J.: Deep residual learning for image recognition. In: Proceedings IEEE Conference on Computer Vision and Pattern Recognition, pp. 770–778 (2016)

30. He, Y., Xiao, L.: Structured pruning for deep convolutional neural networks: a survey. IEEE Trans. Pattern Anal. Mach. Intell. **46**(5), 2900–2919 (2024). https://doi.org/10.1109/TPAMI.2023.3334614

31. Hodgkin, A.L., Huxley, A.F.: A quantitative description of membrane current and its application to conduction and excitation in nerve. J. Physiol. **117**(4), 500 (1952)

32. Hu, Y.Z., Tang, H., Pan, G.: Spiking deep residual networks. IEEE Trans. Neural Netw. Learn. Syst. **34**, 5200–5205 (2021)

33. Huang, G., Liu, Z., Van Der Maaten, L., Weinberger, K.Q.: Densely connected convolutional networks. In: Proceedings of the IEEE Conference on Computer Vision and Pattern Recognition, pp. 4700–4708 (2017)

34. Huang, L.W., Ma, Z., Yu, L., Zhou, H., Tian, Y.: Deep spiking neural networks with high representation similarity model visual pathways of macaque and mouse. In: AAAI Conference on Artificial Intelligence (2023)

35. Izhikevich, E.M.: Simple model of spiking neurons. IEEE Trans. Neural Netw. **14**(6), 1569–1572 (2003)

36. Kim, Y., Panda, P.: Revisiting batch normalization for training low-latency deep spiking neural networks from scratch. Front. Neurosci. **15** (2020)

37. Krizhevsky, A., Sutskever, I., Hinton, G.E.: ImageNet classification with deep convolutional neural networks. In: Advances in Neural Information Processing Systems, vol. 25 (2012)

38. Kushawaha, R.K., Kumar, S., Banerjee, B., Velmurugan, R.: Distilling spikes: knowledge distillation in spiking neural networks. In: 2020 25th International Conference on Pattern Recognition (ICPR), pp. 4536–4543. IEEE (2021)

39. Lechner, M., Hasani, R., Amini, A., Henzinger, T.A., Rus, D., Grosu, R.: Neural circuit policies enabling auditable autonomy. Nat. Mach. Intell. **2**(10), 642–652 (2020)

40. LeCun, Y., Bengio, Y., Hinton, G.: Deep learning. Nature **521**(7553), 436–444 (2015)

41. Lee, C., Sarwar, S.S., Panda, P., Srinivasan, G., Roy, K.: Enabling spike-based backpropagation for training deep neural network architectures. Front. Neurosci. **14** (2019)

42. Li, Y., et al.: Efficient structure slimming for spiking neural networks. IEEE Trans. Artif. Intell. (2024)

43. Li, Y., et al.: Towards efficient deep spiking neural networks construction with spiking activity based pruning. In: Proceedings of the International Conference on Machine Learning (2024)

44. Li, Y., Geller, T., Kim, Y., Panda, P.: SEENN: towards temporal spiking early exit neural networks. In: Advances in Neural Information Processing Systems, vol. 36 (2024)

45. Li, Y., Yin, R., Kim, Y., Panda, P.: Efficient human activity recognition with spatio-temporal spiking neural networks. Front. Neurosci. **17** (2023)

46. Liu, B., Wang, M., Foroosh, H., Tappen, M., Pensky, M.: Sparse convolutional neural networks. In: Proceedings of the IEEE Conference on Computer Vision and Pattern Recognition, pp. 806–814 (2015)

47. Liu, Q., Yan, J., Zhang, M., Pan, G., Li, H.: LITE-SNN: designing lightweight and efficient spiking neural network through spatial-temporal compressive network search and joint optimization. arXiv preprint arXiv:2401.14652 (2024)

48. Liu, Z., Li, J., Shen, Z., Huang, G., Yan, S., Zhang, C.: Learning efficient convolutional networks through network slimming. In: Proceedings of the IEEE International Conference on Computer Vision, pp. 2736–2744 (2017)

49. Lv, C., Xu, J., Zheng, X.: Spiking convolutional neural networks for text classification. In: International Conference on Learning Representations (2023)

50. Ma, G., Jiang, R., Yan, R., Tang, H.: Temporal conditioning spiking latent variable models of the neural response to natural visual scenes. In: Advances in Neural Information Processing Systems, vol. 36 (2024)

51. Ma, X., et al.: Non-structured DNN weight pruning-is it beneficial in any platform? IEEE Trans. Neural Netw. Learn. Syst. **33**(9), 4930–4944 (2022). https://doi.org/10.1109/TNNLS. 2021.3063265

52. Maass, W.: Networks of spiking neurons: the third generation of neural network models. Electron. Colloquium Comput. Complex. **TR96** (1996)

53. Minaee, S., Boykov, Y., Porikli, F., Plaza, A., Kehtarnavaz, N., Terzopoulos, D.: Image segmentation using deep learning: a survey. IEEE Trans. Pattern Anal. Mach. Intell. **44**(7), 3523–3542 (2021)

54. Moser, B.A., Lunglmayr, M.: Quantization in spiking neural networks (2024)

55. Na, B., Mok, J., Park, S., Lee, D., Choe, H., Yoon, S.: AutoSNN: towards energy-efficient spiking neural networks. In: International Conference on Machine Learning, pp. 16253–16269. PMLR (2022)

56. Painkras, E., et al.: Spinnaker: a 1-w 18-core system-on-chip for massively-parallel neural network simulation. IEEE J. Solid-State Circuits **48**(8), 1943–1953 (2013)

57. Park, S., Kim, S., Na, B., Yoon, S.: T2fsnn: Deep spiking neural networks with time-to-first-spike coding. In: 2020 57th ACM/IEEE Design Automation Conference (DAC), pp. 1–6 (2020)

58. Park, S., Yoon, S.: Training energy-efficient deep spiking neural networks with time-to-first-spike coding. arXiv preprint arXiv:2106.02568 (2021)

59. Pei, J., et al.: Towards artificial general intelligence with hybrid Tianjic chip architecture. Nature **572**(7767), 106–111 (2019)

60. Pfeiffer, M., Pfeil, T.: Deep learning with spiking neurons: opportunities and challenges. Front. Neurosci. **12**, 409662 (2018)

61. Roy, K., Jaiswal, A.R., Panda, P.: Towards spike-based machine intelligence with neuromorphic computing. Nature **575**, 607–617 (2019)

62. Rueckauer, B., Liu, S.C.: Conversion of analog to spiking neural networks using sparse temporal coding. In: 2018 IEEE International Symposium on Circuits and Systems (ISCAS), pp. 1–5. IEEE (2018)

63. Schemmel, J., Brüderle, D., Grübl, A., Hock, M., Meier, K., Millner, S.: A wafer-scale neuromorphic hardware system for large-scale neural modeling. In: 2010 IEEE International Symposium on Circuits and Systems (ISCAS), pp. 1947–1950. IEEE (2010)

64. Sengupta, A., Ye, Y., Wang, R.Y., Liu, C., Roy, K.: Going deeper in spiking neural networks: VGG and residual architectures. Front. Neurosci. **13** (2018)

65. Shen, J., Xu, Q., Liu, J.K., Wang, Y., Pan, G., Tang, H.: ESL-SNNS: an evolutionary structure learning strategy for spiking neural networks. In: Proceedings of the AAAI Conference on Artificial Intelligence, vol. 37, pp. 86–93 (2023)

66. Shi, X., Ding, J., Hao, Z., Yu, Z.: Towards energy efficient spiking neural networks: an unstructured pruning framework. In: The Twelfth International Conference on Learning Representations (2023)

67. Shi, X., Hao, Z., Yu, Z.: SpikingResformer: bridging ResNet and vision transformer in spiking neural networks. ArXiv abs/2403.14302 (2024)

68. Simonyan, K., Zisserman, A.: Very deep convolutional networks for large-scale image recognition. In: Proceedings of the International Conference on Learning Representation (2015)

69. Takuya, S., Zhang, R., Nakashima, Y.: Training low-latency spiking neural network through knowledge distillation. In: 2021 IEEE Symposium in Low-Power and High-Speed Chips (COOL CHIPS), pp. 1–3. IEEE (2021)

70. Tan, P.Y., Wu, C.W.: A low-bitwidth integer-STBP algorithm for efficient training and inference of spiking neural networks. In: Proceedings of the 28th Asia and South Pacific Design Automation Conference, pp. 651–656 (2023)

71. Tran, T.D., Le, K.T., Nguyen, A.L.T.: Training low-latency deep spiking neural networks with knowledge distillation and batch normalization through time. In: 2022 5th International Conference on Computational Intelligence and Networks (CINE), pp. 01–06. IEEE (2022)
72. Wang, Y., Xu, Y., Yan, R., Tang, H.: Deep spiking neural networks with binary weights for object recognition. IEEE Trans. Cogn. Dev. Syst. **13**(3), 514–523 (2020)
73. Wei, W., Zhang, M., Qu, H., Belatreche, A., Zhang, J., Chen, H.: Temporal-coded spiking neural networks with dynamic firing threshold: learning with event-driven backpropagation. In: Proceedings of the IEEE/CVF International Conference on Computer Vision, pp. 10552–10562 (2023)
74. Xu, Q., Li, Y., Shen, J., Liu, J.K., Tang, H., Pan, G.: Constructing deep spiking neural networks from artificial neural networks with knowledge distillation. In: Proceedings of the IEEE/CVF Conference on Computer Vision and Pattern Recognition, pp. 7886–7895 (2023)
75. Yao, X., Li, F., Mo, Z., Cheng, J.: GLIF: a unified gated leaky integrate-and-fire neuron for spiking neural networks. In: Advances in Neural Information Processing Systems, vol. 35, pp. 32160–32171 (2022)
76. Yin, R., Li, Y., Moitra, A., Panda, P.: MINT: multiplier-less INTeger quantization for energy efficient spiking neural networks. In: 2024 29th Asia and South Pacific Design Automation Conference (ASP-DAC), pp. 830–835. IEEE (2024)
77. Yin, R., Moitra, A., Bhattacharjee, A., Kim, Y., Panda, P.: SATA: sparsity-aware training accelerator for spiking neural networks. IEEE Trans. Comput.-Aided Design Integr. Circuits Syst. (2022)
78. Yin, W., Kann, K., Yu, M., Schütze, H.: Comparative study of CNN and RNN for natural language processing. arXiv preprint arXiv:1702.01923 (2017)
79. Zhang, H., et al.: SGLFormer: spiking global-local-fusion transformer with high performance. Front. Neurosci. **18** (2024)
80. Zhao, M., et al.: MetaWorm: an integrative data-driven model simulating c. elegans brain, body and environment interactions. bioRxiv (2024)
81. Zhou, C., et al.: Direct training high-performance deep spiking neural networks: a review of theories and methods. arXiv preprint arXiv:2405.04289 (2024)
82. Zhou, Z., et al.: SpikFormer: when spiking neural network meets transformer. ArXiv abs/2209.15425 (2022)
83. Zhu, Y., Yu, Z., Fang, W., Xie, X., Huang, T., Masquelier, T.: Training spiking neural networks with event-driven backpropagation. In: Neural Information Processing Systems (2022)
84. Zou, Z., Chen, K., Shi, Z., Guo, Y., Ye, J.: Object detection in 20 years: a survey. Proc. IEEE **111**(3), 257–276 (2023)

Towards Efficient Fault Detection of Ultra-High Voltage Direct Current Circuit Breakers

Jiayi Wang[1(✉)], Dong Peng[1], Shaoqing Chen[1], Dianbo Zhou[1], Zhenze Long[1], and Botao Cheng[2]

[1] State Grid Sichuan Electric Power Company Electric Power Science Research Institute, Chengdu, Sichuan, China
`{wangjy0515,dpeng04,sqchen01,dianbozhou,zzlong02}@sc.sgcc.com.cn`
[2] State Grid WeiHai Power Supply Company, Weihai, Shandong, China
`jiaowei@sd.sgcc.com.cn`

Abstract. Fault detection on Ultra-High Voltage (UHV) Direct Current (DC) circuit breakers is crucial for the safety and reliability of electrical systems. Existing fault detection algorithms leverage deep neural networks (DNNs) to achieve high detection accuracy under various conditions. However, these methods often introduce considerable delays in fault detection, failing to meet the stringent time requirements for fault detection of UHV DC breakers. To resolve this issue, we propose a training and pruning framework designed to accelerate DNN-based detection models without compromising accuracy. Our framework treats the training of the detection model as a multi-objective optimization problem and utilizes the alternating direction method of multipliers (ADMM) to simultaneously train and prune the detection model. Moreover, since UHV DC breakers are high-value devices, it is infeasible to gather large amounts of fault case data. Therefore, we propose a self-supervised learning module for the proposed framework to pretrain the detection model using normal case data and finetune it using a small amount of fault case data. Experimental results demonstrate that the detection model trained with our framework surpasses baseline models in both mean average precision (98.7%) and inference latency (4ms), providing a more efficient and accurate solution for UHV DC circuit breaker fault detection.

Keywords: Fault detection · Neural network pruning · Self-supervised learning

1 Introduction

In the field of electrical engineering and power systems, the integration of UHV DC breakers represent a significant milestone, seamlessly combining various components. These UHV DC breakers are crucial for managing and protecting the DC power transmission network, making their performance vital to the stability and safety of the entire power system. Consequently, accurately measuring

J. Guo et al. (Eds.): IJCAI 2024, CCIS 2160, pp. 32–42, 2024.
https://doi.org/10.1007/978-981-97-6125-8_3

and evaluating the operation of DC circuit breakers has become a critical area of research in electrical testing. This situation underscores the need for innovative methods and systems to ensure their optimal performance and reliability, highlighting the importance of advancements in fault detection technologies.

Previously, researchers have leveraged classical machine learning algorithms, such as decision trees (DT), support vector machines (SVM), perceptrons, and logistic regression (LR), for fault detection. For instance, Zhao et al. utilized decision trees to classify fault events in UHV DC circuit breakers, achieving moderate accuracy under controlled conditions [17]. Similarly, Chen and Wang employed support vector machines for fault detection, noting improved performance over traditional methods but still facing challenges with varying operational conditions [3]. Despite the advancements, these methods cannot achieve satisfactory detection accuracy under diverse conditions such as various aging stages, different operational situations, and across multiple breaker types. Consequently, researchers have turned to DNNs for enhanced fault detection capabilities. Liu et al. demonstrated the use of convolutional neural networks (CNNs) to improve fault detection accuracy in UHV DC circuit breakers, achieving higher precision compared to classical machine learning models [9]. Moreover, Zhang et al. explored recurrent neural networks (RNNs) for real-time fault detection, reporting significant improvements in accuracy and robustness [15]. However, DNN models are prone to high latency, which is a critical issue for the fault detection of UHV DC breakers, where timely detection and intervention are paramount.

To resolve this issue, we propose a training and pruning framework designed to accelerate DNN-based detection models without compromising accuracy. Our framework treats the training of the detection model as a multi-objective optimization problem and utilizes the Alternating Direction Method of Multipliers (ADMM) to simultaneously train and prune the detection model. This approach optimizes both the model's complexity and performance, ensuring that the detection process is both fast and accurate. Moreover, since UHV DC breakers are high-value devices, it is infeasible to gather large amounts of fault case data. Therefore, we propose a self-supervised learning module for the proposed framework to pretrain the detection model using normal case data and finetune it using a small amount of fault case data. This self-supervised module leverages the inherent patterns in normal operational data to build a robust initial model, which is then refined with limited fault data to enhance fault detection capabilities.

Experimental results demonstrate that the detection model trained with our framework surpasses baseline models in both mean average precision and inference latency. The results highlight the potential of our framework to significantly improve the reliability and operational efficiency of UHV DC breakers.

2 Related Works

In the realm of DC circuit breaker measurement systems, significant advancements have been made particularly in overcoming the challenges associated with traditional methodologies. Historically, these systems have been hindered by a lack of cohesion and efficiency due to the fragmented nature of their measurement modules, as highlighted in various studies [2, 4]. This fragmentation impedes the streamlining of operations and diminishes the effectiveness of data processing and analysis, thereby limiting overall monitoring efficiency. Additionally, traditional approaches struggle to accurately measure the oscillation characteristics of DC circuit breakers, which are crucial for assessing their operational health [7]. This lack of precision prevents a comprehensive evaluation of the breakers' operational states.

Recent shifts in the field, however, have been towards integrating intelligent monitoring systems in electrical engineering [14]. The application of machine learning algorithms in intelligent monitoring has also shown promising results in fault detection and system optimization [6]. Furthermore, novel methods for measuring oscillation characteristics in UHV DC circuit breakers have been developed, emphasizing the need for accurate measurement techniques [18]. These developments highlight the trend towards more integrated and intelligent monitoring solutions in the field. There has been research focusing on advanced diagnostic techniques for DC circuit breakers. These techniques utilize sophisticated sensors and data analytics to diagnose potential issues proactively. For instance, a study by [8] demonstrated the use of ultrasonic sensors to detect mechanical faults in circuit breakers. With the increasing incorporation of renewable energy sources into the power grid, research by [10] explored how DC circuit breakers could be optimized for these new energy systems. Their work highlighted the need for adaptable measurement systems that can handle the variable outputs from renewable sources. The application of thermal imaging in monitoring the health of DC circuit breakers has been an area of interest. A study [11] showed how thermal cameras could be used to detect overheating issues in circuit breakers, which are indicative of potential failures. Moore recently, To capture the rapid transient processes in DC circuit breakers, studies like [16] have developed high-speed data acquisition systems. These systems are designed to capture and analyze transient phenomena that occur during circuit breaker operations, providing crucial insights into their performance. Here's also significant work in predictive maintenance models using AI and machine learning. For example, a study [13] presented a model that predicts circuit breaker failures based on historical performance data, allowing for timely maintenance actions.

Despite these advancements, there remains a gap in developing a fully integrated and highly accurate measurement framework that includes all essential modules, such as intelligent monitoring and optimization prompts. This gap presents an opportunity for further innovation, particularly in enhancing the operational efficiency and accuracy of UHV DC circuit breaker systems. Addressing these prevalent technological inadequacies, this paper introduces a groundbreaking detection algorithm and an integrated measurement system specifically designed for UHV DC circuit breakers. The proposed system represents a significant advancement by addressing and resolving the challenges inherent in existing technologies. By integrating advanced modules for intelligent monitoring and optimization, and improving the accuracy and efficiency of data processing and analysis, this new system offers a comprehensive solution poised to substantially elevate the standards of DC circuit breaker measurement and evaluation.

3   Methodology

3.1   Hardware Design and Data Acquisition

Circuit Monitoring Modeling Module. The circuit monitoring modeling module in the proposed system is designed to construct a comprehensive model for monitoring circuits. This is achieved by analyzing the connections within the circuit and subsequently generating a visual circuit monitoring panel platform. Additionally, the module is equipped with a remote connection interface, enabling the remote monitoring and control of DC circuit breakers. In terms of technical implementation of interface, the module utilizes front-end web technologies like HTML, CSS, and JavaScript to create its interface. It integrates pre-built components using Node-RED, facilitating rapid construction of processes and dashboards. For visualization and monitoring, the module employs Grafana [5], an open-source platform, which is combined with data source integration to create a robust circuit visualization platform. The hardware aspect of the DC circuit breaker includes an Arduino microprocessor for intelligent control. An IGBT is implemented to control the switching of electronic components. This setup allows for the automatic control of the electronic components within the DC circuit breaker through industrial control protocols specific to power grids. These components comprise a knife switch (SH), a circuit breaker (CBB), a DC high-voltage power supply (U), a capacitor bank (c), a Rogowski coil (CT), an oscilloscope (DSO), and a non-linear resistor (F). For enhanced control and operation, the ATK-LORA-01 LoRa module is incorporated to facilitate the pairing with tablets and mobile phones, allowing for more versatile operation of the instrument. In this task, we propose to use a conventional transformer-based model to identify the anomalies within the circuit connections. This model is trained on historical data of circuit behaviors to recognize normal and abnormal patterns, and it is particularly useful for circuit fault detection and maintenance.

Oscillation Test Module. The oscillation test module in our proposed system equips the DC circuit breaker with an intelligent control device, allowing for the input of commands and automated control of the circuit's components. This module performs the oscillation test three times, facilitating precise control over the testing process. Subsequently, the intelligent monitoring module deploys a sensor array to closely monitor various parameters of the DC circuit breaker. These parameters include oscillation frequency (f), capacitance value (C), attenuation coefficient (τ), and current data, all observed during the three oscillation tests. For technical execution, the module integrates an Arduino microprocessor within the circuitry of the DC circuit breaker. In conjunction with an IGBT and a power grid industrial control protocol, it facilitates automatic control over the electronic components of the DC circuit breaker. This automation extends to the operation of the knife switch (SH) and the circuit breaker (CB), including their opening and closing actions. It also manages the discharge of the DC high-voltage power supply (U) and the connection of the Rogowski coil (CT), ensuring that these components operate automatically under a consistent charging voltage from the capacitor bank. The module repeats the auxiliary loop oscillation characteristic test three times. During these tests, an oscilloscope (DSO) is used to record the first (f_1), second (f_2), and third (f_3) oscillation frequencies. The attenuation coefficient (τ) is determined through graphical analysis, and the capacitance values (C_1, C_2, and C_3) are calculated using the capacitor group (c). Moreover, the sensor array, which includes a charge sensor, a laser rangefinder, a time-measuring device, and a current sensor, is employed to monitor the current data accurately.

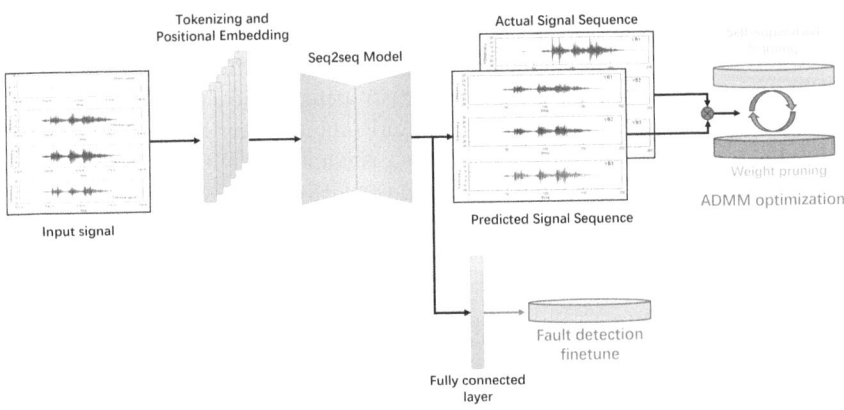

Fig. 1. Overall structure of the proposed training and pruning framework.

3.2   Overall Structure of the Proposed Framework

Given an input diagnosis signal $\mathbf{x} \in \mathbb{R}^N$, where N represents the input size, the training of the fault detection model can be formulated as an optimization problem:

$$\max_{\delta} g(f(\mathbf{x}, \theta)), \tag{1}$$

where $f(\cdot, \theta)$ is a deep neural network classification model with parameters θ. For inference purposes, $f(\cdot, \theta)$ can be simplified to $f(\cdot)$. The function $g(\cdot)$ is the loss function used to optimize δ in relation to $f(\cdot, \theta)$. Existing research methods either employ a small θ for quick inference or a large θ for high detection accuracy. Our proposed method addresses speed and accuracy as a multi-objective optimization problem, utilizing the ADMM optimization framework to achieve both high detection accuracy and fast inference speed simultaneously. The processing pipeline is illustrated in Fig. 1.

Alongside training the parameters θ for accuracy, the ADMM framework also optimizes θ to generate sparse intermediate feature maps and prune redundant parameters. It considers model detection accuracy as the primary optimization objective, with weight pruning as the regularization term. ADMM then iteratively updates the parameters to converge on the optimal solution.

Specifically, following the work of [12], we define the pruning indicator as:

$$\mathcal{R}(\delta) = \begin{cases} 0, & \text{if } \delta \in \mathbf{S}, \\ +\infty, & \text{otherwise} \end{cases} \tag{2}$$

where $\mathcal{R}(\cdot)$ is the indicator function used for weight pruning. In this work, we employ direct magnitude pruning to solve $\mathcal{R}(\cdot)$. Following the standard solving process of ADMM, we introduce auxiliary variables $\mathbf{Z}$. The optimization problem can then be formulated as:

$$\min_{\delta} g(\delta) + \sum_{\mathbf{Z}} \mathcal{R}(\mathbf{Z}),$$
$$s.t. \quad \delta - \mathbf{Z} = \mathbf{0}. \tag{3}$$

In Eq. 3, $\mathbf{Z}$ is the identical variable to θ, and the pruning process $\mathcal{R}(\cdot)$ and accuracy training process $g(\cdot)$ are coupled together, preventing the direct application of stochastic gradient descent methods. Thanks to ADMM, we introduce the augmented Lagrangian variable ρ and decompose Eq. 3 into sub-optimization problems without constraints. For the decomposition of Eq. 3, the first optimization sub-problem is:

$$\min_{\theta} g(\theta) + \frac{\rho}{2}||\theta - \mathbf{Z}^k + \mathbf{U}^k||_F^2 \tag{4}$$

ρ indicates the penalty factor for the constraint, $|| \cdot ||_F^2$ denotes the squared Frobenius distance calculation operation, and $\mathbf{U}^k$ is the dual variable updated iteratively as $\mathbf{U}^k = \mathbf{U}^{k-1} + \theta^k - \mathbf{Z}^k$. This eliminates the constraints of θ and $\mathbf{Z}$ in Eq. 3. In this formulation, θ and $\mathbf{Z}$ can be regarded as two models with the same architecture but different weights. During the iterative solving process, θ and $\mathbf{Z}$ can be modified individually and synchronously updated at the end of each iteration.

Considering $g(\cdot)$ as the objective function of a linear search method, the first term is the loss function, which is differentiable, and the second term is a quadratic regularization term, which is also differentiable and convex. Thus, the problem in Eq. 4 can be solved using stochastic gradient descent methods such as SGD, ADAM, etc.

Next, for Eq. 3, the second optimization sub-problem is:

$$\min_{\mathbf{Z}} \mathcal{R}(\theta) + \frac{\rho}{2}||\theta^{k+1} - \mathbf{Z} + \mathbf{U}^k||_F^2 \tag{5}$$

Since $\mathcal{R}(\cdot)$ is the indicator wrapper of the constraints, the primary task is to satisfy the constraints $\mathbf{S}$ to avoid obtaining a $+\infty$ value. Thus, the optimal solution for the first term $\mathcal{R}(\mathbf{Z})$ is to prune the desired number of weights in $\mathbf{Z}$ to meet the constraints $\mathbf{S}$. For the second term, to achieve the minimal value of the norm distance, the optimal solution is to project the variable $\mathbf{Z}$ onto $\theta^{k+1} + \mathbf{U}^k$. This can be formulated as:

$$\mathbf{Z}^{\mathbf{k+1}} = \{\mathcal{P}_S(\theta^{k+1} + \mathbf{U}^{\mathbf{k}})\} \tag{6}$$

where $\mathcal{P}_S(\theta^{k+1} + \mathbf{U}^k)$ indicates the Euclidean projection of $\theta^{k+1} + \mathbf{U}^k$ onto the subspace S. The calculated auxiliary variable $\mathbf{Z}^{k+1}$ is then used as a known parameter in Eq. 5 for the next iteration. Overall, the solving process of Eq. 5 and Eq. 6 alternates to form an iterative process.

3.3 Self-supervised Loss Function for Accuracy Training

The proposed training and pruning framework requires large amount of training data under fault operation condition. However, it is infeasible to fetch fault data from UHV DC breakers since they are high-value deceives. Therefore, we further propose a self-supervised accuracy training loss function for the proposed framework. By denoting the recorded temporal signal $\mathbf{x}$ as $[x_1, x_2, ..., x_T]$, we leverage sequence-to-sequence modelling and first certain amount of signal segment $[x_1, x_2, ..., x_m]$ to predict the succeeding signal segment $[x_{m+1}, x_{m+2}, ..., x_T]$. The loss function is designed as mean square error between the predicted and ground truth of the succeeding signal segment. In order to match this self-supervised learning architecture, we split the classification model into two parts. The first part is designed by transformer to achieve sequence-to-sequence prediction. The second part is a two-layer fully connected module for final classification output. In this way, the proposed framework can be firstly trained by large amount of data that is captured under normal operation condition. Then small amount of data that is capture under fault operation conditions can be used to finetune the pretrained model.

4   Experimental Results

4.1   Experimental Settings

We construct a comprehensive system as depicted in "Methodology" section. Within this system, the circuit monitoring modeling module employs HTML, CSS, and JavaScript to develop a user interface. It also utilizes Node-RED for the seamless integration of pre-existing components, expediting the creation of processes and dashboards. To further this development, we harness Grafana, which is an open-source platform dedicated to visualization and monitoring. In the realm of hardware, we configure an Arduino microprocessor [1] as an intelligent control device within the DC circuit breaker's circuitry. An Insulated Gate Bipolar Transistor (IGBT) is implemented for the switching of electronic components, facilitating the automated control of these components via an industrial control protocol designed for power grids. The circuit breaker is equipped with an array of electronic components including a knife switch (SH), a circuit breaker (CB), a DC high-voltage power supply (U), a capacitor bank c, a Rogowski coil (CT), an oscilloscope (DSO), and a non-linear resistor (F), all under automated control. Additionally, an ATK-LORA-01 LoRa module is installed to enable the control of the instrumentation through tablets and mobile phones, allowing for remote operation.

Next, the oscillation test module incorporates an Arduino microprocessor into the circuit of the DC circuit breaker. The Arduino microprocessor first activates the IGBT, which in turn closes the CB. Following this, c is completely discharged and safely grounded. Subsequently, the power grid's industrial control protocol is integrated into the circuit model to direct the operation of the CT, which is passed through the DC CB. The lead wire of the conversion reactor is then connected, after which the CT is restored and closed. The signal output end of the CT is connected to the oscilloscope. Once the safe ground connection of the c is removed, control is exerted over the DC circuit breaker to open it, while simultaneously the knife switch is closed via IGBT control, enabling the charging of the c to voltages of 200 V, 400 V, and 600 V in sequence. Then the Rogowski coil captures a minimum of five cycles of the oscillating current, which is displayed on the oscilloscope as a decay curve. A capacitance tester measures the capacitor bank's value, repeated thrice for an average. Under consistent charging voltages, the oscillation characteristic test of the auxiliary loop is performed three times, the oscillation frequency f is determined, and the attenuation time constant τ is derived. In the experiments, calculation results are rounded to two decimal places. Figure 2 represents the diagnosis signal under normal conditions.

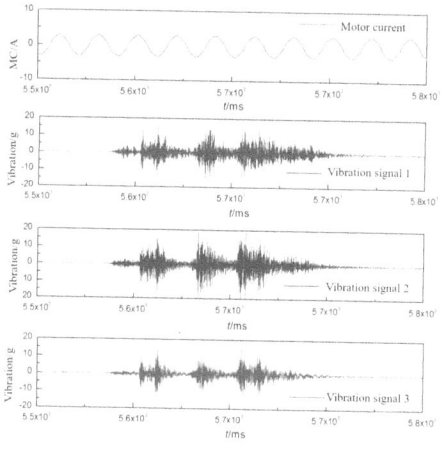

Fig. 2. The motor current and vibration signals.

4.2   Comparison Results

A significant dataset comprising 20,000 data points was half-half segmented into a training set and a testing set. The baselines are set as decision tree (DT), supported vector machine (SVM), logistic regression (LR), long short term memory machine (LSTM) and fully connected network (FC). Notably, the proposed diagnosis method outperforms all the baselines by large margins for both misalignment of contacts (MOC) and fatigue of the operating mechanism spring (FOMS) conditions.

Upon examining Table 1, it is clear that our method achieves a significantly higher average precision (AP) rate for both diagnostic conditions compared to the baseline models. Specifically, our method achieves an AP of 99.20% for MOC condition and 98.15% for FOMS condition. This indicates an improvement of over 6.03% points for the resistor condition and 7.40 points for the shaft condition compared to the next best model, the Long Short-Term Memory (LSTM) network, which scored 94.73% and 92.61%, respectively. The superior performance of our approach can be attributed to its robust feature extraction and anomaly detection capabilities, which leverage advanced transformer architectures optimized for sequence data. Additionally, the self-supervised learning component integrated within the model enhances its ability to distinguish between normal operational patterns and those indicative of specific faults, leading to more accurate and reliable fault diagnosis. These results validate the effectiveness of the proposed method in managing complex diagnostic scenarios in mechanical systems, offering a promising avenue for enhancing predictive maintenance strategies in industrial applications. The high precision of our method not only ensures reliable fault detection but also minimizes the likelihood of false alarms, which is critical for operational efficiency and safety. Our proposed method operates at 4 ms.

Table 1. Comparison results of the proposed method and baselines.

AP (%)	MOC	FOMS
DT	81.43	81.31
SVM	86.46	85.18
LR	86.77	85.40
LSTM	95.25	92.98
FC	93.72	91.51
Ours	**99.20**	**98.15**

Examining Fig. 3, which presents the proposed forecast results for fault diagnosis classification on long-used devices, reveals a nearly perfect alignment between the predicted classifications and the ground truth. The graphical representation shows that for most test set samples, the predicted class labels match the actual class labels, evidenced by the overlapping points. The horizontal axis of the graph represents individual test samples, while the vertical axis represents the class labels, which are binary or discrete values corresponding to different fault conditions. The single outlier, a misclassified loose resistor case, stands out as an exception to the otherwise consistent predictions. This deviation indicates that while the proposed model is highly accurate, there is still a small margin for error, likely due to data variability or slight overfitting to the training data. The model correctly identified 19 out of 20 loose resistor cases, achieving a 95% accuracy rate for these predictions. The overall high prediction accuracy of 98.3% demonstrates the model's robustness and the effectiveness of the proposed method.

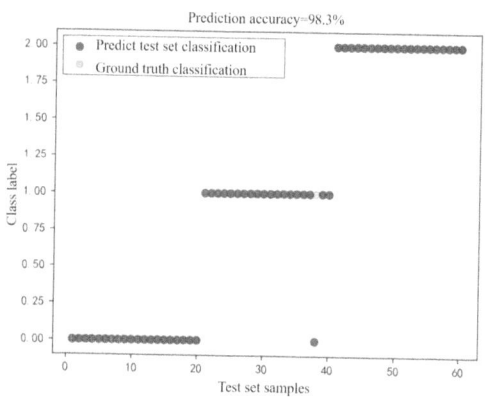

Fig. 3. Experimental results of fault diagnosis classification under aging condition.

5   Conclusion

In this research, we addressed the need for rapid and accurate fault detection in UHV DC breakers. We proposed a training and pruning framework using the ADMM to optimize both model complexity and performance, achieving a high mean average precision of 98.7% and an inference latency of 4 ms. Our framework also incorporates a self-supervised learning module to pretrain the model with normal operational data and fine-tune it with limited fault data. Experimental results confirmed that our approach outperforms baseline models, significantly enhancing the reliability and efficiency of UHV DC breaker fault detection. This improvement not only ensures timely and accurate fault detection but also reduces false alarms, crucial for the stability and safety of power systems.

References

1. Arduino: Arduino User Manual. Arduino (2022). https://docs.arduino.cc/
2. Brown, T., Miller, S.: Challenges in dc circuit breaker measurement systems: a fragmented approach. J. Power Syst. **22**(4), 456–467 (2018). https://doi.org/10.1016/j.jopsys.2018.04.003
3. Chen, L., Wang, Y.: Support vector machine for fault detection in UHV DC circuit breakers. IEEE Trans. Power Deliv. **34**(2), 1234–1241 (2019)
4. Davis, L., Nguyen, H.: Data processing in traditional DC circuit breaker systems: an analysis of inefficiencies. Electr. Eng. Q. **33**(2), 124–135 (2019). https://doi.org/10.1093/eeq/33.2.124
5. Grafana Labs: Grafana: The open observability platform (2023)
6. Johnson, R., Lee, Y.: Application of machine learning in intelligent monitoring of power systems. IEEE Trans. Power Syst. **36**(2), 950–962 (2021). https://doi.org/10.1109/TPWRS.2021.3057612
7. Kim, Y., Patel, D.: Evaluating oscillation characteristics in dc circuit breakers: traditional methods and limitations. IEEE Trans. Industr. Electron. **64**(5), 4102–4111 (2017). https://doi.org/10.1109/TIE.2017.2694341
8. Lee, J., Nguyen, T.: Advanced diagnostic techniques using ultrasonic sensors for dc circuit breakers. J. Electr. Eng. **58**(4), 205–213 (2019)
9. Liu, J., et al.: Convolutional neural networks for fault detection in UHV DC circuit breakers. IEEE Trans. Power Syst. **35**(3), 2567–2575 (2020)
10. Martinez, A., Lopez, B.: Optimization of DC circuit breakers for renewable energy integration. In: Proceedings of the International Conference on Renewable Energy Systems, pp. 112–119 (2022)
11. Patel, R., Kumar, S.: Thermal imaging for fault detection in DC circuit breakers. Int. J. Power Syst. **62**(1), 134–140 (2020)
12. Ren, A., et al.: ADMM-NN: an algorithm-hardware co-design framework of DNNs using alternating direction methods of multipliers. In: Proceedings of the Twenty-Fourth International Conference on Architectural Support for Programming Languages and Operating Systems, pp. 925–938 (2019)
13. Robinson, M., Ghosh, A.: Predictive maintenance models for DC circuit breakers using AI. In: Proceedings of the 2023 Conference on Artificial Intelligence in Power Systems, pp. 45–52 (2023)
14. Thompson, J., Garcia, A.: The rise of intelligent monitoring in electrical engineering. Int. J. Electr. Eng. Innov. **12**(1), 22–34 (2020). https://doi.org/10.1080/ijeei.2020.1029384
15. Zhang, H., et al.: Recurrent neural networks for real-time fault detection in UHV DC circuit breakers. IEEE Trans. Industr. Electron. **38**(1), 123–132 (2021)
16. Zhao, L., Wang, Y.: High-speed data acquisition systems for DC circuit breakers. J. Power Energy Eng. **67**(3), 300–307 (2022)
17. Zhao, W., et al.: Decision tree-based fault classification in UHV DC circuit breakers. J. Electr. Eng. **30**(4), 567–574 (2018)
18. Zhao, X., Wang, H.: Novel techniques for measuring oscillation characteristics in UHV DC circuit breakers. Int. J. Electr. Power Energy Syst. **125**, 106789 (2023). https://doi.org/10.1016/j.ijepes.2023.106789

Robust Autonomous Unmanned Aerial Vehicle System for Efficient Tracking of Moving Objects

Zhiwei Dong[1], Yang Yong[2], Zining Wang[3], Song-Lu Chen[1], and Xu-Cheng Yin[1(✉)]

[1] University of Science and Technology Beijing, Beijing, China
{songluchen,xuchengyin}@ustb.edu.cn
[2] SenseTime Research, Shenzhen, China
yongyang@sensetime.com
[3] Beihang University, Beijing, China
wangzining@buaa.edu.cn

Abstract. The autonomous unmanned aerial vehicle (AUAV) system has gained increasing attention due to its wide range of applications in various fields. However, integrating complex deep learning perception algorithms with autonomous navigation system on limited computing resources of UAV poses a significant challenge. In this paper, we propose a solution by leveraging the co-design of software and hardware in a heterogeneous computing system on the UAV, maximizing hardware resources including sensors. Building upon an existing autonomous navigation system, we integrate and optimize deep learning perception algorithms to create an autonomous, robust, and stable AUAV system for tracking moving objects. By achieving autonomy control with the limited resources on the UAV, we extend the usability, offering new possibilities for various domains such as agriculture, search and rescue, and infrastructure inspection.

Keywords: Autonomous Unmanned Aerial Vehicle · Object Tracking · Efficient AI model

1 Introduction

Unmanned aerial vehicles (UAV) or drone have emerged as versatile tools with applications spanning various fields. In agriculture, UAV are revolutionizing precision farming management by carrying sensors such as multi-spectral or thermal cameras. These cameras capture high-resolution images, enabling farmers to assess crop growth, detect pests and diseases, and optimize irrigation practices. For search and rescue missions, UAV provide invaluable support through rapid aerial reconnaissance. Equipped with real-time imagery and video capabilities, they aid in locating stranded individuals and guiding rescue operations. UAV also play a vital role in aerial photography, allowing photographers to capture stunning perspectives and aerial views. In infrastructure inspection, UAV facilitate the assessment of bridges, buildings, and power lines, reducing the risks associated with manual inspections. Furthermore, UAV find utility in geological exploration and weather monitoring, enabling researchers to gather data from remote and inaccessible areas. Overall, UAV continue to redefine the possibilities in

J. Guo et al. (Eds.): IJCAI 2024, CCIS 2160, pp. 43–50, 2024.
https://doi.org/10.1007/978-981-97-6125-8_4

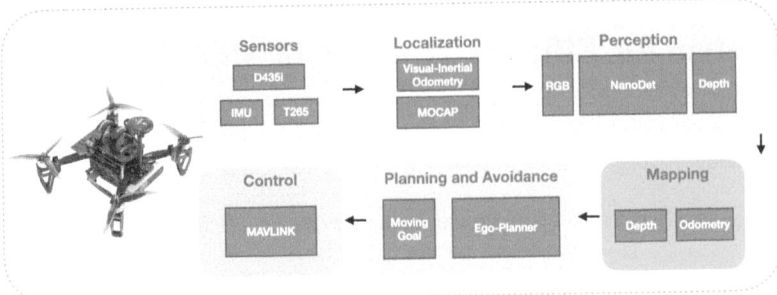

Fig. 1. The overall framework of our method. The six different modules include hardware module sensors and five software modules for localization, perception, mapping, planning and avoidance, and control, with descriptions of the sensors included or the specific functional packages used within the modules.

numerous domains, enhancing efficiency, safety, and data collection capabilities. Along with the rapid development of deep learning, UAV have become an important deep learning platform (Fig. 1).

In recent years, significant research efforts have been directed toward enhancing the intelligence and autonomy of UAVs. Researchers have focused on developing lightweight perception algorithms, precise localization methods, real-time mapping techniques, obstacle avoidance algorithms, and efficient flight control communication protocols. A notable study by [8] proposes an autonomous navigation system, that explores the utilization of various sensors, including LiDAR and cameras, to collect information about the UAV's surroundings. By employing real-time mapping, path planning, and obstacle avoidance algorithms, the system achieves effective obstacle recognition, path planning, and autonomous navigation for the UAV. This work represents a significant contribution to the advancement of UAV autonomy and highlights the potential for intelligent and self-guided UAV systems in various applications.

However, in practical applications, autonomous UAV systems require autonomous navigation systems to integrate with perception algorithms, typically based on deep learning. Nonetheless, the limited computing resources in UAV hardware systems pose significant challenges in deploying both autonomous navigation systems and complex perception algorithms. To address this, we have optimized the existing autonomous navigation system through a software and hardware co-design approach that leverages the heterogeneous computing resources available in UAV systems. This optimization enables a robust autonomous unmanned aerial vehicle system for tracking objects.

2   Related Works

2.1   UAV Hardware System

The hardware system of a drone includes basic components, flight controllers, onboard computers, and sensors. Specifically, the basic components consist of the frame, motors, propellers, and batteries, which form the main body of the drone and provide support for robotic form of drones. The flight controller is responsible for receiving and processing data from certain sensors, and it controls the motors to perform flight actions such as takeoff, landing, hovering, etc. It is mainly supported by an MCU (Microcontroller Unit). The onboard computer, with higher performance compared to the flight controller, is used to receive and process complex sensor data, perceive and make decisions, and communicate with the flight controller. Various types of sensors are commonly used, and drones are often equipped with multiple sensors. Common sensors include GPS, barometers, IMUs (Inertial Measurement Units), as well as various vision sensors such as LiDAR, RGB cameras, or infrared cameras.

2.2   UAV Software System

Based on the mentioned hardware system above, an autonomous drone system requires five essential modules: perception, localization, mapping, path planning and obstacle avoidance, and control.

Perception

The perception module relies primarily on vision or other sensors, including barometers, optical flow sensors, monocular, RGB or stereo cameras, infrared or near-infrared sensors, depth or LiDAR, as well as the fusion of multiple cameras or sensors. It encompasses the processing of sensor data using traditional or deep learning algorithms. For example, [5] is a lightweight detection solution that provides the ability to perceive specific types of objects and bounding box information using RGB images. Many perception algorithms are based on deep learning to handle complex sensor.

Localization

The localization module relies on both sensors and the results from the perception module, because with sensors alone may not provide direct localization capabilities. Localization methods include the use of IMU, which measures the drone's inertia to calculate the distance traveled in various directions and determine the drone's position. However, IMU errors accumulate over time and are generally not used in isolation. Compasses also assist in determining the orientation.

Additionally, common GPS systems can be used for drone localization, but outdoor GPS localization is typically accurate to the meter-level, and drones may experience significant drift during hovering. RTK (Real-Time Kinematic) technology addresses this issue by setting up a fixed RTK base station, allowing drones to achieve centimeter-level localization by performing differential calculations between GPS and RTK signals. Network RTK can be achieved without the need for a dedicated RTK base station by leveraging mobile network base stations with RTK capabilities, enabling centimeter-level outdoor positioning.

VIO (Visual Inertial Odometry) and LIO (Laser Inertial Odometry) are visual and LiDAR-based odometry methods, respectively. They track objects within the field of view to estimate the drone's relative position. LIO is relatively costly, while VIO currently performs well in indoor environments with clearly identifiable objects and has lower cost. Intel's RealSense T265 is a camera with an integrated computing stick that provides visual inertial odometry directly.

MOCAP (Motion Capture) involves attaching specific tracking markers to objects to obtain their positions through motion capture. Drones can employ MOCAP systems indoors, which offer higher accuracy but also come with higher costs. Lastly, the fusion of multiple sensors further enhances localization accuracy.

Mapping

The mapping module relies on perception and localization. It creates global or local maps based on the environment perceived at specific localization points. Mapping can be achieved by fusing data from depth point clouds, LiDAR point clouds, RGB data from stereo cameras, and other sources with localization data. In the case of outdoor autonomous driving vehicles, there are now high-precision maps available in certain areas, which can be fused with localization and perception data to get better map quality.

Path Planning and Obstacle Avoidance

Efficient and safe drone path planning with obstacle avoidance algorithms is a crucial component of autonomous UAV systems. In recent years, researchers have proposed various innovative path planning methods to enhance the flight capabilities and application scenarios of drones.

Based on classical search algorithms such as the A* algorithm, VFH*, and Dijkstra's algorithm, guidance for drone flight is provided by searching for the shortest or optimal paths in a graph. For example, a drone path planning method based on the 3DVFH* algorithm has been proposed in [1], which considers the influences of obstacles to achieve efficient path planning and obstacle avoidance. Additionally, [7] optimizes the A* algorithm by incorporating robot kinematics, improving the planning speed.

Sampling-based methods like the Rapidly-exploring Random Trees (RRT) algorithm and the Probabilistic Roadmap (PRM) algorithm construct feasible paths by sampling and connecting points in the configuration space. [6] combines machine learning techniques to improve the efficiency and adaptability of path planning by learning the features of existing paths.

In addition to traditional path planning methods, deep learning algorithms enable drones to learn complex flight patterns and path planning strategies from large datasets. [3] presents a drone path planning method based on deep reinforcement learning. This approach utilizes neural networks to learn flight strategies and optimizes path planning using reinforcement learning algorithms.

Control

The control module relies on the onboard computer, which makes the final decision based on perception algorithms and the surrounding environment. [4] and [2] can be used to send to the flight controller for controlling the drone's attitude, velocity, acceleration, heading, and other parameters.

3   Method

In this section, we begin by presenting an overview of the methodology and algorithms employed in this vanilla solution. Furthermore, we delve into the optimization process for performance enhancement on a resource-constrained UAV.

3.1   Vanilla Solution

Based on an existing autonomous navigation system by [7], which consists of a mapping module, path planning, and obstacle avoidance module. We enhanced the system by incorporating the Intel NCS2(Neural Compute Stick 2)in combination with OpenVINO for executing perception algorithms by [5] to generate moving goals. The RealSense T265 camera provides accurate and robust localization information.

Through MAVLink, the autonomous navigation system can send commands to the flight controller, enabling control of the drone's position and ensuring that it follows the planned trajectory and avoids obstacles during autonomous flight. These components form our vanilla solution.

3.2   Solution Optimization

However, simply combining these modules will not achieve the objective of a stable object tracking AUAV system. The drone will not be able to accurately locate objects in the physical world, and the flight commands will not be sent to the drone in real-time and with precision. We need to organically integrate and optimize these modules.

First, we improved the Ego-planner, which was originally designed for moving along predefined waypoints and couldn't continuously track moving objects. We observed issues such as stuck and program variable inconsistency during continuous updating goals. To address this, we modified the source code of Ego-planner to enhance its stability in continuous planning scenarios and ensured it didn't get stuck in failure loops during obstacle avoidance.

Furthermore, to enhance mapping and planning efficiency, we adjusted the inflation value in different directions and the mapping resolution to accommodate the non-spherical obstacle traversability of the drone and save more resources for perception algorithms.

Despite the fast execution of various modules in Ego-planner, the target information required for planning was slow, becoming the bottleneck. This meant that the UAV couldn't plan and issue accurate flight commands in a timely manner. To address this, we needed fast updates of planning targets, mapping, and localization information. While the RealSense T265 provided 200 Hz localization information, the other two components were considerably slower.

For planning targets, the perception algorithm received sensor inputs and detected objects. By using the camera's intrinsic parameters, we estimated the real-world coordinates based on the detected bounding boxes. Nonetheless, with only a monocular camera and non-spherical moving objects, accurately estimating the object's distance and calculating its coordinates proved challenging. To resolve this, we utilized the depth camera in the RealSense D435i to estimate the depth value of the central region of the object in the RGB camera, allowing us to estimate its real position. However, this alignment process slowed down the frame rate of the RealSense camera as it required additional calculations to align the depth and RGB images. This slowdown affected the data speed required for mapping. To optimize this, we aligned only the two corner points of the RGB detection results to the depth camera, rather than aligning the entire image, thereby speeding up this time-consuming step.

Table 1. Main results of our optimizing steps. "Vanilla" represents the direct combination of modules that does not work properly. "Organic" represents the optimization for moving object tracking. "PID" and "predict" respectively refer to the introduction of PID control and path prediction.

Method	Score	Stable Avoidance
Vanilla	–	No
Organic	0.79	No
Organic w/PID	0.93	No
Organic w/predict	0.96	Yes

Additionally, the perception algorithm wasn't solely dedicated to running deep neural networks but also involved a significant amount of time for image reshaping. To optimize this, we trained the deep neural network using native low-resolution camera images to minimize the reshaping time. We also employed quantization techniques to ensure the model ran on a low bit, preventing the perception algorithm from becoming a bottleneck during Ego-planner execution.

Through the optimization of the Ego-planner, perception algorithms, and the coordination of sensors and processors, we successfully achieved object tracking with the drone. We designed a metric to represent the stability of tracking by sampling the distance between the UAV and the tracked object at a fixed frequency, then calculating the average. When the distance is exactly 1 m, the highest score is 1.

$$score = 1 - \frac{|distance - 1|}{4}$$

While the tracking was accomplished, we still observed relatively low stability. Upon analysis, we identified two main issues. Firstly, the drone required time for perception and final control, resulting in an inability to track objects closely. Secondly, in cases where tracking was lost, the drone might lose sight of the target, leading to an incomplete tracking.

To address the first issue, we introduced PID control, a widely-used control algorithm that provides feedback control based on the deviation between the desired setpoint and the system's current output. By designing a PID system, the drone could achieve more stable tracking.

To tackle the second issue, we introduced a position prediction method to anticipate the target's position after it disappears. Specifically, we marked the trajectory of the object and set a goal point in the direction of the object's movement, rather than a point along the line connecting the drone and the object. This allowed the drone to perform evasive maneuvers and keep the tracked object in its view even if the object vanished laterally due to obstacles.

By incorporating these improvements, we further optimized the performance of the tracking system, ultimately achieving an average 0.96 obstacle avoidance performance and a stable and robust autonomous tracking system (Fig. 2).

Fig. 2. The real-world execution of our tracking system.

4   Experiments

In this section, we introduce the setup and how our optimization approach has improved tracking performance.

4.1   Experiment Setup

We utilized the PX4 Vision Dev Kit V1.5 as our drone, which is a cost-effective development kit widely employed in UAV development. The kit includes a Pixhawk 6C flight controller, which serves as the core control unit for the drone. The onboard computer is equipped with an Intel®Atom x5-z8350 processor capable of running at up to 1.92 GHz.

In terms of sensors, we incorporated the RealSense T265 and RealSense D435i cameras for indoor localization and perception. Additionally, we integrated an Intel NCS2 to facilitate the execution of deep learning-based perception algorithms. The NCS2 provides dedicated computational resources specifically tailored for accelerating and optimizing the performance of these algorithms.

Regarding the simulated world, we set up a tunnel along the path that obstructs the drone's flight. The moving object passes through the tunnel from below, and the drone needs to pass around the obstacle during the tracking process. The moving object follows a predefined pattern and passes through the tunnel twice while circling around it. We calculate the average score whole process at 30 Hz.

4.2   Main Results

Table 1 illustrates the performance improvements of our step-by-step optimization approach on the autonomous tracking system. The vanilla solution was not able to run directly, but through our final optimization scheme, we achieved an average score of 0.96.

5   Conclusion

By co-designing the software and hardware systems of the drone, we have effectively utilized the heterogeneous resources of the drone system, resulting in a stable and robust autonomous tracking system for moving object. Through the deployment of deep learning perception algorithms on resource-constrained drone systems and the optimization of overall system performance, we have expanded the scenarios of drone systems and demonstrated the feasibility of achieving complex autonomous control with limited resources.

Disclosure of Interests. The authors have no competing interests to declare that are relevant to the content of this article.

References

1. Baumann, T.: Obstacle avoidance for drones using a 3DVFH* algorithm. Spring Term **67** (2018)
2. Kříž, V., Gabrlik, P.: UranusLink - communication protocol for UAV with small overhead and encryption ability. IFAC-PapersOnLine **48**, 474–479 (2015)
3. Li, Y., Zhang, S., Ye, F., Jiang, T., Li, Y.: A UAV path planning method based on deep reinforcement learning. In: 2020 IEEE USNC-CNC-URSI North American Radio Science Meeting (Joint with AP-S Symposium), pp. 93–94. IEEE (2020)
4. Meier, L., et al.: MAVLink: micro air vehicle communication protocol. Tillgänglig (2013). http://qgroundcontrol.org/mavlink/start. Accessed 22 May 2014
5. Lyu, R.: NanoDet-Plus: super fast and high accuracy lightweight anchor-free object detection model (2021). https://github.com/RangiLyu/nanodet
6. Yang, K., Keat Gan, S., Sukkarieh, S.: A gaussian process-based RRT planner for the exploration of an unknown and cluttered environment with a UAV. Adv. Robot. **27**(6), 431–443 (2013)
7. Zhou, X., Wang, Z., Ye, H., Xu, C., Gao, F.: EGO-planner: an ESDF-free gradient-based local planner for quadrotors. IEEE Robot. Autom. Lett. **6**(2), 478–485 (2020)
8. Zhou, X., Zhu, J., Zhou, H., Xu, C., Gao, F.: EGO-swarm: a fully autonomous and decentralized quadrotor swarm system in cluttered environments. In: 2021 IEEE International Conference on Robotics and Automation (ICRA), pp. 4101–4107. IEEE (2021)

Efficient Fintuning with Limited Data

Entity Augmentation for Efficient Classification of Vertically Partitioned Data with Limited Overlap

Avi Amalanshu$^{(\boxtimes)}$, Viswesh Nagaswamy, G. V. S. S. Prudhvi, and Yash Sirvi

Autonomous Ground Vehicle Research Group,
Indian Institute of Technology Kharagpur, Kharagpur 721302, WB, India
avi.amalanshu@kgpian.iitkgp.ac.in

Abstract. Vertical Federated Learning (VFL) is a machine learning paradigm for learning from vertically partitioned data (i.e. features for each input are distributed across multiple "guest" clients and an aggregating "host" server owns labels) without communicating raw data. Traditionally, VFL involves an "entity resolution" phase where the host identifies and serializes the unique entities known to all guests. This is followed by private set intersection to find common entities, and an "entity alignment" step to ensure all guests are always processing the same entity's data. However, using only data of entities from the intersection means guests discard potentially useful data. Besides, the effect on privacy is dubious and these operations are computationally expensive. We propose a novel approach that eliminates the need for set intersection and entity alignment in categorical tasks. Our Entity Augmentation technique generates meaningful labels for activations sent to the host, regardless of their originating entity, enabling efficient VFL without explicit entity alignment. With limited overlap between training data, this approach performs substantially better (e.g. with 5% overlap, 48.1% vs 69.48% test accuracy on CIFAR-10). In fact, thanks to the regularizing effect, our model performs marginally better even with 100% overlap.

Keywords: Federated Learning · Vertical Federated Learning · Sample Efficiency

1 Introduction

Federated Learning (FL) [13] is a recent distributed machine learning strategy. FL aims to achieve communication efficiency and data privacy by never communicating the raw data. In FL, data-owning participants ("guests") train models on their local data, coordinated and aggregated by a label-owning "host". FL typically implies a "horizontal" distribution, where a participant holds its own set of samples within a global dataset. Vertical Federated Learning (VFL) is a variant where parties holding different *features* of the same samples collaborate

---

A. Amalanshu, V. Nagaswamy, G. V. S. S. Prudhvi and Y. Sirvi—Equal contribution.

J. Guo et al. (Eds.): IJCAI 2024, CCIS 2160, pp. 53–65, 2024.
https://doi.org/10.1007/978-981-97-6125-8_5

without pooling data to learn joint representations. This is essential for sensitive cross-institution collaborations, such as in healthcare, emphasizing the importance of aligning records to the same entities for cohesive, privacy-preserving model training.

VFL effectively splits the parameters of a global model across the network. The host has the deeper layers and makes a prediction at each training/inference iteration. For the prediction to be meaningful, all guests must have passed their features of the same entity. But, this means they must discard data on entities not known to all participants– potentially valuable for training local models. In systems with a small intersection, there may be insufficient samples to train a VFL model effectively, hindering VFL's scalability.

For example, cameras and traffic sensors at an intersection may struggle to detect crashes if the number of frames where the crash is visible to all cameras is small. The entity alignment process introduces significant computational overhead, hampering real-world VFL deployment at scale, affecting overall efficiency. Other challenges include data skew, where data distribution across entities varies drastically, and privacy risks during alignment despite VFL's principle of avoiding direct data sharing. This raises the question: are PSI and entity alignment truly necessary during training? (Fig. 1).

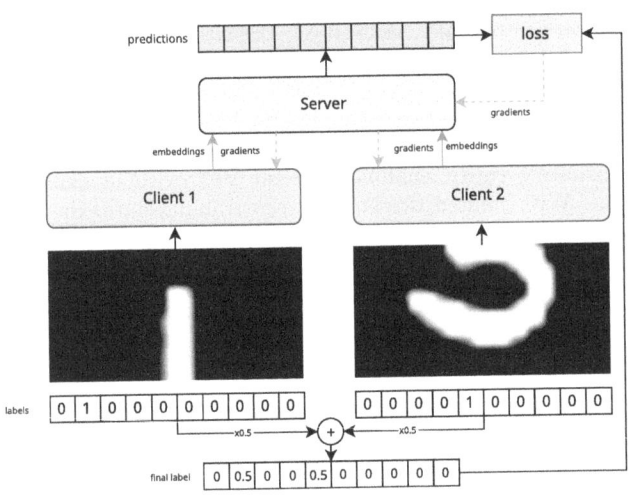

Fig. 1. Example forward pass with entity augmentation. Both clients forward activations from arbitrary inputs to the host, which is aware of the identity of said inputs. Half the features in the host input correspond to the number 1 and the other half correspond to 0. The interpolated label is their weighted average.

We introduce *Entity Augmentation*, a strategy for VFL that eliminates the need for PSI and entity alignment. Instead of agreeing on a single entity (or batch), the host computes a weighted average of labels for all entities processed by any guest. The weights are proportional to the total dimension of the input vector corresponding to each entity's features. Hosts may calculate meaningful losses for any activations received, as long as each corresponds to labelled entities.

In this paper, we:

- Propose Entity Augmentation, a novel strategy that interpolates labels for all entities sent by all guests, weighted by their contribution to the host input, synthesizing semantically coherent labels for guest activations.
- Demonstrate that VFL with Entity Augmentation achieves performance on par (better on some datasets) with VFL with entity alignment.

These empirical results indicate that Entity Augmentation is a viable alternative to traditional FL pipelines, offering substantial improvements in data utilization, computational efficiency, and ease of deployment.

2   Background

2.1   VFL Participants

Guests. Consider a consortium $\mathcal{G}$, comprising participants each with a distinct feature set. For a guest $i \in \mathcal{G}$, the dataset is $\mathcal{D}_i = \{\mathbf{x}_j \in \mathbb{R}^{|F_i|} : j \in \{1, 2, ..., |\mathcal{S}_i|\}\}$, where:

- $\mathcal{S}_i$ is the set of unique entities recorded in $\mathcal{D}_i$.
- F_i captures the attributes of these entities observed by guest i.
- Entities are considered samples from a distribution X.

The **guest model** $m_i(\cdot; \theta_i) : \mathbb{R}^{|F_i|} \to \mathbb{R}^{\text{out}_i}$ is defined by parameters θ_i.

These models aim to encode the features F_i of entities $\mathbf{x} \in \bigcap_{i=1}^{|\mathcal{G}|} \mathcal{S}_i$ for the host h to utilize in predictions, without sharing their model parameters or direct data features, including labels.

Host. The host h coordinates the training process, holding the label set $\mathcal{L} = \{\mathbf{y}_j \in \mathbb{R}^{\text{out}} : j \in \{1, 2, ..., |\mathcal{S}_h|\}\}$, where $\mathcal{S}_h$ is the set of unique entities with labels. A crucial intersection $|\mathcal{S}_\mathcal{G} \cap \mathcal{S}_h| > 0$ ensures shared entities for training.

The host model $m_h(\cdot; \theta_h) : \mathbb{R}^{\text{out}_1} \times \mathbb{R}^{\text{out}_2} \times ... \times \mathbb{R}^{\text{out}_{|\mathcal{G}|}} \to \mathbb{R}^{\text{out}}$ is parameterized by θ_h, aiming to minimize expected loss for optimal parameters $\theta = (\theta_1, \theta_2, ..., \theta_{|\mathcal{G}|}, \theta_h)$.

2.2   Entity Alignment

In VFL, coherence during training is ensured through data synchronization, formalized as $\mathcal{S}_\mathcal{G} = \bigcap_{i=1}^{|\mathcal{G}|} \mathcal{S}_i$. This uses a private set intersection (PSI, [12,14]) multiparty computation, preserving privacy while identifying intersecting entities across $\mathcal{G}$.

Following PSI, the host h processes $\mathcal{S}_{\mathcal{G}}$, ensuring uniform model training across the federated network. This step is vital for coherent aggregation of model updates, reflecting the collective knowledge of $\mathcal{G}$.

Without proper alignment, i.e., if $\mathcal{S}_{\mathcal{G}}$ is not established, issues like data inconsistency ($\mathcal{S}_i \not\subseteq \mathcal{S}_{\mathcal{G}}$ for any i) arise, leading to degraded model performance from training on non-corresponding entities. Additionally, without alignment, the federated model faces privacy vulnerabilities and inefficiencies in learning. Thus, Entity Alignment is crucial in vertical federated learning.

3   Related Work

3.1   Entity Resolution in Federated Learning

In the absence of unique IDs, the task of resolving common entities between datasets based on their features is called Entity Resolution. In 2017, Hardy et al. [5] introduced one of the first privacy-preserving strategies for learning from vertically partitioned data. The work proposes a pipeline of entity resolution, distributed logistic regression, and Paillier encryption to maintain privacy without noise addition. The authors demonstrate this works under certain entity resolution error assumptions without impacting model performance. This suggests certain errors do not alter optimal classifier performance.

Nock et al. [15] investigate the empirical impact of entity resolution errors on FL. The authors provide bounds on deviations in classifier performance due to these errors, and demonstrate the benefits of using label information with entity resolution algorithms.

3.2   Data Augmentation for Classification Generalization

CutMix [21] is a data augmentation technique used in image classification to enhance deep learning model training by combining parts of different images and their corresponding labels. Unlike traditional methods that process each image individually, CutMix creates new training examples by patching segments from multiple images together.

Given two images A and B, and their corresponding one-hot encoded labels $\mathbf{y}_A$ and $\mathbf{y}_B$, the CutMix process involves:

1. Randomly selecting a region R within image A.
2. Replacing region R in image A with the corresponding region from image B to generate a new training image A'.
3. Combining the labels proportionally to the number of pixels of each class present in the new image, resulting in a mixed label $\mathbf{y}' = \lambda \mathbf{y}_A + (1 - \lambda)\mathbf{y}_B$, where λ is the ratio of the remaining area of image A to the area of the original image.

Mathematically, for a region R with bounding box coordinates (r_x, r_y, r_w, r_h), the new training image A' is represented as:

$$A' = \begin{cases} B_{r_x:r_x+r_w, r_y:r_y+r_h} & \text{for } (i,j) \in R \\ A_{i,j} & \text{otherwise} \end{cases} \quad (1)$$

Here, (i, j) is the pixel location in the images. The label mixing coefficient λ is typically sampled from a Beta distribution, which controls the strength of the mixing.

CutMix improves model robustness and generalization by forcing the network to learn regionally informative features, rather than relying on specific patterns in the training set. This generates diverse examples within each mini-batch, helping to prevent overfitting.

3.3 Sample Efficient Vertical Federated Learning

Work on sample efficiency is scarce, despite its absence greatly limiting the applicability of VFL to carefully designed systems with significant overlap in sample spaces.

Sun et al. propose a method [17] to solve this problem. Following a few epochs of VFL training on aligned data, guests cluster their remaining datasets based on gradients received during the aligned training. The authors experimentally show that this approach is performant. However, as suggested by Amalanshu et al. [1] this is a form of privacy-breaching label inference attack.

In that paper, the authors present an unsupervised method of training guest models independently from host models, hence allowing them to exploit data outside the intersection without breaching privacy. However, task-relevant transfer learning still uses aligned datasets.

4 Proposed Method

VFL typically assumes that the input datasets for each model are "aligned," meaning that records are consistent across entities indexed in $\left(\bigcap_{i=1}^{|\mathcal{G}|} \mathcal{S}_i \right) \cap \mathcal{S}_h$. We propose a novel training approach for categorical tasks that allows each dataset to be sized $\min_{i \in \{1,...,|\mathcal{G}|\}} |\mathcal{S}_i \cap \mathcal{S}_h|$, or $\max_{i \in \{1,...,|\mathcal{G}|\}} |\mathcal{S}_i \cap \mathcal{S}_h|$ if guests may reuse data.

Extending the idea of the CutMix regularization, we propose entity augmentation for training the owner model. We construct artificial entity samples by combining features from various entities and averaging their labels. This approach enables training on a minimal subset of samples.

There are various ways such a scheme might be implemented. For instance, entity augmentation may be precomputed before training begins— the host may inform the guests which order to process their entities, and memoize the corresponding augmented labels. Alternatively, the augmented labels could be computed at training time as long as the host is aware of the identities of all the entities whose encoded features it has just received. Algorithm 1 outlines one way of achieving the latter for models trained via gradient-based algorithms.

Using a queue to store the latest activations and sample IDs, we also achieve some fault tolerance– if a guest fails to send an activation, the host simply uses the last one received. We outline the procedure for entity alignment and augmentation in categorical tasks.

The proposed method optimizes data use, enhancing the robustness and generalization of the learned models. Empirical results demonstrating the effectiveness of our approach, including in scenarios with deliberate sample misalignment, are presented in Sect. 5.

5   Experiments

To evaluate the effectiveness of the proposed algorithm, we conduct experiments on six different real-world datasets using three distinct architecture models in a SplitNN fashion. [2,4]. The experiments are divided into the following setups: (1) aligned data setup, where the dataset is entity-aligned; and (2) misaligned data setup, where the dataset is entity-augmented/misaligned. This division helps us mimic real-world scenarios where data may not always be perfectly aligned between clients.

We hope to demonstrate the following:

1. Entity Augmentation leads to meaningful learning, that is, Entity Augmentation allows us to exploit data outside the intersection $S_\mathcal{G} \cap S_h$ (namely, members of $\bigcup_{i=1}^{|\mathcal{G}|} (S_i \cap S_h)$).
2. Training on datasets with Entity Augmentation and without alignment outperform that on aligned datasets if there are sufficiently long-range semantic correlations.

We also provide a brief comparison to few-shot VFL [17] in Table 1.

5.1   Datasets

We use the following datasets and architectures for our experiments:

- **Computer Vision (CV) Datasets:** MNIST [10] and CIFAR-10 split into two guests. [9] with ResNet-18, ResNet-56 [6], and ResNeXt-29 (8x64d) [19].
- **Tabular Datasets:** Parkinsons [16] and Credit Card [20].
- **Multiview Datasets:** Handwritten Digits [3] and Caltech-7 [11].

The tabular and multiview datasets are divided evenly across four guests.

Algorithm 1. Neural Network Training with Entity Augmentation

---

Require: $\mathcal{D}_i \forall i \in \{1, 2, \ldots, |\mathcal{G}|, h\}$: Datasets of guests $i \in \mathcal{G}$ and host h
Require: $\mathcal{S}_i \ \forall i \in \{1, 2, \ldots, |\mathcal{G}|\}$: Serialized sets of of entities for which guests i have features
Require: $\mathcal{S}_h$: Set of entities for which the label owner has labels
Require: Label set $\mathcal{L} = \{\mathbf{y}_j \in \mathbb{R}^c : \mathbf{y}_j$ is the one-hot label for entity $\mathbf{x}_j\}$
Require: $\text{optim}_i \forall i \in \{1, 2, \ldots, |\mathcal{G}|, h\}$: parameter optimizer for each participant
Guest training iteration (for guest i)

  1: Retrieve the features $\mathbf{x}_{j,i}$ of the next entity $\mathbf{x}_j$ in its dataset
  2: Calculate guest model output $\mathbf{a}_i \leftarrow m_i(\mathbf{x}_{j,i}; \theta_i)$
  3: Send $\mathbf{a}_i$ and sample ID j to host
  4: Receive loss gradient $\nabla_{\mathbf{a}_i} \ell$ from the host
  5: Perform backpropagation to obtain $\nabla_{\theta_i} \ell$
  6: Calculate weight update $\theta_i \leftarrow \text{optim}_i(\nabla_{\theta_i} \ell, \theta_i)$

Server executes

  1: Initialize empty activation queues Q_i and label queues $Q_{\text{label},i}$ for each guest.
  2: **repeat**
  3:     **for** all guests $i \in \mathcal{G}$ in parallel **do**
  4:       Initiate guest training iteration   ▷ send $\mathbf{a}_i, j$
  5:       Add $\mathbf{a}_i$ to Q_i and j to $Q_{\text{label},i}$
  6:     **end for**
  7:     Read $\hat{\mathbf{a}}_i \forall i$ from the top of each Q_i
  8:     Calculate prediction $\mathbf{y} \leftarrow m_h(\hat{\mathbf{a}}_1, \ldots, \hat{\mathbf{a}}_{|\mathcal{G}|}; \theta_h)$
  9:     Read $\mathbf{j}_i \forall i$ from the top of each Q_{label_i}
 10:     Retrieve label $\mathbf{y}_{j_i} \forall j_i$ read
 11:     Form label $\mathbf{y} = \dfrac{\sum_{i=1}^{|\mathcal{G}|} w_i \mathbf{y}_{j_i}}{\sum_{i=1}^{|\mathcal{G}|} w_i}$ where w_i is the dimension of $\mathbf{a}_i$ ▷ Entity Augmentation
 12:     Compute loss ℓ
 13:     Perform backpropagation to obtain $\nabla_{\theta_h} \ell$ and $\nabla_{\mathbf{a}_i} \ell \forall i \in \{1, 2, \ldots, |\mathcal{G}|\}$
 14:     Send all gradients to their respective participants.
 15:     Calculate weight update $\theta_h \leftarrow \text{optim}_h(\nabla_{\theta_h} \ell, \theta_h)$
 16:     **for** all guests $i \in \mathcal{G}$ in parallel **do**
 17:       Complete guest training iteration
 18:     **end for**
 19: **until** convergence or a fixed number of iterations

5.2 Model Details

Models Used for VFL Datasets

Handwritten. Guests: linear(120) $\rightarrow$ linear(70) $\rightarrow$ ReLU; Hosts: linear(280) $\rightarrow$ linear(120) $\rightarrow$ LeakyReLU$\rightarrow$ linear(40) $\rightarrow$ linear(10)

CalTech-7. Guests: linear(512) $\rightarrow$ linear(256) $\rightarrow$ ReLU; Hosts: linear(1024) $\rightarrow$ linear(512) $\rightarrow$ linear(256) $\rightarrow$ LeakyReLU $\rightarrow$ linear(128) $\rightarrow$ linear(7)

Credit Card. Guests: linear(5) → linear(2) → ReLU; Hosts: linear(22) → linear(10) → linear(8) → linear(4) → linear(1)

Parkinsons. Guests: linear(94) → linear(47) → ReLU; Hosts: linear(94) → linear(47) → LeakyReLU → linear(22) → linear(10) → LeakyReLU → linear(1)

Guest-Host Model Splits for ResNet-Like Models

For all our CV models (ResNet-18, ResNet56, ResNeXt-29 8x64), each guest owns its own CNN filter as well as half of the first fully connected layer. The remaining fully connected layers are owned by the host.

5.3   Nomenclature

We will use the following terminology for the remainder of the paper

- **Aligned Data**: Refers to entity-aligned/private set intersection data. For example, in the case of two clients, each client inputs corresponding parts of the same image into their respective models.
- **Misaligned Data**: Refers to intentionally misaligned data– the members and order of the "misaligned" sample space are different for each guest. In this case, clients input parts of different images into their respective models.

5.4   Experimental Setup

Exploiting Data Outside the Intersection. To evaluate the effect of entity augmentation, we propose an experiment where the dataset is divided into $x\%$ entity-aligned data and $\frac{(100-x)}{2}\%$ misaligned data for two clients. That is to say, we have $x\%$ of the dataset aligned between the two guests. where corresponding parts of the data are assigned to each client. The remaining $(100 - x)\%$ is shuffled and **split evenly** between the two clients, i.e. each client gets a slice from a totally non-overlapping subset of the sample space. We attempt to train a split neural network with just the aligned data and investigate the impact on performance when the misaligned data is also used via Entity Augmentation.

Entity Alignment vs Misaligned Augmentation. To test the hypothesis that training on misaligned data can outperform aligned data given long-range semantic correlations, we conduct experiments on fully aligned and intentionally misaligned data. For each dataset, we train models on both aligned and misaligned data. We compare the performance of the models to assess if misaligned data with sufficient long-range semantic correlations can lead to better learning outcomes. The results of these experiments demonstrate the impact of data alignment on model performance and the improved performance of entity augmentation.

5.5   Implementation Details

For the CV datasets, we apply the proposed algorithm using ResNet and ResNeXt architectures. For tabular and multiview datasets, we employ the SplitNN architecture. Each experiment is run for 60 epochs, with two guests for the CV and tabular datasets. For multiview datasets, we set the number of guests to be equal to the number of views. We implement our models in PyTorch and train them to minimize binary cross entropy loss. The PyTorch implementation internally calculates a sigmoid. We use the Adam optimizer with $\beta_1 = 0.9, \beta_2 = 0.999$. We use a learning rate of 0.001 for all CV experiments, 0.1 for both multiview datasets, and 5×10^{-4} for both tabular datasets.

Table 1. We compare our method to the results on vanilla VFL and 5-shot VFL due to Sun et al. [17] using the same model. We measure accuracy when a certain number of training samples (denoted in the table as $|\cap \mathcal{S}|$) overlap between the guests, and the remaining samples are split evenly between the two. The host is assumed to know labels for all samples. Entity Augmentation cannot exploit as many samples as few-shot VFL but significantly more than standard VFL, and as a result is performant without requiring guests to guess private labels.

Method	Samples Used	Privacy	Accuracy (%) at $|\cap\mathcal{S}|$			
			256	512	1024	2048
Entity Aug. (Ours)	$\bigcup\limits_{i=1}^{|\mathcal{G}|} \mathcal{S}_i \cap \mathcal{S}_h$	✓	67.82	73.35	73.87	74.25
Few-shot VFL [17]	$\bigcup\limits_{i=1}^{|\mathcal{G}|} \mathcal{S}_i$	✗	78.93	83.03	85.68	87.23
Standard VFL [17]	$\mathcal{S}_h \cap \left(\bigcap\limits_{i=1}^{|\mathcal{G}|} \mathcal{S}_i \right)$	✓	31.47	35.33	42.71	50.75

6   Results and Discussions

Entity Alignment vs Misaligned Augmentation. Our experiments with entity augmentation, as shown in Tables 2 and 3, demonstrate that our method achieves comparable results on the MNIST dataset and improved performance on the CIFAR, Handwritten, Caltech-7, Credit Card and Parkinson's datasets. This is not unexpected since Entity Augmentation is functionally a form of CutMix, which has been shown to have a regularizing effect. [21]

MNIST, with its single color channel and simpler, well-defined shapes, presents fewer long-range feature variations compared to datasets with complex imagery. For instance, a straight line in the top quarter could ambiguously belong to a 5 or 7. Thus, performance gains from CutMix are less pronounced on MNIST.

Table 2. Accuracy comparison between entity aligned and entity misaligned data with Entity Augmentation on MNIST and CIFAR datasets.

Dataset	Architecture	Accuracy	
		Aligned	*Misaligned*
CIFAR10	ResNet-18	72.92%	74.34%
	ResNet-56	77.09%	79.12%
	ResNeXt-29 8x64	81.08%	82.06%
MNIST	ResNet-18	99.25%	98.20%
	ResNet-56	99.34%	98.44%
	ResNeXt-29 8x64	99.12%	98.43%

Table 3. Accuracy comparison between training on entity-aligned data vs entity augmented misaligned data on the view-partitioned datasets Handwritten and Caltech-7, and the vertically partitioned tabular datasets Credit Card and Parkinsons.

Dataset	Aligned	Misaligned
Handwritten	98.25%	98.63%
Caltech-7	98.98%	98.98%
Credit Card	81.55%	81.95%
Parkinsons	86.34%	87.22%

Exploiting Data Outside the Intersection. From the results of our experiment in Table 3, it is visible that when only a tiny entity-aligned dataset is available, using entity misaligned/augmented data (i.e., with no private set intersection) along with it for training provides better performance compared to training only on the aligned dataset. These results clearly support our claim that entity-misaligned/augmented data is helpful for training and results in better performance than only using entity-aligned data, resulting in seamless integration of diverse data sources, reduced data wastage, and enhanced model learning efficiency (Table 4).

Table 4. Accuracy comparison between training a ResNet–18 on only a small intersection of entity-aligned data vs that entity-aligned data combined with entity augmented misaligned data on MNIST and CIFAR datasets.

Dataset	Accuracy	
	Aligned	*Aligned + Misaligned*
CIFAR10 ($x = 5\%$)	48.1%	69.48%
MNIST ($x = 5\%$)	97.1%	98.37%
CIFAR10 ($x = 10\%$)	54.34%	70.4%
MNIST ($x = 10\%$)	97.92%	98.5%

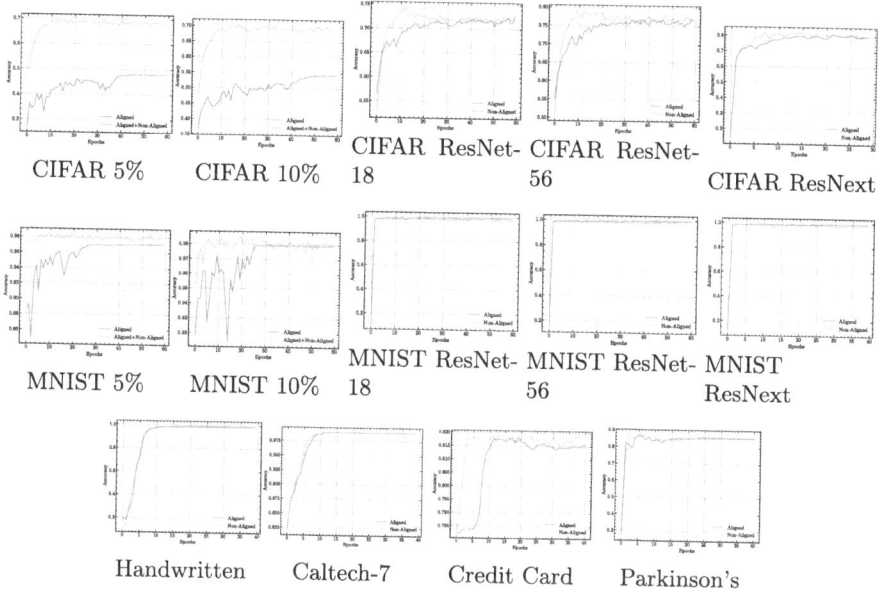

CIFAR 5%   CIFAR 10%   CIFAR ResNet-18   CIFAR ResNet-56   CIFAR ResNext

MNIST 5%   MNIST 10%   MNIST ResNet-18   MNIST ResNet-56   MNIST ResNext

Handwritten   Caltech-7   Credit Card   Parkinson's

Fig. 2. Training Curves for CIFAR, MNIST, Handwritten, Caltech-7, Parkinson's, and Credit Card datasets. Significant convergence improvements are observed with our method on CIFAR and MNIST. The efficacy extends to datasets like Handwritten, Caltech-7, Credit Card, and Parkinson's.

More Efficient Training. Figure 2 reveal that Entity Augmentation not only boosts the skyline performance of VFL models, but also allow them to converge substantially faster. Experiments using only $x\%$ aligned data plateaus at a much lower accuracy *and* at a far earlier epoch. A similar trend may be seen in our experiments on fully aligned vs fully misaligned data. Another interesting phenomenon is the stability of training– the test accuracy is qualitatively smoother and more stable wherever Entity Augmentation is used.

7   Future Work

The proposed method shows promising results for training pipelines where the label can be represented in a one-hot encoded fashion. Subsequently, we seek to extend the idea of generating synthetic labels for regressive tasks. In this light, Verma et al. [18] investigate the potential of swapping weights in the penultimate layer to create samples through inference. Expanding upon this, Hwang et al. [7] use linear interpolation and constrained sampling for data augmentation. Furthermore, Jiang et al. [8] employ Gaussian Mixture Models to facilitate the generation of synthetic and continuous sensor data. Our future endeavours will focus on incorporating such augmentation techniques within the Vertical Federated Learning (VFL) framework. This integration seeks to optimize the utilization of data that lies beyond the confines of the Private Set Intersection, thereby enhancing the efficiency and effectiveness of the VFL pipeline for regressive tasks.

8   Conclusion

This work presents Entity Augmentation, a strategy for generating semantically meaningful labels for guest activations without entity alignment. We interpolate labels weighted by features to synthesize labels for training. We subsequently demonstrate that our pipeline achieves performance on par with traditional FL approaches that require entity alignment. Our evaluations on the CIFAR10 and MNIST datasets showed improved results across various baseline architectures, and we achieved competitive results on Handwritten, Caltech-7, Parkinsons and Credit Card datasets. In future, we seek to extend the augmentation technique to regressive tasks and experiment with Gaussian mixture models and constrained sampling.

References

1. Amalanshu, A., Sirvi, Y., Inouye, D.I.: Decoupled vertical federated learning for practical training on vertically partitioned data (2024). arXiv:2403.03871
2. Ceballos, I., Sharma, V., Mugica, E., Singh, A., Roman, A., Vepakomma, P., Raskar, R.: Splitnn-driven vertical partitioning. arXiv:2008.04137 (2020)
3. Dua, D., Graff, C.: UCI machine learning repository (2017). http://archive.ics.uci.edu/ml
4. Gupta, O., Raskar, R.: Distributed learning of deep neural network over multiple agents. J. Netw. Comput. Appl. **116**, 1–8 (2018). https://doi.org/10.1016/j.jnca.2018.05.003
5. Hardy, S., et al.: Private federated learning on vertically partitioned data via entity resolution and additively homomorphic encryption. arXiv:1711.10677 (2017)
6. He, K., Zhang, X., Ren, S., Sun, J.: Deep residual learning for image recognition. arXiv:1512.03385 (2015)
7. Hwang, S.H., Whang, S.E.: RegMix: data mixing augmentation for regression. arXiv:2106.03374 (2022)
8. Jiang, X., Yao, L., Yang, Z., Song, Z., Shen, B.: Gaussian mixture model and double-weighted deep neural networks for data augmentation soft sensing. In: 2023 IEEE 12th Data Driven Control and Learning Systems Conference (DDCLS), pp. 1914–1919 (2023). https://doi.org/10.1109/DDCLS58216.2023.10166693
9. Krizhevsky, A.: Learning multiple layers of features from tiny images. Technical report (2009)
10. LeCun, Y., Cortes, C., Burges, C.: MNIST handwritten digit database. ATT Labs **2** (2010). http://yann.lecun.com/exdb/mnist
11. Li, F.F., Andreeto, M., Ranzato, M., Perona, P.: Caltech 101 (2022). https://doi.org/10.22002/D1.20086
12. Lu, L., Ding, N.: Multi-party private set intersection in vertical federated learning. In: 2020 IEEE 19th International Conference on Trust, Security and Privacy in Computing and Communications (TrustCom), pp. 707–714 (2020). https://api.semanticscholar.org/CorpusID:231916141

13. McMahan, B., Moore, E., Ramage, D., Hampson, S., Arcas, B.A.: Communication-efficient learning of deep networks from decentralized data. In: Singh, A., Zhu, J. (eds.) Proceedings of the 20th International Conference on Artificial Intelligence and Statistics. Proceedings of Machine Learning Research, vol. 54, pp. 1273–1282. PMLR (2017). https://proceedings.mlr.press/v54/mcmahan17a.html

14. Morales, D., Agudo, I., Lopez, J.: Private set intersection: a systematic literature review. Comput. Sci. Rev. **49**, 100567 (2023). https://doi.org/10.1016/j.cosrev.2023.100567, https://www.sciencedirect.com/science/article/pii/S1574013723000345

15. Nock, R., et al.: Entity resolution and federated learning get a federated resolution. arXiv:1803.04035 (2018)

16. Sakar, C.O., et al.: A comparative analysis of speech signal processing algorithms for Parkinson's disease classification and the use of the tunable Q-factor wavelet transform. Appl. Soft Comput. **74**, 255–263 (2019)

17. Sun, J., et al.: Communication-efficient vertical federated learning with limited overlapping samples. In: Proceedings of the IEEE/CVF International Conference on Computer Vision (ICCV), pp. 5203–5212 (2023)

18. Verma, V., et al.: Manifold mixup: better representations by interpolating hidden states. arXiv:1806.05236 (2019)

19. Xie, S., Girshick, R., Dollár, P., Tu, Z., He, K.: Aggregated residual transformations for deep neural networks. arXiv:1611.05431 (2017)

20. Yeh, I.C., Lien, C.H.: The comparisons of data mining techniques for the predictive accuracy of probability of default of credit card clients. Expert Syst. Appl. **36**(2), 2473–2480 (2009)

21. Yun, S., Han, D., Oh, S.J., Chun, S., Choe, J., Yoo, Y.: CutMix: regularization strategy to train strong classifiers with localizable features. arXiv:1905.04899 (2019)

CafeLLM: Context-Aware Fine-Grained Semantic Clustering Using Large Language Models

Ryan Yuki Huang[1,2] 🆔 and Colin Robert Small[2(✉)] 🆔

[1] Brown University, Providence, RI 02912, USA
ryan_y_huang@brown.edu
[2] ModernVivo Inc., Seattle, WA 98164, USA
colin@modernvivo.com

Abstract. Text clustering is crucial for users like researchers aiming to organize large collections of textual data. However, textual data are often unstructured and esoteric in many domains, presenting unique challenges that conventional named entity recognition (NER) or clustering methods fail to address. Here, we present CafeLLM, a Context-Aware Fine-grained clustering method that uses Large Language Models (LLMs) to cluster terms or phrases from these specialized textual datasets based on a given context. CafeLLM leverages the robustness of LLMs to generalize efficiently from textual data, enabling the clustering of semantically identical text values without the need for extensive labeled training data. The approach works in two phases: extraction and clustering. In the extraction phase, each text is reframed by extracting key information based on the user-provided context. In the clustering phase, texts are paired in an iterative process to determine if they belong in the same cluster. Overall, we empirically demonstrate that CafeLLM is effective in clustering fine-grained and specialized textual datasets, providing users with a tool to automate and streamline the organization of such data. By addressing the challenge of efficient generalization from limited resources, CafeLLM contributes to advancing real-world AI applications in natural language processing.

Keywords: Text Clustering · Large Language Models (LLMs) · Semantic Analysis

1 Introduction

Text clustering is a fundamental task in natural language processing (NLP) that plays a pivotal role in organizing and extracting meaningful insights from vast collections of textual data [12]. By grouping similar words or documents together based on their content, text clustering facilitates various downstream applications, including document organization [1], information retrieval [13], and recommendation systems [3] (Fig. 1).

Current text clustering methods employ pre-trained embedding models such as word2vec [15] and Bidirectional Encoder Representations from Transformers

J. Guo et al. (Eds.): IJCAI 2024, CCIS 2160, pp. 66–81, 2024.
https://doi.org/10.1007/978-981-97-6125-8_6

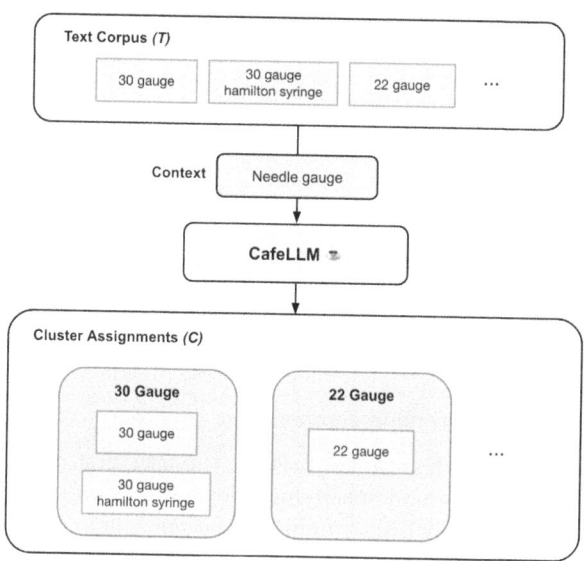

Fig. 1. CafeLLM Framework Overview. CafeLLM takes in a fine-grained text corpus T and the context to extract underlying meanings of text. Text with the same meaning form clusters in C.

(BERT) [4]. Once these representations of text are computed, clustering algorithms like K-means, fuzzy C-means, or hierarchical clustering are commonly utilized to partition the texts into coherent groups [18]. However, these frameworks can only cluster textual data based on the representation extracted by the model. In practice, many users want to cluster data based on the underlying meaning of the text, or in other words, by what is signified in its context. For example, consider the scenario where two patients express similar experiences of hair loss but word it differently [7]:

– "My hair is falling out in huge amount".
– "My shower drain is full of hair every time".

Pre-trained embedding models, while adept at capturing surface-level semantic features of text, often fail to fully discern these similarities in texts that require understanding of nuanced meanings. Furthermore, these prior methods fail to consider the context by which the user is interested in clustering the text. For example, OpenAI's GPT-4 Turbo model [17] embeds the statement "my head hurts when I get out of bed in the morning" more closely to "my stomach hurts when I get out of bed in the morning" than "I get headaches every morning" by cosine similarity, which would be undesired if a user is interested in grouping statements according to patients' chief complaints.

With rapid advancements in natural language processing (NLP), particularly with Large Language Models (LLMs), there's been a paradigm shift in how we are able to approach text processing. LLMs have been cited to handle a wide array of natural language tasks, including comprehension, summarization, and reasoning [22].

1.1 Our Contribution

In this paper, we present CafeLLM, a framework that uses LLMs to cluster a set of texts given a context by which those texts should be grouped. To define this task formally, let T be a set of terms or phrases t such that $T = \{t_1, t_2, ..., t_n\}$ and C be a set of term/phrase clusters c, initially empty as $C = \emptyset$. Our task is to iteratively assign each $t \in T$ to a cluster $c \in C$ according to their semantic meaning or to create a new cluster c if t does not belong in the existing clusters $c \in C$.

CafeLLM is built on two main components:

1. Context-Based Text Extraction. Here, the user first defines the context by identifying the objective and specifying relevant keywords by which to cluster. For example, if a user wishes to cluster patient chief complaint data into like groups, they would define context as "patient affliction" to extract the disease that the patient is complaining about. After the context is defined, we prompt the LLM to extract relevant information from each terms or phrases t in the corpus based on this user-provided context. For example, we may ask the LLM to <Extract the {patient affliction} from {"My hair is falling out in huge amount."}>. This allows the language model to identify and extract specific information, such as the patient affliction in the given example, from unstructured text data. By first distilling the original terms and phrases down to what is relevant to the provided context, we help the model focus on the following clustering task.

2. LLM Clustering. After the extraction task, we use pairwise comparisons to evaluate whether two values should be in the same cluster. This is achieved by asking the LLM whether $< t$ is equal to a $t \in C$ based on {context}>. Here, we iteratively prompt this to the LLM until t either finds an equivalent pre-clustered value, $t \in C$, or until no more comparisons can be made.

To reduce computational costs of these pairwise comparisons, we employ two key strategies. First, every unclustered value t is only compared to one representative value $t \in c$ per cluster c. Furthermore, to make the methodology more deterministic, we use the first value t that was placed into a cluster c as the representative value for comparison. The other strategy employed here is a heuristic ordering of pairwise comparisons. Specifically, let t_{uc} denote an unclustered value and $t_{c,i}$ denote the representative value of cluster c_i. In this strategy, the unclustered t_{uc} and every $t_{c,i}$ are first embedded using a pre-trained embedder. Then, we perform $t_{uc} : t_{c,i}$ comparisons in ascending order of the cosine similarity of $emb(t_{uc})$ and $emb(t_{c,i})$. Even though pre-trained embedding themselves can only capture semantics and not underlying meanings, we find experimentally that using this heuristic can decrease computation times by 36.4% on average across the datasets used in this paper.

To evaluate our framework, we used two main datasets, the "Patient Comments and Specialist Types" (*PCAST*) dataset from [7] and a new dataset curated from extracting needle gauges (*NG*) used in published preclinical animal trials for drug discovery. Additionally, we present ablation studies to analyze the generalizability of the CafeLLM framework across a variety of LLM models.

Overall, we make the following contributions:

1. We introduce CafeLLM, a Context-Aware Fine-Grained clustering framework that uses LLMs to understand the underlying meaning of texts in context for more purposeful groupings.
2. We demonstrate the robustness of LLMs to effectively cluster large sets of textual data.
3. We offer a solution for users to fully automate the clustering of noisy and unstructured text data without needing extensive prior knowledge, such as the number of clusters.

2   Related Works

Pre-trained Embeddings. Presently, pre-trained embedding models remain a popular choice when paired with algorithms such as K-means to accomplish text clustering. This workflow has been employed for fine-grained datasets in various fields from neuroscience to music [6,16,20,21]. Notably, Gu et al. have used this framework to cluster similar datasets to this paper [6]. They used a BERT model and then DBSCAN to cluster named-entities in their medical term dataset, grouping together terms like "difficulty breathing" and "difficult to breathe". However, these methods often lack mechanisms to deal with more noisy text that can affect the representation extracted from the pre-trained embedding model [5]. To extract necessary information from noisy texts, studies have used pre-trained Name Entity Recognition (NER) models [8,11]. However, they often fail with unstructured or esoteric terms and can only be used for domain-specific tasks that they are trained on. In contrast, CafeLLM is able to extract key information from any unstructured text without any pre-trained models an d automatically form new clusters from a text corpus.

LLMs Paired with Embedding Models. Other prior works have stacked LLMs on top of the above approach to fix issues present in pre-trained embedding models. A recent method by Zhang et al. have used LLMs to fix clusters made by using classical clustering algorithms on text embeddings extracted by a pre-trained embedder [23]. First, it uses an entropy-based sampling strategy to prompt the LLM with triplet tasks, refining the clustering perspective; then, it determines clusters through hierarchical clustering and guidance from an LLM. Viswanathan et al. have discovered that LLMs can help in correcting clusters made by embedding models and in extracting features before clustering [19]. It is demonstrated in both studies that LLMs are particularly effective in guiding clustering decisions and in information extraction. Yet, these methodologies still in-large rely on the representation from the pre-trained embedding model. They alo don't consider the context of the text corpus, which is vital for extracting and, subsequently, clustering underlying meanings in text [9].

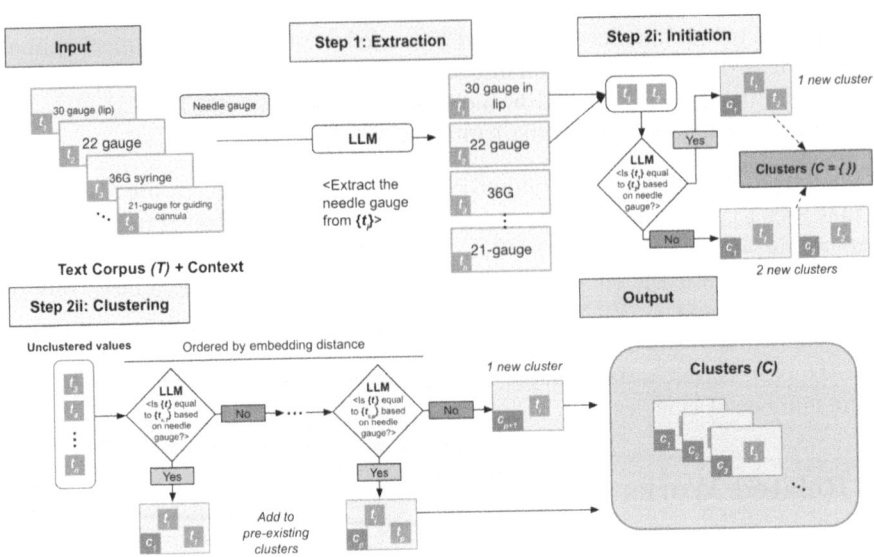

Fig. 2. CafeLLM Workflow. Starting with a set of text and a context like "needle gauge", we prompt an LLM to extract the needle gauge from all $t \in T$. Then, in the initiation step, we populate the set of clusters C (initially $\emptyset$) by evaluating whether the first two text values are equal based on needle gauge via LLM prompting. This sets up the pairwise comparison in the clustering step, where we cluster $t_3, ..., t_n$ by comparing each with a representative values $t_{c,i}$ in each $c \in C$. This results in the output, including all newly formed clusters.

LLM-Based Clustering. The sole use of LLMs for clustering has been studied by Kwon et al., who built a framework to cluster images based on a text criteria using Vision Language Models (VLMs) and LLMs [10]. They use a text criteria like "image location", a set of images, and the number of clusters as input for their framework. Then, their framework is able to output all the images that belong to each cluster, demonstrating that LLMs are able to cluster groups of texts into predetermined clusters. Moreover, they show that the use of a criteria can help group texts in a way that is more interpretable and that satisfies user needs. However, much like a handful of prior methods, a core issue is that this framework requires foresight about the dataset to predetermine how many clusters exist in the dataset–a requirement that CafeLLM removes altogether.

3   Approach

This section introduces the details of the CafeLLM framework, which works in two phases as shown in Fig. 2. The first phase involves an extraction step: each text is denoised and extracted to represent its meaning in context. Then, the text is clustered using pairwise comparisons ordered by embedding similarity.

3.1   Context-Based Extraction

Here, we show how our framework is able to turn unstructured, noisy text into text that captures its meaning in context by taking advantage of an LLM's ability to extract information. The extraction task uses an LLM extraction prompt P_E that takes in a text value t from the corpus T and the context as input. Then, it outputs t_E, the corresponding text value that has been properly extracted and structured. This extraction task is performed on all $t \in T$ (Algorithm 1).

Algorithm 1. Extraction Algorithm

Input: Text corpus T, Extracted text set T_E (initially $\emptyset$), Extraction prompt P_E, context $\mathcal{X}$
Output: T_E
1: **for** t in T **do**
2:     T_E.append($P_E(t, \mathcal{X})$)
3: **end for**
4: **return** T_E

In this task, P_E = <Extract the {context} from {t}>. However, to further refine the extraction task, we use chain-of-thought (CoT) prompting by providing in-context examples for the LLM. The precise prompting for each dataset is provided in Table 6 and Table 5.

3.2   Clustering with Heuristics

After we populate the extracted text set T_E, we group texts together to form clusters. Note that, unlike many other text clustering tasks, CafeLLM does not have information about (1) the number of clusters and (2) what the cluster labels should be. The set of clusters C is initially empty $\emptyset$, and to cluster all T_E, CafeLLM uses pairwise comparisons to determine if text values are suitable for grouping. A naive approach using this strategy would be to compare every unique pair in T_E to determine cluster assignments, but this would always require $\binom{|T_E|}{2}$ comparisons. Therefore, to remove unnecessary comparisons, CafeLLM breaks down the problem into two subparts.

Initiation. Since the cluster set C is empty, we initially consider the first two texts $t_1, t_2 \in T_E$. We use the pairwise comparison prompt P_C to determine if the two texts are semantically equal, where

$$P_C = <t_i \text{ is equal to } t_j \text{ based on } \{\text{context}\} \text{ (True/False)}>$$

The prompt takes in t_1, t_2, and the context and outputs a boolean (True/False). If true, then t_1 and t_2 should be in the same cluster, and we form a cluster c_1 containing t_1 and t_2. Otherwise, we form two separate clusters c_1 and c_2 containing t_1 and t_2, respectively.

As shown in Algorithm 2, while populating the cluster assignment set C, we also provide labels for newly formed clusters in a dictionary L. We assign the first value to enter a cluster as the label, which is useful for interpreting cluster assignments and for clustering other values in the following subpart.

Algorithm 2. Cluster Initiation Algorithm

Input: Extracted text set T_E, Clusters set C (initially $\emptyset$), Cluster Labels L, Comparison prompt P_C, context $\mathcal{X}$

Output: C, L

1:   first, second $\leftarrow T_E[1], T_E[2]$
2:   equal$\leftarrow P_C(\mathcal{X},$first,second$)$
3: **if** equal **then**
4:     $C[c_1] = [$first, second$]$
5:     $L[c_1] = $ first
6: **else**
7:     $C[c_1] = [$first$]$
8:     $L[c_1] = $ first
9:     $C[c_2] = [$second$]$
10:    $L[c_2] = $ second
11: **end if**
12: **return** C, L

Clustering Entire Corpus. After the initiation phase, C is no longer empty. Thus, instead of naively comparing every pair in T_E, we can iteratively compare every unclustered t_i with every cluster label $t_{c,j} \in L$ corresponding to each cluster c. This ensures that we don't redundantly compare t_i with two values in the same cluster, which should result in the same answer like comparing $t_i = $ "22 gauge" with "30 gauge (mice)" and "30G". Furthermore, we can stop comparing when an equal value is found from L, as it indicates that we found a cluster to place t_i in.

To further reduce computation, we can heuristically order the values in L to find an equal value $t_{c,j} \in L$ more efficiently, if it exists. CafeLLM uses embedding as a heuristic, comparing the unclustered text t_i to the label with the closest embedding. While pre-trained embeddings themselves cannot effectively cluster, in practice, we have found that it can help remove unnecessary comparisons with texts that are disparate from t_i.

To perform these comparisons, the P_C prompt is used as shown in the heuristic clustering algorithm (Algorithm 3), where SortByEmbbeding(S, t) denotes a function to sort a set S by embedding similarity to text t.

4   Experiments

We now present experimental results to show the effectiveness of CafeLLM to cluster fine-grained textual datasets. In this study, we use two main datasets as shown in Fig. 3:

Algorithm 3. Heuristic Clustering Algorithm

Input: Extracted text set T_E, Clusters set C (initially $\emptyset$), Cluster Labels L, Comparison prompt P_C, context $\mathcal{X}$
Output: C, L

1:   $p \leftarrow$ length of C
2:   **for** t in $T_E[3:]$ **do**
3:      SortByEmbedding(L, t)
4:      PairFound $\leftarrow$ False
5:      $j \leftarrow 1$
6:      **while** not PairFound or $j >$ length of L **do**
7:        equal$\leftarrow P_C(\mathcal{X}, t, L[j])$
8:        **if** equal **then**
9:          PairFound $\leftarrow$ True
10:         break
11:        **end if**
12:        $j = j + 1$
13:      **end while**
14:      **if** PairFound **then**
15:        $C[j]$.append(t)
16:      **else**
17:        $C[c_{p+1}] = [t]$
18:        $L[c_{p+1}] = t$
19:      **end if**
20: **end for**
21: **return** C, L

- *PCAST* contains 6662 text values with 25 different ground truth categories. Each text entails patient comments about their symptoms, and the categories are the type of issue [7]. For example, a text: ground truth pair is
  - "My entire body is freezing.": "Feeling cold"
  We use this dataset to evaluate the framework's ability to cluster a larger text corpus with phrases that are more nuanced.
- *NG* contains 314 needle gauge values extracted from various clinical trials. The text values are assigned to 68 different categories. An example text: ground truth pair is
  - "19 g syringe needle": "19 Gauge"
  This dataset serves to test whether CafeLLM can properly equate noisy texts containing numerical values.

4.1 CafeLLM Effectiveness

First, we examine the effectiveness of CafeLLM to cluster textual datasets that considers the context. Using the *PCAST* and *NG* datasets, we measure four values–V Measure, Completeness, Homogeneity, and Rand Index–by comparing labels created by the framework and ground truth labels from each respective dataset. To account for run-to-run consistency, we take an average of three runs for each evaluation. Here, we evaluate the clusters created from five systems:

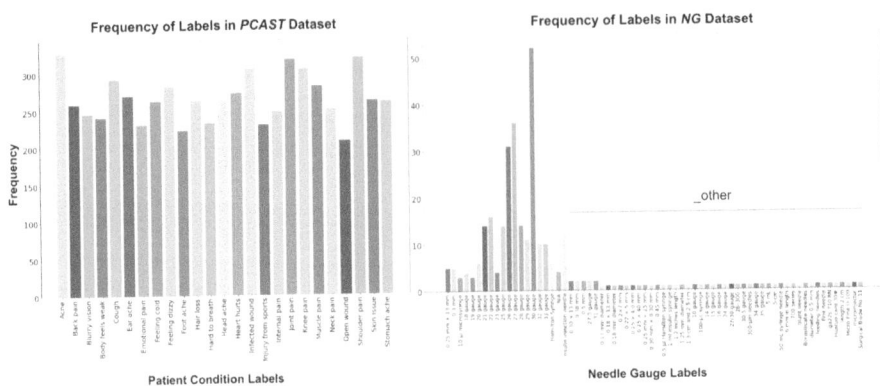

Fig. 3. *PCAST* and *NG* Datasets. Here, we display information about the two datasets used to evaluate CafeLLM. We show the frequency of each label in the *PCAST* dataset on the left, while the right chart shows frequencies for the *NG* dataset. To simplify *NG*, we group all values not in the top 25 frequencies into "_other".

1. *LLM Prompting (LLM)*. To illustrate the necessity for building a complex LLM-based clustering scheme, we compared the results to those obtained from a single LLM prompt. The specific prompt is discussed in Table 4.
2. *Extraction+LLM Prompting (Extract+LLM)*. To show that the clustering step in CafeLLM is necessary, we add the extraction step from CafeLLM to the LLM Prompting system.
3. *Embedding+K-Means (EmbK)*. As previously mentioned, using a pre-trained embedder with a method like K-means is commonly used for clustering. This benchmark serves to compare results with the state-of-the-art method.
4. *Extraction+Embedding+K-Means (Extract+EmbK)*. Much like Extraction + LLM Prompting, this system serves as a comparison to determine the necessity of CafeLLM's clustering step.
5. *CafeLLM*. Finally, this represents the entire framework of CafeLLM, including extraction and clustering steps.

The results from this experiment are shown in Table 1. Furthermore, a confusion matrix was constructed (Fig. 4) to show the percentages of each ground truth label that was correctly grouped by CafeLLM. Looking at the results for the *NG* dataset, we can observe that CafeLLM significantly outperforms the other two benchmarks across all measures. With a V Measure of 0.974 and Rand Index of 0.953, we find that the granularity of clusters and the overall clustering assignments are similar to the original dataset. On the other hand, for the *PCAST* dataset, CafeLLM clusters with moderate completeness and high homogeneity, indicating that the CafeLLM-generated clusters are not perfect and that CafeLLM creates clusters with a higher fidelity than those provided in the *PCAST* dataset. Because CafeLLM doesn't have prior knowledge about the ground truth labels, we observe that it can create more discrete, detailed groups than the dataset labels describe. This phenomenon can be seen in the confusion

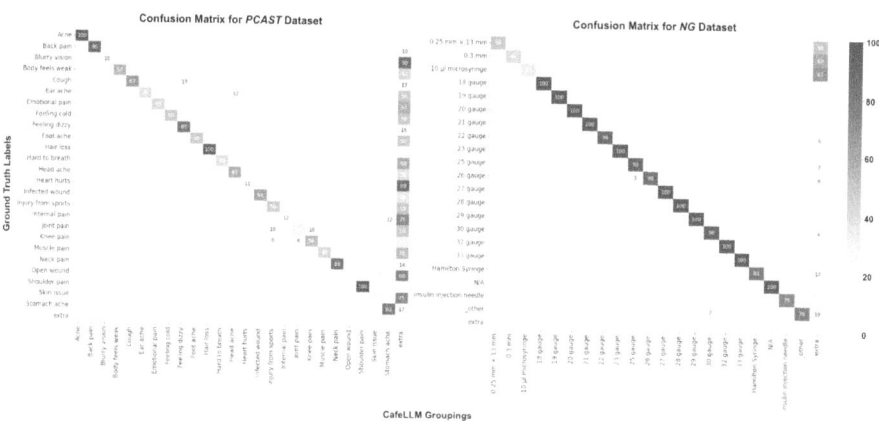

Fig. 4. Confusion Matrix for CafeLLM Clusters. Shown here is the confusion matrix for both datasets with "extra" including all new clusters created by CafeLLM that were not originally present in the model.

matrix. For the *PCAST* confusion matrix, the "extra" category contains extra clusters that CafeLLM created that are nonexistent in the original dataset. For example, CafeLLM separated out patient comments about "skin rashes" from the "skin issue" cluster.

As previously mentioned, there are two key issues in prior methods: (1) the presence of noisy or unstructured text that can change the representation and (2) the lack of consideration to the context. CafeLLM solves these issues with the extraction step, which purposefully extracts context-based information from each term or phrase and can often remove noise from textual data. However, this raises the question of whether using extracted values for other text clustering methods can solve the aforementioned issues to yield comparable results to CafeLLM. In other words, we seek to evaluate whether the clustering step in CafeLLM is still required. To do this, we compare the results from CafeLLM to the performance of using Embedding+K-Means and LLM Prompting after extraction. Albeit not significantly, it is interesting to note that the completeness of pairing the extraction step with Embedding+K-means is greater than that of CafeLLM in both datasets. This further illustrates how noisy texts can significantly change the representation extracted by the embedding model. However, even though the extraction step can alleviate issues in prior methods, CafeLLM still performs better than the other two frameworks in every other metric, suggesting the importance of the clustering step and revealing that CafeLLM is more effective than current state-of-the-art methods.

4.2 Embedding as a Heuristic

In order to optimize the efficiency of the clustering process, CafeLLM employs an embedding-based heuristic to reduce the number of pairwise comparisons

Table 1. Metrics measured from running CafeLLM on the *PCAST* and *NG* datasets. Each value was taken from an average of three separate runs.

Metrics from *PCAST* and *NG* Datasets					
Dataset	Framework	V Measure	Completeness	Homogeneity	Rand Index
PCAST	CafeLLM	**0.830**	0.733	**0.955**	**0.523**
	EmbK	0.691	0.724	0.662	0.287
	LLM	0.624	0.742	0.538	0.202
	Extract+EmbK	0.732	**0.763**	0.704	0.349
	Extract+LLM	0.644	0.756	0.560	0.228
NG	CafeLLM	**0.974**	0.959	**0.989**	**0.953**
	Emb+K-Means	0.760	0.963	0.628	0.613
	LLM	0.874	0.938	0.819	0.820
	Extract+EmbK	0.798	**0.979**	0.674	0.643
	Extract+LLM	0.902	0.936	0.870	0.865

required, thereby accelerating the determination of semantic similarity between texts. To measure the efficacy of using this heuristic, we measure $\mathcal{M}$, defined here as the number of comparisons it takes for an unclustered value t to find a clustered pair $t_{c,i}$ that is contextually similar in meaning, assuming that there exists this equal pair. This is an especially vital measure because, as shown in step 2ii of Fig. 2, our algorithm can stop early once this equal pair is found and add unclustered t to the cluster containing $t_{c,i}$; otherwise, further computation and calls to the LLM has to be made.

In order to reduce unnecessary computation, CafeLLM incorporates an embedding based ordering, where $t_{c,i}$ values that are closer in the embedding space are compared first. Thus, here, we assess the number of comparisons $\mathcal{M}$ with and without the heuristic to determine whether the use of an embedding-based ordering actually reduces computation in CafeLLM. To measure $\mathcal{M}$, we logged every decision made by the LLM. Overall, we find that this heuristic is fairly effective at reducing $\mathcal{M}$ and, therefore, computation. Notably, it can be especially effective for datasets containing more nuanced phrases with a 42.9% decrease in $\mathcal{M}$ when used in the *PCAST* dataset and a 26.5% decrease in $\mathcal{M}$ when used in the *NG* dataset (Table 2).

Table 2. Average $\mathcal{M}$ measured in both datasets taken from three different runs of CafeLLM.

Scenario	*PCAST* Avg. $\mathcal{M}$	*NG* Avg. $\mathcal{M}$
With Heuristic	**33.1**	**21.5**
Without Heuristic	47.3	27.2

4.3   Ablation Studies

In this section, we present an ablative analysis on the design choices of the LLM used in CafeLLM. The underlying decision made in CafeLLM relies on API calls to an LLM model in both the extraction and clustering step. Thus, we compare the performance of CafeLLM when replacing the LLM used in these steps with various OpenAI models (GPT-4, GPT-4o, and GPT-3.5) and two others: Llama 3 from Meta [14] and Claude 3 Opus from Anthropic [2]. As displayed in Table 3, CafeLLM typically performs the same regardless of the LLM model in the *PCAST* dataset. However, using GPT-4 results in better performance for the *NG* dataset, demonstrating its ability to compare numerical values. Yet, overall, it is evident that all LLM models can achieve comparable results, which illustrates that the CafeLLM framework is robust and isn't reliant on the choice of the pre-trained LLM. Furthermore, since CafeLLM can achieve comparable performance with more affordable models like GPT-3.5, it offers a cost-effective alternative for those seeking to reduce expenses without significantly compromising performance.

Table 3. The effect of the LLM model on CafeLLM's performance on the *PCAST* and *NG* datasets, evaluated on four metrics.

Ablation Study for *PCAST* and *NG* Datasets					
Dataset	LLM Model	V Measure	Completeness	Homogeneity	Rand Index
PCAST	GPT-4	**0.830**	0.733	**0.955**	0.523
	GPT-4o	0.816	0.720	0.941	0.522
	GPT-3.5	0.805	0.710	0.929	0.475
	Llama 3	0.825	**0.735**	0.948	**0.538**
	Claude 3 Opus	0.820	0.731	0.935	0.514
NG	GPT-4	**0.974**	0.959	**0.989**	**0.953**
	GPT-4o	0.965	0.949	0.981	0.942
	GPT-3.5	0.962	0.951	0.975	0.939
	Llama 3	0.959	**0.969**	0.951	0.932
	Claude 3 Opus	0.948	0.951	0.943	0.900

5   Conclusion

In this paper, we introduce CafeLLM, a novel tool for users to automatically cluster textual data that considers the context without requiring any prior insight into the dataset. Specifically, given a set of fine-grained terms or phrases and the context to cluster them, our framework is able to effectively place them into groups based on their semantic similarity in context. By leveraging LLMs to understand nuanced text, the framework can first extract context-relevant information from each value in the dataset. Then, we find here that using pairwise comparison is particularly efficacious at determining semantic similarities between text, which is used to decide whether two text values are in the same cluster. To reduce computations, we employ a heuristic ordering to determine which representative value $t_{c,i}$ an unclustered value t should compare with first based on embedding similarity. Experiments show that the use of this embedding-based heuristic can significantly reduce the number of pairwise comparisons, making CafeLLM more computationally efficient.

To improve the current CafeLLM framework, we outline here two key next steps to address some limitations.

1. *Computational Efficiency.* A key limitation to CafeLLM is that performing pairwise comparisons, even with the embedding-based heuristic, can be computationally expensive and can require large numbers of API calls. A possible solution is to use less expensive LLM models, as outlined in the ablation studies. However, a more practical solution might be to employ some variation of k-nearest neighbors to stop the pairwise comparisons early for each unclustered value t.

2. *Considering the Cluster Granularity.* Another limitation to CafeLLM is that we don't consider how granular the clusters have to be. This issue is evident in the results shown for CafeLLM's performance on the *PCAST* dataset. Many clusters separated into more detailed clustered than intended by the ground truth labels. Arguably, this might have also been an issue because of the existence of different ground truth labels at different levels of detail of the same disease type like "skin issue" and "acne". However, to mitigate this issue altogether, we can modify the prompt in the extraction step by specifically stating how granular the clusters should be, either through explicit language or by example.

Overall, this paper highlights a new tool that performs better than state-of-the-art clustering methods, requires no knowledge about the ground truth clusters, and considers the context by which the user intends to cluster. We believe that it can be used for various applications, including and not limited to comments from people like patients, noisy numerical values, and survey answers. In the future, we hope to make CafeLLM a computationally efficient tool that can cluster textual data in a way that captures the granularity and that considers the context–all without user insight or intervention.

6 Supplementary Prompts

Table 4. Prompt to get clusters from a single LLM prompt

LLM Prompting
Two needle gauges are equal if they have the same quantity gauge. Help me put these values into clusters based on equivalent needle gauges.

Table 5. Prompt to extract context-relevant information from the *NG* dataset

NG CoT Extraction
Needle gauge is a quantity measuring the gauge of a needle in a biopsy. You will be given a list of input data containing needle gauges. For each value, extract the needle gauge from the input data. For example, given the input: [5-gauge, 1.25 mm diameter, 21 gauge (human study), 10G, 6 mm in length], you could extract the needle gauge for each value as follows: 5-gauge : 5 gauge   1.25 mm diameter : 1.25 mm   21 gauge (human study) : 21 gauge

Table 6. Prompt to extract context-relevant information from the *PCAST* dataset

PCAST CoT Extraction
You will be given a list of complaints from patients. Extract the disease from the following valuse. Please provide your answer in a format like: "cancer". There is always a possible value to extract; however, if you believe there is none, please respond with "N/A". For example, given the following value: "I used to be out of breath after going up a dozen of stairs, but now I struggle to breath even when I sit down.", you could extract the disease as follows: "hard to breathe"   Another example is "My head hurts whenever I try to do something." where the answer would be "headache"   Another example is "When i'm driving my eyes see in double" where the answer would be "blurry vision"

Acknowledgments. This work was supported by ModernVivo Inc.

References

1. Aggarwal, C.C., Zhai, C.: A survey of text clustering algorithms. In: Aggarwal, C., Zhai, C. (eds.) Mining Text Data. Springer, Boston (2012). https://doi.org/10.1007/978-1-4614-3223-4_4
2. Anthropic: The Claude 3 Model Family: Opus, Sonnet, Haiku. Anthropic (2024). https://www.anthropic.com/news/claude-3-family
3. Beregovskaya, I., Koroteev, M.: Review of clustering-based recommender systems. arXiv (2020). https://doi.org/10.48550/arXiv.2109.12839
4. Devlin, J., Chang, M., Lee, K., Toutanova, K.: BERT: pre-training of deep bidirectional transformers for language understanding. arXiv (2019). https://arxiv.org/abs/1810.04805
5. Doval, Y., Vilares, J., Gómez-Rodríguez, C.: Towards robust word embeddings for noisy texts. arXiv (2020). https://doi.org/10.48550/arXiv.1911.10876
6. Gu, K., Vosoughi, S., Prioleau, T.: SymptomID: a framework for rapid symptom identification in pandemics using news reports. ACM Trans. Manag. Inf. Syst. **12**(4), 1–17 (2021). https://doi.org/10.1145/3462441
7. Jahin, M.A.: Patient Comments and Specialist Types Dataset. Mendeley Data, V1 (2024). https://doi.org/10.17632/2twgjzpn82.1
8. Jehangir, B., Radhakrishnan, S., Agarwal, R.: A survey on named entity recognition—datasets, tools, and methodologies. Nat. Lang. Process. J. **3**, 100017 (2023). https://doi.org/10.1016/j.nlp.2023.100017
9. Juneja, P., Jain, H., Deshmukh, T., Somani, S., Tripathy, B.K.: Context aware clustering using glove and K-means. Int. J. Softw. Eng. Appl. **8**(4), 21–38 (2017). https://doi.org/10.5121/ijsea.2017.8403
10. Kwon, et al.: Image clustering conditioned on text criteria. arXiv (2024). https://doi.org/10.48550/arXiv.2310.18297
11. Lajčinová, B., Valábek, P., Spišiak, M.: Named entity recognition for address extraction in speech-to-text transcriptions using synthetic data. arXiv (2024). https://doi.org/10.48550/arXiv.2402.05545
12. Li, H.: Text clustering. In: Liu, L., Özsu, M.T. (eds.) Encyclopedia of Database Systems. Springer, Boston (2009). https://doi.org/10.1007/978-0-387-39940-9_415
13. Liu, X., Croft, W.B.: Cluster-based retrieval using language models. In: Proceedings of the 27th Annual International ACM SIGIR Conference on Research and Development in Information Retrieval (2004). https://doi.org/10.1145/1008992.1009026
14. Meta: Introducing Meta Llama 3: The most capable openly available LLM to date. Meta (2024). https://ai.meta.com/blog/meta-llama-3/
15. Mikolov, T, Chen, K., Corrado, G., Dean J.: Efficient estimation of word representations in vector space. arXiv (2013). https://arxiv.org/abs/1301.3781
16. Ning, H., Chen, Z.: Fusion of the word2vec word embedding model and cluster analysis for the communication of music intangible cultural heritage. Sci. Rep. **13**, 22717 (2023). https://doi.org/10.1038/s41598-023-49619-8
17. OpenAI: GPT-4 technical report. arXiv (2023). https://arxiv.org/abs/2303.08774
18. Subakti, A., Murfi, H., Hariadi, N.: The performance of BERT as data representation of text clustering. J. Big Data (2022). https://doi.org/10.1186/s40537-022-00564-9
19. Viswanathan, V., et al.: Large language models enable few-shot clustering. arXiv (2023). https://doi.org/10.48550/arXiv.2307.00524

20. Wehrli, S., Arnrich, B., Irrgang, C.: German text embedding clustering benchmark. arXiv (2024). https://doi.org/10.48550/arXiv.2401.02709
21. Xu, Q., Gu, H., Ji, S.: Text clustering based on pre-trained models and autoencoders. Front. Comput. Neurosci. **17** (2024). https://doi.org/10.3389/fncom.2023.1334436
22. Yin, Z., et al.: Do large language models know what they don't know? arXiv (2023). https://doi.org/10.48550/arXiv.2305.18153
23. Zhang, Y., Wang, Z., Shang, J.: ClusterLLM: large language models as a guide for text clustering. In: Proceedings of the 2023 Conference on Empirical Methods in Natural Language Processing (2023). https://doi.org/10.18653/v1/2023.emnlp-main.858

Adapter-Based Contextualized Meta Embeddings

James O'Neill[1] and Sourav Dutta[2(✉)] (iD)

[1] DynamoFL Ireland, Dublin, Ireland
`james@dynamofl.com`
[2] Huawei Ireland Research Centre, Dublin, Ireland
`sourav.dutta2@huawei.com`

Abstract. This paper introduces MetaLoRA and MetaUniPELT, two meta-embedding approaches that extends Low Rank Adaptation (LoRA) and adapters for fine-tuning and combining multiple pretrained models. We find that both models improve performance across a range of monolingual and multilingual tasks, outperforming baselines such as fully fine-tuned single models, simple concatenation of pretrained embeddings with classification layer fine-tuning and soft-voting ensembles. On the XGLUE benchmark, we find a 1.7 test score increase over the best fully-fine tuned model and a 0.24 increase over the best fully-fine tuned ensemble on sentence classification tasks. Our results underscore the potential of parameter-efficient fine-tuning of ensembles as efficient and effective alternatives to full fine-tuning and standard ensemble methods.

Keywords: LoRA · Adapter · Meta Embedding · Multilingual

1 Introduction

Traditionally, the two primary approaches in utilizing pretrained language models (PLMs) [4,5,7,23] for downstream tasks has been to either fully fine-tuning (FT) the entire model or only fine-tuning a task-specific classification layer (CFT) while the remaining layers are frozen. However, both of these approaches have their respective limitations, such as (1) significant computational costs and catastrophic forgetting [13] of pretrained knowledge during full FT and (2) suboptimal performance in the case of CFT.

Parameter efficient tuning (PEFT) methods [9,10,14,15,19,24] have led to a good trade-off between FT and CFT by only tuning a small fraction of the total number of parameters. However, when the downstream task is semantically far from the self-supervised pretraining task (e.g., masked language modeling), adapters struggle to meet similar performance to FT. Hence, this work aims to bridge that gap by extending PEFT methods to ensembled PLMs where the

---

J. O'Neill—Work done while author was at Huawei Ireland Research Centre, Dublin, Ireland.

J. Guo et al. (Eds.): IJCAI 2024, CCIS 2160, pp. 82–90, 2024.
https://doi.org/10.1007/978-981-97-6125-8_7

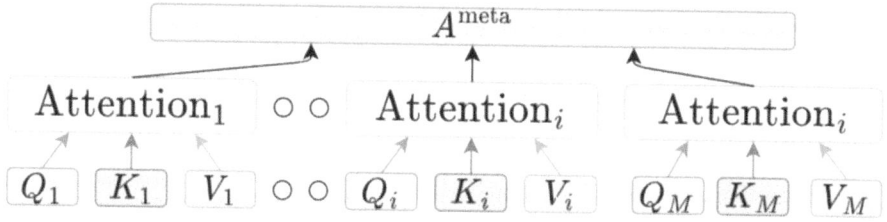

Fig. 1. MetaLoRA Meta-Embeddings

total number of parameters being tuned is still significantly less than full FT of a single model, while having the benefit of being highly parallelizable at inference time (Fig. 1).

In this paper we propose a meta-embedding method that harnesses the advantages of multiple pretrained models while mitigating the shortcomings of conventional fine-tuning strategies. We propose to integrate features from multiple pretrained models and only fine-tune a small fraction (<12.5% for UniPELT and <15% for LoRA) parameters in each of the models within the ensemble using PEFT methods. This encourages the models to adapt their embeddings to be more task-specific while benefiting from interdependent features, while still retaining the valuable knowledge gained during pretraining. These fine-tuned meta-embeddings are concatenated and processed through a classifier for both sentence-level and token-level tasks. We find that our proposed PEFT-based ensemble approach outperforms ensemble baselines and single fully-finetuned models with a relatively small number of tunable parameters for sentence-level tasks and outperforms standard ensembling on token-level tasks in both monolingual and multilingual settings.

Therefore, we aim to create an overall meta-embedding architecture, which is desirable compared to deeper networks with an equivalent number of parameters. Such shallower meta-architectures, as enabled by LoRA, offer faster inference times while maintaining high performance. This not only addresses the practical concerns associated with deploying large models in real-world applications but also enhances the efficiency of NLP systems, making them more accessible and cost-effective.

2 Related Research

In this section, we revise related research on the two main aspects of this work, (1) PEFT methods that improve efficiency and scalability of PLMs by reducing the number of trainable parameters and (2) Contextualized Meta-Embeddings (CMEs) methods that combine multiple embedding representations for improved generalization.

2.1   Parameter Efficient Fine-Tuning

PEFT methods have recently gained significant attention, as they offer a promising way to improve the efficiency and scalability of PLMs by reducing the number of trainable parameters.

Adapters. Adapter tuning is a popular PEFT approach that adds a small number of additional parameters to the PLMs that are tunable and task-specific while the underlying pre-trained PLM parameters are kept frozen. The original **bottleneck adapters** [9] places another tunable feedforward layer in front of the pretrained feedforward layer output of each self-attention block. Recently there has been variants that experiment with the placement of adapters within the self-attention block [11,20,21].

Low-Rank Adaptation (**LoRA**) [10] fine-tuning is another popular PEFT method that involves factorizing the weight matrices in the PLM into low-rank matrices. The low-rank matrices are then trained on the downstream task and merged with the original weight matrices after training, thus inference speed is not increased after training. Generalized LoRA (**GLoRA**) [3] extends LoRA by using a modular layer-wise structure search that incorporates a more generalized prompt module design per layer, allowing for flexibility in fine-tuning. Other methods such as **Prefix tuning** (PT) [14] instead fine-tunes a prefix of continuous input vectors that is prepended to the input prompt for large PLMs. Thus, unlike typical adapters, the fine-tuning is happening at the very *input* to the model while the model parameters are frozen. Lastly, **UniPELT** combines prefix tuning, bottleneck adapters and LoRA submodules in a unified setup, also using a gating mechanism that activates which submodule to use throughout training.

2.2   Contextualized Meta-embeddings

CMEs combine multiple contextualized embeddings to produce a stronger representation for downstream tasks. [12] pioneered meta-embeddings by training an LSTM sentence encoder on top of a set of dynamically combined word embeddings. [22] propose a GCCA based multi-view sentence encoder that combines domain-specific and generic sentence embeddings for unsupervised Duplicate Question Detection. [17] have used multi-task learning via a meta-embedding reconstruction loss that is used as a secondary loss to the main supervised task loss. [18] propose sentence meta-encoders in the multilingual setting and show that such frozen generic sentence embeddings provides significant benefits in supervised sentence classification when using CFT. A principled approach for meta-embeddings was explored in [8]. [1] have also surveyed the SoTA in meta-embeddings for various tasks. However, these works do not explore the use of PEFT for ensemble-based models, specifically meta-embeddings.

3   Methodology

This section provides a description of our proposed approach, highlighting the effectiveness of LoRA or adapters in fine-tuning multiple PLMs for meta-embeddings, referred to as *MetaLoRA* and *MetaUniPELT*. However, in our description we assume the use of MetaLoRA for simplicity. Before describing MetaLoRA, we introduce how LoRA freezes pretrained model weights and injects trainable low-rank decomposition (LRD) matrices into each layer for a *single* model and learns the residual from the fixed pretrained weight. Assume $\mathbf{W}_0, \boldsymbol{b}_0$ are the pretrained weights and bias of the model, and let f be a linear layer. Thus $f(\boldsymbol{x}) = \mathbf{W}_0\boldsymbol{x} + \boldsymbol{b}_0$ and $\boldsymbol{x} \in \mathbb{R}^d$ is the layer input and during training $\mathbf{W}_0$ and $\boldsymbol{b}_0$ are frozen (or not updated). The learning process is then given as Eq. 1 where $\Delta\mathbf{W}$ is the learnable LRD weights.

$$f(x) = \mathbf{W}_0\boldsymbol{x} + \Delta\mathbf{W}\boldsymbol{x} + b_0 = \mathbf{W}_{\text{LoRA}}\boldsymbol{x} + b_0 \tag{1}$$

3.1   MetaLoRA

We now describe how LoRA can be applied to an ensemble of PLMs for simultaneous LoRA fine-tuning of meta-embeddings. To begin, the pretrained model weights of each model are frozen in the ensemble, preventing the pretrained knowledge from being destructed during fine-tuning. Then, trainable LRD matrices are inserted into each layer of each model in the ensemble. During fine-tuning, only the LRD matrices of each model are trained to minimize the loss on the downstream task, while the remaining pretrained weight matrix remains frozen. In the forward-pass the outputs of each fine-tuned model are concatenated to produce the meta-embedding, before applying the classifier on top of this embedding. Equation 2 shows the formulation of MetaLoRA for n models in the ensemble, where Concat is the concatenation operator and $g(\cdot)$ applies a concatenation of projected LoRA linear outputs for the final meta-embedding. Here, $\mathbf{W}_{\text{LoRA}}^i$ and b_0^i are the LRD weights and bias of the i-th pretrained model in the ensemble and $\boldsymbol{x}^1, \boldsymbol{x}^2 \ldots \boldsymbol{x}^n$ are the input embeddings corresponding to n different tokenizers that are associated with each n models (the number of tokenizers is less than the number of models if more than one model shares the same tokenizer).

$$g(\boldsymbol{x}^1, \boldsymbol{x}^2 \ldots \boldsymbol{x}^n) = \text{Concat}(\mathbf{W}_{\text{LoRA}}^1\boldsymbol{x}^1 + \boldsymbol{b}_0^1,$$
$$\mathbf{W}_{\text{LoRA}}^2\boldsymbol{x}^2 + \boldsymbol{b}_0^2, \ldots, \mathbf{W}_{\text{LoRA}}^n\boldsymbol{x}^n + \boldsymbol{b}_0^n) \tag{2}$$

Once the PLMs have been MetaLoRA fine-tuned, the final meta-embedding can be used for downstream tasks. In preliminary experiments, UniPELT produced the strongest results of PEFT methods (not including LoRA), hence we used MetaUniPELT in our experimental framework.

We note that when using meta-embeddings for token-level tasks, as in MetaLoRA, we must assume that the tokenizers for each model within the ensemble are the same. This is because having different sub-tokenization vocabularies via the same or varying tokenization schemes can lead to misaligned predictions. Thus, the models we experiment with for token-level tasks share the same tokenizer. We focus our token-level experiments on a shared tokenizer across all models, although Myer's algorithm [16] can be used to align different tokenizers[1]. We now describe our baseline models and empirical findings.

---

[1] see https://github.com/explosion/tokenizations.

Table 1. Zero-shot Accuracy performance of baselines with varying Layer Mean Pooling on XNLI. The column heading denotes the indices of the subset of model layers that have been used for mean-pooling to get the representations. For example "1:-1" represents the mean between the first and last hidden layers.

Model	Mean	1:-1	1,2,3:-1,-2,-3	1	-1
Single Model					
XLM-R$_{\text{Large}}$	79.25	77.25	78.13	72.15	75.81
InfoXLM$_{\text{Large}}$	79.58	78.13	79.45	69.41	77.81
Multilingual-E5$_{\text{Large}}$	79.68	78.59	79.40	73.52	78.19
Ensemble Full-FT					
Ensemble-FT	82.60	79.53	81.93	73.90	80.41
BagEnsemble-FT	82.08	79.15	81.37	73.91	80.93
Ensemble Classification-FT					
Ensemble-CFT	75.45	70.41	72.51	68.45	71.89
SME-CFT	78.19	72.51	74.91	70.58	77.64
Proposed					
Meta-FT	83.37	79.14	81.58	75.81	81.80
MetaLoRA	79.72	78.14	79.53	73.32	78.83
MetaUniPELT	79.50	78.43	79.71	74.04	79.11

4   Experimental Results

Model Baselines. Below we list a description of the baselines we use in our experiments. **Single Models** - we use XLM-R$_{\text{Large}}$ [6], InfoXLM$_{\text{Large}}$ [4] and Multilingual-E5$_{\text{Large}}$ [25] as the single model FT baselines. These are also the underlying models that we use for all other ensembles, including MetaLoRA and MetaUniPELT. **Ensemble-FT:** a fully fine-tuned ensemble that outputs averaged logits across each n models logit output, using n classification layers. **BagEnsemble-FT:** the same as Ensemble-FT except each model learns with on a unique subset of the training data using random sampling without replacement [2] e.g 3 models that each only observe one third of the training data each. **Ensemble-CFT:** this is Ensemble-FT but we only fine-tune the classification layer and the remaining weights of each model are frozen. **Sentence Meta-Encoder** (SME-CFT) [18]: this is a meta-embedding of PLM embeddings with a single classification layer for CFT that takes the meta-embedding as input. It is similar to Ensemble-CFT except the concatenation of embeddings is done prior to passing to a *single* classification layer. **Meta-FT:** a fully fine-tuned meta-embedding i.e. no PEFT methods, but also use concatenation of ensemble embeddings to a single classification layer.

Table 2. Fine-Tuning XLM-R$_{\text{Large}}$ Results on News Classification. Test Accuracy on English and Zero-Shot Results for German, Spanish, French, and Russian.

	de	en	es	fr	ru	Avg.
XLM-R$_{\text{Large}}$	83.82	92.71	83.01	78.00	78.53	83.21
InfoXLM$_{\text{Large}}$	83.89	92.65	83.28	78.12	78.51	83.28
Multilingual-E5$_{\text{Large}}$	80.51	90.89	79.52	75.47	70.52	79.37
Ensemble-FT	87.09	93.08	85.71	80.69	80.67	85.45
BagEnsemble-FT	86.92	92.90	85.56	80.57	80.82	85.35
Ensemble-CFT	83.22	92.48	82.68	77.45	78.13	82.79
SME-CFT	82.33	91.90	82.10	77.14	77.52	82.19
Meta-FT	87.22	93.21	85.84	80.64	80.63	85.51
MetaLoRA	87.31	93.24	85.98	80.72	80.65	**85.57**
MetaUniPELT	84.69	92.81	84.981	81.49	82.87	85.37

Sentence-Level Tasks. Here we analyse two of the sentence-level tasks from the XGLUE benchmark, namely XNLI and News Classification. Table 1 shows the zero-shot test results for varying sentence representations used as apart of the concatenated meta-embedding. Consistently we find that concatenating "Mean" pooled embeddings outperforms different combinations. We find performance varies as a function of which layers are chosen for meta-embeddings but mean pooling all layers consistently outperforms subsets of layers for XNLI. Lastly, we find MetaUniPelt outperforms single model FT baselines, SME-CFT is a few percentage points away from ensemble-based FT models. Observe, in Table 1, the column heading denote the indices of the subset of model layers that are used for mean-pool representation. For example "1:-1" is the mean between the first and last hidden layers, and "Mean" includes all the layers.

From Table 2 we find that both zero-shot (non-english) and standard (english) test results improve over the best single FT model baseline by 2.29% and 1.53% respectively using MetaLoRA, while MetaUniPELT achieves similar performance. In fact, MetaLoRA achieves the best performance and outperforms baselines.

Token-Level Tasks. Our main finding on Named Entity Recognition (NER) and Part-of-Speech (POS) tagging as token-level tasks, based on the average performance is reported as Token Avg. in Table 3 and in Table 4 respectively. We find that since the input-output compression ratio (i.e., forcing the model to compact sentences into a fixed size vector representation) is less when compared to sentence-level tasks, the benefit of meta-embeddings are diminished somewhat for token predictions. We posit, this is a reason why not fully fine-tuning ensemble approaches for token-level tasks leads to performance degradation. Moreover, POS and NER tasks are semantically far from the PLM pretraining objective. Hence, PEFT methods that do not directly update attention matrices suffer in performance. From Table 3 we find that largest gains in performance over base-

Table 3. Fine-Tuning Results on Named Entity Recognition. Test F1 score on English and Zero-Shot Results in German, Spanish and Dutch.

	de	en	es	nl	Avg.
XLM-R$_{Large}$	72.27	92.74	76.44	81.00	80.61
InfoXLM$_{Large}$	71.89	91.49	75.12	81.82	80.08
Multilingual-E5$_{Large}$	68.13	86.13	72.18	74.38	74.45
Ensemble-FT	72.83	92.91	77.01	81.82	81.15
BagEnsemble-FT	71.91	93.04	78.84	82.15	**81.49**
Ensemble-CFT	49.12	84.31	58.13	57.45	62.25
SME-CFT	40.39	81.33	55.35	55.52	58.15
Meta-FT	72.42	91.84	77.80	81.89	80.99
MetaLoRA	67.30	85.18	71.82	67.05	72.84
MetaUniPELT	67.14	86.62	71.03	65.74	72.63

lines are made when evaluating on English, the language each model is trained on. This suggests that while PEFT methods result in models that generalize better than baselines in the supervised learning case for token-level tasks, they may lack some parameters to preserve zero-shot performance on the remaining languages it has not been trained on. Table 5 provides the zero-shot POS performance for the competing approaches across different languages.

Overall Results. Finally, Table 4 shows the average sentence-level, token-level and the overall average task *understanding* scores on the XGLUE benchmark for our proposed for our proposed MetaLoRA and MetaUniPELT and baselines. While the average token-level task score is lower, we find that based on the

Table 4. XGLUE benchmark zero-shot results. Sent Av. is the average XGLUE test-set score on sentence-level tasks and Token Av. is for token-level tasks.

Model	XNLI	NC	NER	PAWSX	POS	QAM	QADSM	WPR	Sent. Av.	Token Av.	Average
Single Model											
XLM-R$_{Large}$	79.25	83.21	80.61	89.23	80.38	69.82	71.05	73.27	77.64	80.50	78.35
InfoXLM$_{Large}$	79.58	83.28	80.08	90.83	80.33	69.82	71.6	73.68	78.13	80.21	78.65
Multilingual-E5$_{Large}$	79.68	79.37	74.45	89.37	76.19	70.53	71.71	74.47	77.70	75.32	77.11
Ensemble Full-FT											
Ensemble-FT	82.6	85.45	81.15	90.50	80.93	70.28	72.94	74.88	79.46 ( )	81.05 ( )	79.86 ( )
BagEnsemble-FT	82.08	85.35	**81.49**	91.52	80.86	70.06	71.33	74.09	79.07 ( )	**81.18** ( )	79.60 ( )
Ensemble Classification-FT											
Ensemble-CFT	75.45	82.79	62.25	88.43	72.40	69.02	70.25	73.77	76.62 (↓)	67.34 (↓)	74.30 (↓)
SME-CFT	78.19	82.19	65.68	88.31	74.51	71.39	72.56	75.37	78.00 (↓)	70.10 (↓)	76.02 (↓)
Proposed											
Meta-FT	**83.37**	85.51	80.99	90.54	**81.21**	70.28	**73.57**	74.88	**79.70** ( )	81.10 ( )	**80.05** ( )
MetaLoRA	79.72	**85.57**	72.84	**92.62**	75.35	70.41	72.68	**76.62**	79.60 ( )	74.10 (↓)	78.73 ( )
MetaUniPELT	79.5	85.37	72.63	92.42	75.52	**70.81**	72.43	76.42	79.49 ( )	74.07 (↓)	78.14 (↓)

Table 5. POS Tagging F1 scores on English and Zero-Shot on 17 languages.

	en	ar	bg	de	el	es	fr	hi	it	nl	pl	pt	ru	th	tr	ur	vi	zh	Avg.
XLM-R$_{Large}$	96.37	69.66	89.77	91.92	87.99	89.49	**90.70**	71.86	93.06	88.91	84.83	90.47	86.55	57.44	72.71	64.09	57.82	63.27	80.38
InfoXLM$_{Large}$	95.91	68.24	**90.41**	91.59	88.07	89.81	91.28	71.21	92.73	89.11	83.62	91.08	86.95	57.90	72.88	63.57	57.71	63.81	80.33
Multilingual-E5$_{Large}$	92.42	58.65	81.18	80.68	77.23	78.07	81.18	58.50	80.87	82.27	74.40	82.62	77.23	54.30	67.80	53.29	54.90	57.08	71.81
Ensemble-FT	97.52	70.51	90.36	92.09	88.37	89.88	**91.21**	72.51	93.44	88.73	85.69	91.29	86.99	57.58	73.46	64.73	58.42	64.00	80.93
BagEnsemble-FT	97.42	70.65	90.18	92.68	88.23	89.07	91.18	72.50	93.87	88.27	85.40	91.62	86.23	57.30	74.80	63.29	59.90	62.91	80.86
Ensemble-CFT	94.19	59.31	81.94	80.73	78.33	78.73	79.83	60.81	81.07	82.01	75.49	82.84	78.02	54.80	67.62	54.40	55.01	58.15	72.40
SME-CFT	93.12	59.95	81.81	80.59	78.51	78.16	80.14	59.69	80.82	81.54	75.80	83.01	77.76	54.16	67.33	53.11	55.28	47.46	71.57
Meta-FT	97.49	70.91	90.63	92.21	88.70	90.04	91.59	72.82	93.71	88.90	85.70	91.29	87.02	58.04	73.62	65.03	58.57	63.91	**81.21**
MetaLoRA	85.43	61.67	84.79	86.11	82.08	84.86	84.68	70.51	88.56	84.46	79.90	86.02	81.38	49.18	72.45	67.15	55.30	51.76	75.35
MetaUniPELT	85.59	62.01	85.05	86.28	82.04	84.76	84.90	71.11	88.36	84.68	79.64	85.77	81.69	49.82	72.78	67.08	55.93	51.81	75.52

zero-shot cross-lingual performance that both MetaLoRA and MetaUniPELT improve over all baselines for sentence-level tasks and slightly improve performance over all tasks when compared to fully-finetuned single models.

5 Conclusion

This work presented parameter-efficient meta-embedding models, namely MetaLoRA and MetaUniPELT. We find that these models outperform baselines on sentence embedding tasks and also outperforms classification only fine-tuned ensembles for token-level tasks. To our knowledge, this is the first focused study on how PEFT can be used in the context of ensembles. In future work, we look to improve the alignment between these models input tokenization and corresponding token embeddings for token level tasks, including generative models, not only discriminatively pretrained models. In conclusion, we find that contextualized meta-embeddings can outperform alternative ensemble approaches and full fine-tuned single models with only few tunable parameters being used.

References

1. Bollegala, D., O'Neill, J.: A survey on word meta-embedding learning. arXiv preprint arXiv:2204.11660 (2022)
2. Breiman, L.: Bagging predictors. Mach. Learn. **24**, 123–140 (1996)
3. Chavan, A., Liu, Z., Gupta, D., Xing, E., Shen, Z.: One-for-all: generalized LoRA for parameter-efficient fine-tuning. arXiv preprint arXiv:2306.07967 (2023)
4. Chi, Z., et al.: InfoXLM: an information-theoretic framework for cross-lingual language model pre-training. arXiv preprint arXiv:2007.07834 (2020)
5. Conneau, A., et al.: Unsupervised cross-lingual representation learning at scale. arXiv preprint arXiv:1911.02116 (2019)
6. Conneau, A., et al.: Unsupervised cross-lingual representation learning at scale. In: Proceedings of the 58th Conference of the Association for Computational Linguistics, ACL 2020, Virtual Conference, 6–8 July 2020, pp. 8440–8451 (2020). http://arxiv.org/abs/1911.02116
7. Devlin, J., Chang, M.W., Lee, K., Toutanova, K.: BERT: pre-training of deep bidirectional transformers for language understanding. arXiv preprint arXiv:1810.04805 (2018)

8. Dutta, S., Assem, H.: Enhanced sentence meta-embeddings for textual understanding. In: Hagen, M., et al. (eds.) ECIR 2022. LNCS, vol. 13186, pp. 111–119. Springer, Cham (2022). https://doi.org/10.1007/978-3-030-99739-7_13

9. Houlsby, N., et al.: Parameter-efficient transfer learning for NLP. In: International Conference on Machine Learning, pp. 2790–2799. PMLR (2019)

10. Hu, E.J., et al.: LoRA: low-rank adaptation of large language models. arXiv preprint arXiv:2106.09685 (2021)

11. Karimi Mahabadi, R., Henderson, J., Ruder, S.: Compacter: efficient low-rank hypercomplex adapter layers. In: Advances in Neural Information Processing Systems, vol. 34, pp. 1022–1035 (2021)

12. Kiela, D., Wang, C., Cho, K.: Dynamic meta-embeddings for improved sentence representations. arXiv preprint arXiv:1804.07983 (2018)

13. Kirkpatrick, J., et al.: Overcoming catastrophic forgetting in neural networks. Proc. Natl. Acad. Sci. **114**(13), 3521–3526 (2017)

14. Li, X.L., Liang, P.: Prefix-tuning: optimizing continuous prompts for generation. arXiv preprint arXiv:2101.00190 (2021)

15. Mao, Y., et al.: UniPELT: a unified framework for parameter-efficient language model tuning. arXiv preprint arXiv:2110.07577 (2021)

16. Myers, E.W.: An O (ND) difference algorithm and its variations. Algorithmica **1**(1–4), 251–266 (1986)

17. Neill, J.O., Bollegala, D.: Meta-embedding as auxiliary task regularization. arXiv preprint arXiv:1809.05886 (2018)

18. Patel, R.N., Burgin, E., Assem, H., Dutta, S.: Efficient multi-lingual sentence classification framework with sentence meta encoders. In: 2021 IEEE International Conference on Big Data (Big Data), pp. 1889–1899. IEEE (2021)

19. Pfeiffer, J., Kamath, A., Rücklé, A., Cho, K., Gurevych, I.: AdapterFusion: non-destructive task composition for transfer learning. arXiv preprint arXiv:2005.00247 (2020)

20. Pfeiffer, J., et al.: AdapterHub: a framework for adapting transformers. arXiv preprint arXiv:2007.07779 (2020)

21. Pfeiffer, J., Vulić, I., Gurevych, I., Ruder, S.: MAD-X: an adapter-based framework for multi-task cross-lingual transfer. arXiv preprint arXiv:2005.00052 (2020)

22. Poerner, N., Schütze, H.: Multi-view domain adapted sentence embeddings for low-resource unsupervised duplicate question detection. In: Proceedings of the 2019 Conference on Empirical Methods in Natural Language Processing and the 9th International Joint Conference on Natural Language Processing (EMNLP-IJCNLP), pp. 1630–1641 (2019)

23. Radford, A., Narasimhan, K., Salimans, T., Sutskever, I., et al.: Improving language understanding by generative pre-training. arXiv (2018)

24. Rebuffi, S.A., Bilen, H., Vedaldi, A.: Learning multiple visual domains with residual adapters. In: Advances in Neural Information Processing Systems, vol. 30 (2017)

25. Wang, L., et al.: Text embeddings by weakly-supervised contrastive pre-training. arXiv preprint arXiv:2212.03533 (2022)

Advancements in Multimodal Systems

MADP: Multi-modal Sequence Learning for Alzheimer's Disease Prediction with Missing Data

Yudie Wang[1], Zirui Wang[2], Huiyun Gong[3], Sanwang Wang[4,5], Mingzhe Li[6], and Jian Dong[7(✉)]

[1] State Key Laboratory of Complex and Critical Software Environment, Beihang University, Beijing 100191, China
yudiewang@buaa.edu.cn
[2] Shenyuan Honors College, Beihang University, Beijing 100191, China
zrayking_buaaer@buaa.edu.cn
[3] School of Computer Science and Engineering, Beihang University, Beijing 100191, China
gonghuiyun@buaa.edu.cn
[4] Department of Psychiatry, Renmin Hospital of Wuhan University, Wuhan 430060, China
sanwangwang@whu.edu.cn
[5] Peking University Sixth Hospital, Peking University Institute of Mental Health, NHC Key Laboratory of Mental Health (Peking University), National Clinical Research Center for Mental Disorders (Peking University Sixth Hospital), Beijing 100191, China
[6] Peking-Tsinghua Center for Life Sciences and PKU-IDG/McGovern Institute for Brain Research, Beijing 100191, China
dylmzh@pku.edu.cn
[7] China Electronics Standardization Institute, Beijing 10007, China
dongjian@cesi.cn

Abstract. Alzheimer's disease prediction is essential for enabling early diagnosis and timely intervention. These proactive measures are critical in slowing disease progression and improving the quality of life for affected individuals. A significant challenge in this context is the substantial amount of missing data, which arises due to the variable health status of subjects or other unpredictable circumstances. Moreover, existing methods struggle to accurately model the disease progression and fail to capture the effects of interactions among various factors on disease changes. To bridge this gap, we propose an end-to-end multi-modal sequence learning framework for Alzheimer's disease prediction with missing data (MADP). Rather than employing fixed-value padding or interpolation, MADP introduces a learnable mechanism designed to address data missing and guide the model to learn the multi-modal features for subsequent disease modeling. Furthermore, we model the static composition and dynamic evolution information in the process of disease progression respectively to decompose complex disease information. An extensive group of experiments on Tadpole dataset demonstrates that the proposed MADP achieves more favorable performance.

J. Guo et al. (Eds.): IJCAI 2024, CCIS 2160, pp. 93–103, 2024.
https://doi.org/10.1007/978-981-97-6125-8_8

Keywords: Alzheimer's Disease Prediction · Sequence Learning ·
Missing Data · Disease Modeling

1   Introduction

Alzheimer's disease (AD) is the predominant cause of dementia and creates an
enormous social and economic burden [20]. Alzheimer's disease prediction facilitates early diagnosis and intervention, enhances patients' quality of life and
allows healthcare systems to allocate resources more efficiently. With the rapid
development of deep learning models [14,16,17,29], Many approaches [1,10,13]
for computer-aided disease prediction have been implemented, resulting in favorable outcomes.

The employment of multi-modal data [11,21] in predicting Alzheimer's disease [6,18,23,27,30] is becoming increasingly widespread, as these data provide
supplementary insights into a patient's condition [1,15,23,30]. During the collection of long-term longitudinal data, various factors such as deteriorating health,
transfer to different treatment facilities or withdrawal from the study lead individuals to interrupt their follow-up. These issues result in substantial omissions
in disease data. The existing methods [15,27] use fixed value completion, interpolation completion and other strategies to complete the data. However, these
approaches ignore the informational potential of the missing data. Consequently,
we adopt a new learnable method to fill in the missing data.

Existing methods for Alzheimer's disease prediction can be categorized into
two primary groups: classified-based AD prediction [5,22,28] and time series
forecasting-based AD prediction [15,27]. Classified-based AD prediction usually deal with static data, ignoring the time series characteristics of the data.
Time series forecasting-based AD prediction are highly effective in capturing the
dynamic nature of disease progression by modeling temporal variations in disease
evolution. Therefore, this paper adopts time series forecasting-based AD prediction type and propose an end-to-end multi-modal sequence learning framework
for Alzheimer's disease prediction with missing data (MADP). Because of the
advantage of time series forecasting, several recent works [15,27] have proposed
using brain networks or other multi-modal disease data as historical inputs to
predict future disease states. However, these methods do not resolve the challenge
of modeling complex disease progression. Some methods [2] try to use Ordinary
Differential Equations (ODE) for disease prediction, but oversimplified assumptions make the model unable to accurately capture real-world disease dynamics.
And it is difficult to solve feasible solutions for complex problems. Therefore, we
model the inherent attributes and evolution information of the composite disease information separately, allowing the model to understand and predict the
disease trajectory in detailed.

To address the issues mentioned above, we concentrate in this paper on multi-
modal sequence learning for disease prediction with missing data, and the main
contributions are summarized as follows:

- To address the challenges posed by missing multi-modal data, we introduce
  the multi-modal embedding module, which optimally utilizes the available

data and enhances the model's stability and robustness in dealing with incomplete or anomalous data.

- In response to the complexities of modeling Alzheimer's disease, we propose the classified information predictor, which model the static composition and dynamic evolution information of the process of disease progression respectively to decompose complex disease information.
- We validate MADP on the Tadpole dataset, which achieves superior performance.

2   Related Work

2.1   Classified-Based AD Prediction

Most works for Alzheimer's disease prediction belong to classified-based AD prediction [4,9,12,22,25,26,30,31]. These methods only make predictions about the current state and are essentially a classification task. They employ historical longitudinal data or cross-sectional data as model inputs for diagnosing Alzheimer's disease at the current time point. Some of these studies exclusively utilize Magnetic Resonance Imaging (MRI) data for predicting Alzheimer's disease [22,25,26]. However, more research make multi-modal data aligned to reveal more complete latent information, where extensive techniques are applied to better extract the correlation and complementary relationship between different modalities [4,9,12,30,31].

2.2   Time Series Forecasting-Based AD Prediction

Compared with classified-based AD prediction, only a few methods [2,5,27] utilize longitudinal data for long-term disease prediction, which belong to time series forecasting-based AD prediction. These methods are based on long-term time series forecasting and present more challenges to model design and data modeling. Certain studies apply mathematical approaches like ODE [2] to diseases modeling while others predict future disease state indirectly by modeling the change of experimentally-verified biomarkers [7]. However, data scarcity and the presence of missing values are pressing issues that necessitate resolution. TR-GAN [5] completes missing sessions of MRI datasets, which can deal with variant input sequence length and flexibly generate future variant sessions. Some studies [27] integrate Long Short-Term Memory (LSTM) [8] with fusion modules to automatically capture complementary information and learn the latent representation. Contrary to these methods, our approach introduces a learnable mechanism for imputing missing data and predicts the disease trajectory by modeling the inherent attributes and evolution information separately.

3   Method

3.1   Overall Framework

An overview of our proposed framework is illustrated in Fig. 1. To achieve a holistic understanding of Alzheimer's disease, MADP employs a robust time series

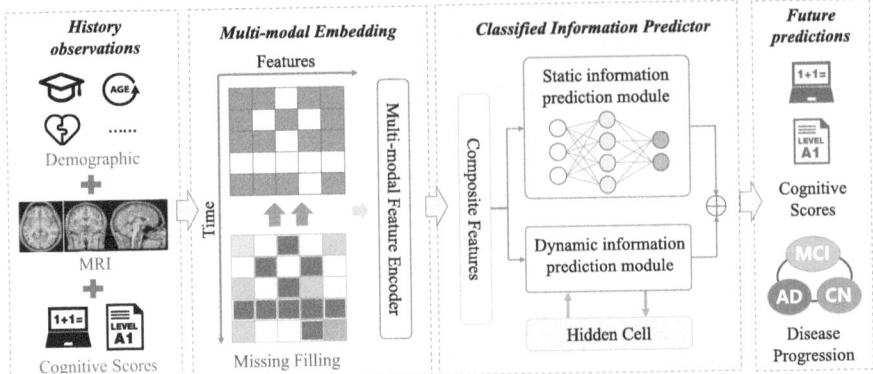

Fig. 1. Overview of MADP. MADP utilizes individuals' multi-modal data as input, addressing missing values and integrating features via the multi-modal embedding module. Subsequently, the classified information predictor models composite features to predict the future cognitive scores.

prediction model that integrates several modalities. Specifically, MADP utilizes MRI, demographic and cognitive assessment scores as key inputs to predict the future disease states. For the problem of insufficient utilization of multi-modal missing data, we use multi-modal embedding module to fill the missing values and learn the correlation between different modal data. For the difficulty of disease modeling, we propose classified information predictor to decompose composite disease information.

3.2   Formulation

Assuming the total number of individuals to be N and each individual containing T historical visits, we denote the v-th modality data as $X^v = \{X_1^v, X_2^v, \ldots, X_T^v\}$, where $X_t^{(v)} \in \mathbb{R}^{n_t \times d_v}$ represents the feature matrix of v-th modality at t-th visit, which consists of n_t individuals and d_v features. Since our study is based on MRI, cognitive assessment and demographics, we denote them respectively as $X^{(1)}, X^{(2)}, X^{(3)}$. By concatenating the three modalities data, we get historical observations $X \in \mathbb{R}^{N \times T \times D}$, where D denotes the number of the input features. Let $Y \in \mathbb{R}^{N \times F \times D'}$, $Y = \{Y_1, Y_2, \ldots, Y_F\}$, where we aim to predict F subsequent time points. D' represents the number of cognitive scores that need to be predicted. In this article, $D' = 1$, which means only Alzheimer's disease assessment scale-cognitive section(ADAS-13) is predicted. Given historical observations with T visits, we aim to predict the individuals' disease states at F future moments. MADP adopts an auto-regressive framework, which predicts future disease states by frame-by-frame prediction.

3.3   Multi-modal Embedding

To address the challenges arising from missing multi-modal data, we introduce a multi-modal embedding module. This module is designed to leverage incomplete datasets by incorporating missing data rather than discarding it prematurely. It enhances the stability and robustness of the model when dealing with incomplete or anomalous data. The module ensures that the inherent information within the missing components is utilized to a greater extent. It improves the overall efficacy of the modeling process.

Specifically, for historical observations X, we use the learnable parameters $X' \in \mathbb{R}^{N \times T \times D}$ to automatically fill in missing values in X. It allows the model to process and interpolate missing data efficiently. This can provide more accurate results than static, non-learning interpolation strategies such as mean and median padding.

$$X_{fill} = \begin{cases} X\,(X_t^v \neq \mathrm{NaN}), \\ X'\,(X_t^v = \mathrm{NaN}), \end{cases} \tag{1}$$

The filling principle is shown in formula 1. When X is missing, X' is used to fill. Data from different modality provide unique information about the disease. In order to build a comprehensive and accurate disease prediction model, we use the full connected layer as the multi-modal feature encoder $E_{encoder}$ to fuse multi-modal features and obtain historical composite features $X_{encoder} \in \mathbb{R}^{N \times T' \times D_e}$ of the individuals. D_e denotes the dimension size encoded by multi-modal feature encoder. Since MADP is an auto-regressive temporal prediction model, $T' = 1$.

$$X_{encoder} = E_{encoder}(X_{fill}), \tag{2}$$

3.4   Classified Information Predictor

In response to the complex evolution of Alzheimer's disease (AD), we develop a novel module named classified information predictor (CIP). The predictor comprises two distinct modules: the static information prediction module and the dynamic information prediction module. By bifurcating the prediction process into static and dynamic components, our approach effectively simplifies the overall predictive modeling of AD progression, allowing for a more nuanced understanding and anticipation of disease trajectories. We input the encoded features $X_{encoder}$ into CIP and get the future predictions $Y' \in \mathbb{R}^{N \times T' \times D_p}$, where D_p denotes the feature dimension.

Static Information Prediction Module. The module focuses on processing information that is intrinsic to the individual, such as genetic factors, baseline clinical data and other biomarkers that do not change significantly over time. These information usually remain relatively stable throughout the course of the disease. However, they provide an important reference for the underlying risk and initial state of the disease. We use the fully connected layers E_{static} to predict $X_{static} \in \mathbb{R}^{N \times T' \times D_p}$ that remain stable over the course of the disease but have a non-negligible impact on the condition.

$$X_{static} = E_{static}(X_{encoder}), \tag{3}$$

Dynamic Information Prediction Module. In contrast to static information prediction module, the dynamic information prediction module deals with disease features that evolve over time, such as cognitive decline, changes in physical and psychological conditions and biomarker data that are checked periodically. The module predicts dynamic changes, enabling it to map the time trajectory and rate of disease progression. We use LSTM as the dynamic information prediction module $LSTM_{dynamic}$ for predicting dynamic changes $X_{dynamic} \in \mathbb{R}^{N \times T' \times D_p}$ in disease evolution and update hidden cell to record history information.

$$X_{dynamic} = LSTM_{dynamic}(X_{encoder}), \tag{4}$$

We fuse the results of the static information prediction module and the dynamic information prediction module to get the final predictions $Y_{pred} \in \mathbb{R}^{N \times T' \times D'}$

$$Y_{pred} = X_{static} + X_{dynamic}, \tag{5}$$

3.5   Training

By stacking the predictions Y_{pred} for all future time points, we get the future predictions $Y' \in \mathbb{R}^{N \times F \times D'}, Y' = \{Y'_1, Y'_2, \ldots, Y'_F\}$. Subsequently, we employ Mean Squared Error (MSE) loss to guide the learning process of MADP.

$$MSE = \frac{1}{NF}(Y - Y')^2, \tag{6}$$

4   Experiment

4.1   Datasets and Metrics

Datasets. We use the Tadpole [19] dataset to verify our model. The Tadpole dataset is extracted from the Alzheimer's Disease Neuroimaging Initiative (ADNI) [11], where involves predicting the symptoms related to Alzheimer's disease (AD) within 1–5 years. In our experiments, we focus on predicting disease states at specific time points, using image data(MRI/PET/DTI etc.), cognitive test data, demographic statistics. The dataset comprises 12,742 records from 1,737 individuals, categorized at baseline as follows: 417 individuals with Cognitively Normal (CN) status, 872 individuals with Mild Cognitive Impairment

(MCI), 342 individuals diagnosed with Alzheimer's disease (AD), and 106 individuals exhibiting Subjective Memory Complaints (SMC). Detailed information about the Tadpole dataset is provided in Table 1. We only show the statistics of data at a interval of 12 months, but the real time interval of data is 6 months, which means that the dataset contains a total of 21 visits. BL means Baseline visit. The date when the individual takes the first examination is called Baseline, and follow-up visits are named by the duration from the baseline time point. For example, M06 denotes the visit when the individual was examined 6 months after the first visit.

Table 1. Number of observed individuals for different data sources at different visits in the Tadpole datasets. Image data consist of Magnetic Resonance Imaging (MRI), Positron Emission Tomography (PET) and Diffusion Tensor Imaging (DTI). Demographics data includes age, gender, ethic and education. The dataset also includes scale data such as Alzheimer's disease assessment scale-cognitive section (ADAS-13) and Minimum Mental State Examination (MMSE).

Type	BL	M12	M24	M36	M48	M60	M72	M84	M96	M108	M120
MRI	1721	1392	1125	455	341	171	163	39	32	11	1
PET	893	4	558	26	324	89	68	58	46	34	17
DTI	217	150	73	14	0	0	0	4	1	0	0
Demographics	1737	1737	1737	1737	1737	1737	1737	1737	1737	1737	1737
Scale	1723	1458	1269	799	627	328	233	175	129	95	64

Metrics. The prediction performance of the model is evaluated by Mean Absolute Error (MAE) and Mean Squared Error (MSE). The computational formulas for these indicators are presented in Eq. 7 and Eq. 8. $Y_{k,t}$ and $\hat{Y}_{k,t}$ denote the corresponding ground truth and prediction at t-th time point, where k means the number of individuals. N_t denotes the number of observed individuals at t-th time. For both MAE and MSE, the lower value indicates the better performance.

$$MAE = \frac{1}{N_t T} \sum_{t=1}^{T} |Y_{k,t} - \hat{Y}_{k,t}|, \tag{7}$$

$$MSE = \frac{1}{N_t T} \sum_{t=1}^{T} (Y_{k,t} - \hat{Y}_{k,t})^2, \tag{8}$$

4.2 Implementation Details

We use three types of data: MRI, cognitive assessment and demographics. Since the brain structure of AD patients changes only at specific locations, we use data from the hippocampus, whole brain, entorhinal cortex, fusiform gyrus, and middle temporal gyrus instead of whole brain MRI data. Demographics take into account race, age, marital status and education. Only ADAS-13 is used for cognitive assessment data. The dataset was partitioned into training and testing sets at a ratio of 9:1. Our model utilizes data from the initial 11 visits as historical observations to forecast cognitive scores for the subsequent 10 visits. The multi-modal feature encoder is composed of a fully connected layer, the static information prediction module is composed of a Multi-Layer Perceptron (MLP) [14], and the dynamic information prediction module is structured as a two-layer LSTM [8] network. Besides, we set the batch size and initial learning rate to 1 and 1×10^{-3}, respectively.

As shown in Table 2, MADP is compared with three classical time series prediction models: Recurrent Neural Network (RNN) [24], Long Short-Term Memory (LSTM) [8] and Gate Recurrent Unit (GRU) [3]. LSTM and GRU are both variations of RNN, which are designed to solve vanishing gradients when dealing with long sequences prediction. Through the mechanism of forgetting and memory, LSTM and GRU are able to effectively capture temporal dependencies within time series data, resulting in enhanced predictive performance compared to RNN. By comprehensively utilizing incomplete multi-modal disease data and accurately modeling complex disease processes, MADP demonstrates superior performance over LSTM, achieving enhancements of 16.67% and 22.10% in MSE and MAE, respectively.

Table 2. Comparison of MADP with other time series forecasting models.

Model	MSE	MAE
LSTM [8]	0.6921	1.1376
GRU [3]	0.7056	1.2265
RNN [24]	0.7744	1.1855
Ours (MADP)	**0.5767**	**0.8862**

4.3   Ablation Study

In this paper, classified information predictor, multi-modal feature encoder and missing filling module are sequentially removed from MADP. As shown in Table 3, ablation experiments are conducted on the Tadpole to demonstrate the contribution of each module to the prediction performance.

Table 3. Ablation studies on the components of MADP.

Model	MSE	MAE
MADP	**0.5767**	**0.8862**
MADP-Classified Information Predictor	0.6193	0.9089
MADP-Multi-modal Feature Encoder	0.6921	1.1376
MADP-Missing Filling	1.1521	2.6636

Initially, the absence of the classified information predictor within MADP leads to an omission in modeling the disease's inherent features, consequently diminishing the accuracy of predictions. Furthermore, removal of the multimodal feature encoder hampers the model's ability to discern interactions among multi-modal features, impairing model performance. Lastly, as shown in Table 3, the contribution of the missing filling module is significant. This module enhances the utilization of missing data by substituting it with learnable parameters rather than prematurely discarding it.

5   Conclusion

In this paper, we introduce MADP, an end-to-end multi-modal sequence learning framework for Alzheimer's disease prediction with missing data. MADP employs learnable parameters to complete multi-modal missing data. Furthermore, MADP models the static composition and dynamic evolution information in the process of disease progression to decompose complex disease information. Experiments results demonstrate that our proposed method yields superior performance, effectively utilizing available data and enabling a detailed understanding and prediction of the disease trajectory.

Acknowledgments. This work was supported by the National Key Research and Development Program of China (2023YFC2506800).

Disclosure of Interests. Jian Dong is a member of China Electronics Standardization Institute. The authors have no competing interests to declare that are relevant to the content of this article.

References

1. Archetti, D., et al.: Multi-study validation of data-driven disease progression models to characterize evolution of biomarkers in Alzheimer's disease. NeuroImage Clin. **24**, 101954 (2019)
2. Bossa, M.N., Sahli, H.: A multidimensional ode-based model of Alzheimer's disease progression. Sci. Rep. **13**(1), 3162 (2023)
3. Chung, J., Gulcehre, C., Cho, K., Bengio, Y.: Empirical evaluation of gated recurrent neural networks on sequence modeling. arXiv preprint arXiv:1412.3555 (2014)
4. Cosmo, L., Kazi, A., Ahmadi, S.-A., Navab, N., Bronstein, M.: Latent-graph learning for disease prediction. In: Martel, A.L., et al. (eds.) MICCAI 2020. LNCS, vol. 12262, pp. 643–653. Springer, Cham (2020). https://doi.org/10.1007/978-3-030-59713-9_62
5. Fan, C.C., et al.: TR-GAN: multi-session future MRI prediction with temporal recurrent generative adversarial network. IEEE Trans. Med. Imaging **41**(8), 1925–1937 (2022)
6. Giorgio, J., et al.: A robust and interpretable machine learning approach using multimodal biological data to predict future pathological tau accumulation. Nat. Commun. **13**(1), 1887 (2022)

7. Zheng, H., et al.: Data-driven causal model discovery and personalized prediction in Alzheimer's disease. NPJ Digit. Med. (137) (2022)

8. Hochreiter, S., Schmidhuber, J.: Long short-term memory. Neural Comput. **9**(8), 1735–1780 (1997)

9. Huang, Y., Chung, A.C.S.: Edge-variational graph convolutional networks for uncertainty-aware disease prediction. In: Martel, A.L., et al. (eds.) MICCAI 2020. LNCS, vol. 12267, pp. 562–572. Springer, Cham (2020). https://doi.org/10.1007/978-3-030-59728-3_55

10. Iddi, S., et al.: Predicting the course of Alzheimer's progression. Brain Inform. **6**, 1–18 (2019)

11. Jack, C.R., Jr., et al.: The Alzheimer's disease neuroimaging initiative (ADNI): MRI methods. J. Magn. Reson. Imaging Official J. Int. Soc. Magn. Reson. Med. **27**(4), 685–691 (2008)

12. Ko, W., Jung, W., Jeon, E., Suk, H.I.: A deep generative-discriminative learning for multimodal representation in imaging genetics. IEEE Trans. Med. Imaging **41**(9), 2348–2359 (2022). https://doi.org/10.1109/TMI.2022.3162870

13. Koval, I., et al.: Ad course map charts Alzheimer's disease progression. Sci. Rep. **11**(1), 8020 (2021)

14. LeCun, Y., Bengio, Y., Hinton, G.: Deep learning. Nature **521**(7553), 436–444 (2015)

15. Liang, W., et al.: Modeling Alzheimers' disease progression from multi-task and self-supervised learning perspective with brain networks. In: Greenspan, H., et al. (eds.) MICCAI 2023. LNCS, vol. 14220, pp. 310–319. Springer, Cham (2023). https://doi.org/10.1007/978-3-031-43907-0_30

16. Liu, X., et al.: A meaningful learning method for zero-shot semantic segmentation. Sci. China Inf. Sci. **66**(11), 210103 (2023)

17. Ma, Y., et al.: Transductive relation-propagation with decoupling training for few-shot learning. IEEE Trans. Neural Netw. Learn. Syst. **33**(11), 6652–6664 (2021)

18. Maheux, E., et al.: Forecasting individual progression trajectories in Alzheimer's disease. Nat. Commun. **14**(1), 761 (2023)

19. Marinescu, R.V., et al.: TADPOLE challenge: accurate Alzheimer's disease prediction through crowdsourced forecasting of future data. In: Rekik, I., Adeli, E., Park, S.H. (eds.) PRIME 2019. LNCS, vol. 11843, pp. 1–10. Springer, Cham (2019). https://doi.org/10.1007/978-3-030-32281-6_1

20. Masters, C.L., Bateman, R., Blennow, K., Rowe, C.C., Sperling, R.A., Cummings, J.L.: Alzheimer's disease. Nat. Rev. Dis. Primers **1**(1), 1–18 (2015)

21. Nichols, E., et al.: Global, regional, and national burden of Alzheimer's disease and other dementias, 1990–2016: a systematic analysis for the global burden of disease study 2016. Lancet Neurol. **18**(1), 88–106 (2019)

22. Pan, X., et al.: Multi-view separable pyramid network for ad prediction at mci stage by 18 F-FDG brain pet imaging. IEEE Trans. Med. Imaging **40**(1), 81–92 (2020)

23. Qiu, S., et al.: Multimodal deep learning for Alzheimer's disease dementia assessment. Nat. Commun. **13**(1), 3404 (2022)

24. Rumelhart, D.E., Hinton, G.E., Williams, R.J.: Learning representations by back-propagating errors. Nature **323**(6088), 533–536 (1986)

25. Song, X., et al.: Multicenter and multichannel pooling GCN for early ad diagnosis based on dual-modality fused brain network. IEEE Trans. Med. Imaging **42**(2), 354–367 (2023). https://doi.org/10.1109/TMI.2022.3187141

26. Tang, X., Zhang, C., Guo, R., Yang, X., Qian, X.: A causality-aware graph convolutional network framework for rigidity assessment in parkinsonians. IEEE Trans. Med. Imaging **43**(1), 229–240 (2024). https://doi.org/10.1109/TMI.2023.3294182
27. Xu, L., et al.: Multi-modal sequence learning for Alzheimer's disease progression prediction with incomplete variable-length longitudinal data. Med. Image Anal. **82**, 102643 (2022)
28. Zhang, H., et al.: Classification of brain disorders in rs-fMRI via local-to-global graph neural networks. IEEE Trans. Med. Imaging **42**(2), 444–455 (2022)
29. Zhao, X., et al.: Temporal speciation network for few-shot object detection. IEEE Trans. Multimed. **25**, 8267–8278 (2023)
30. Zheng, S., et al.: Multi-modal graph learning for disease prediction. IEEE Trans. Med. Imaging **41**(9), 2207–2216 (2022)
31. Zhu, Q., et al.: Deep multi-modal discriminative and interpretability network for Alzheimer's disease diagnosis. IEEE Trans. Med. Imaging **42**(5), 1472–1483 (2023). https://doi.org/10.1109/TMI.2022.3230750

Multi-modal Spatiotemporal Forecasting via Cross-Scale Operator Learning and Spatial Representation Aggregation

Yajun Gao[1], Tianrui Ma[2], Chujie Xu[1], and Miao Wang[3]

[1] State Key Laboratory of Complex and Critical Software Environment, Beihang University, Beijing 100191, China
{yajungao,chujie_xu}@buaa.edu.cn
[2] School of Computer Science and Engineering, Beihang University, Beijing 100191, China
19374191@buaa.edu.cn
[3] Intelligent Game and Decision Lab, Beijing 100071, China
mercury.miao@nudt.edu.cn

Abstract. The vertically integrated liquid (VIL) is one of the effective indicators for assessing severe weather caused by strong convection, and accurate forecasting is crucial. In highly complex and interconnected atmospheric systems, the evolution of VIL is often potentially linked to other physical factors such as cloud cover, water vapor, and temperature. However, most previous studies have used various time series prediction methods that only relied on the statistical patterns of observed VIL variables, neglecting the correlations between VIL and other physical backgrounds. This limitation makes it difficult to achieve reliable and accurate predictions that align with the overall atmospheric dynamics. Therefore, we fully utilize the physical spatiotemporal data obtained from satellites and propose a novel multi-modal spatiotemporal forecasting model. This model includes a Cross-scale Operator Learner (COL) and a Spatial Representation Aggregator (SRA), which extracts and integrates physical background information to align model predictions with real physical processes. The COL could discover a common nonlinear operator from correlated multi-modal data. It explores various nonlinear functions that map the discrete input space to hidden physical spatial space, thereby obtaining an atmospheric spatial representation of atmospheric evolution processes. The SRA integrates the atmospheric spatial representation and VIL's spatial representation, generating an enhanced spatiotemporal representation with both VIL spatial details and atmospheric physical background. This representation can realize temporal embedding better and improve the model's accuracy in predicting VIL. We refined the SEVIR dataset to ensure complete and aligned modalities, and conducted extensive experiments demonstrating that our model outperforms other state-of-the-art models.

Keywords: Multi-modal · Spatiotemporal forecasting · Cross-scale Operator learning · Spatial Representation Aggregation

J. Guo et al. (Eds.): IJCAI 2024, CCIS 2160, pp. 104–118, 2024.
https://doi.org/10.1007/978-981-97-6125-8_9

1   Introduction

Spatiotemporal forecasting for the vertically integrated liquid (VIL) aims to mine the complex evolution law of VIL and to predict VIL in the future. The existing methods usually take historical observations as the input and pay attention to the accurate learning of its statistical law to achieve reliable prediction. Focusing on short-term and long-term spatial dependencies in historical data, ConvLSTM [1], E3D-LSTM [2], and PredRNN [3] based methods combine convolutional neural networks and recurrent neural networks to realize spatiotemporal information coupling. Considering that recurrent-based methods can only be trained and deduced in sequential order and are computationally inefficient, a series of models based on encoder-decoder structures, including SimVP [4], SimVP-V2 [5] and TAU [6], are proposed, which show robustness in spatiotemporal prediction. In addition to data-driven models, some methods focus on mathematical prior knowledge in dynamic systems, and propose prediction models based on operator learning methods to elucidate hidden dynamic information, so as to achieve prediction results aligned with the real world.

However, these methods ignore the influence of other physical factors on the evolution of VIL, such as cloud cover, water vapor, and temperature. Within the intricate and interlinked atmospheric system, such oversight can result in predictions that deviate markedly from real-world physical phenomena, as illustrated in Fig. 1. Therefore, some researchers put forward the use of multi-modal data to achieve the gain of physical and other background information. These approaches utilize early-fusion, intermediate-fusion mechanisms, or complex feature extraction and association strategies to achieve effective multi-modal information extraction and fusion. However, current methods primarily engage multi-modal inputs at the feature level and lack guidance based on mathematically stable mechanisms, such as nonlinear operators that can describe dynamic systems. Consequently, they fail to achieve prediction results that align with real complex dynamic systems.

To address this challenge, we introduce a novel multi-modal spatiotemporal forecasting model that leverages physical spatiotemporal data acquired from satellites to achieve efficient information gain. To align predictions with actual physical processes, a Cross-scale Operator Learner (COL) and a Spatial Representation Aggregator (SRA) are introduced into the proposed model for efficient extraction and integration of physical background information. Inspired by the DeepONet [7] framework - a universal deep operator network - COL is engineered to identify a common nonlinear operator within the associated multi-modal data. This operator explores various nonlinear functions, mapping discrete input space to hidden physical spatial space, thereby capturing a dynamic atmospheric space representation of evolutionary processes. Subsequently, the SRA integrates the above atmospheric spatial representation with VIL's spatial representation to generate an enhanced spatiotemporal representation with both VIL spatial details and the atmospheric physical background, thus realizing temporal embedding better.

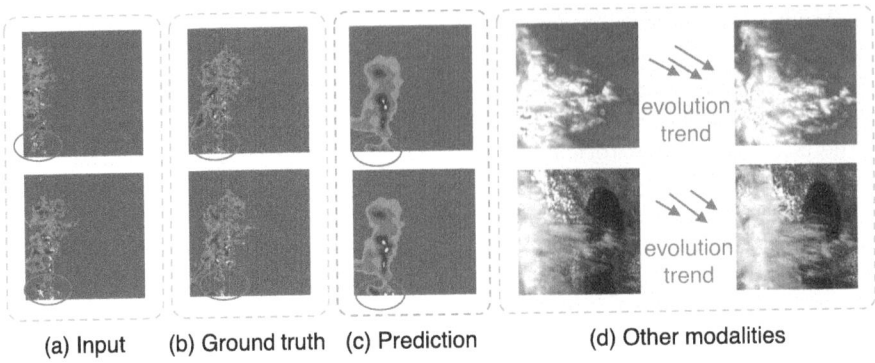

(a) Input   (b) Ground truth   (c) Prediction   (d) Other modalities

Fig. 1. The predictions deviate significantly from the visual presentation of real-world physical phenomena.

To the best of our knowledge, this is the first work to introduce multi-modal data from an operator learning perspective in the VIL forecasting task, attempting to extract spatial representations of atmospheric evolution and efficiently integrate them with VIL spatial details. Our main contributions are as follows:

- We propose a novel multi-modal spatiotemporal forecasting model that extracts and integrates physical background information to align model predictions with real physical processes.
- A Cross-scale Operator Learner (COL) is introduced to learn a general nonlinear operator from discrete multi-scale input data, ultimately yielding a spatial representation of the atmospheric evolution.
- To further generate an enhanced spatiotemporal representation, a Spatial Representation Aggregator (SRA) is designed to integrate VIL spatial details with the atmospheric physical background, thereby enriching the temporal embedding.
- Extensive experiments on the SEVIR [8] dataset demonstrate that the proposed model significantly outperforms existing state-of-the-art models.

2 Related Work

Our method implements a multi-modal spatiotemporal forecasting model based on operator learning to achieve results aligned with the real physical world. Therefore, we will discuss single-modal spatiotemporal forecasting in Sect. 2.1 and multi-modal spatiotemporal forecasting in Sect. 2.2. Operator learning in forecasting is discussed in Sect. 2.3.

2.1 Single-Modal Spatiotemporal Forecasting

In the field of single-modal spatiotemporal forecasting tasks, existing methods usually employ strategies that either couple or decouple spatiotemporal information for feature extraction. For example, ConvLSTM [1] and E3D-LSTM [2] integrate 2D and 3D convolutional neural networks [9] (CNNs) respectively into Long Short-Term Memory [10](LSTM) networks to effectively capture spatial correlations over single or multiple time steps. Additionally, architectures such as PredRNN [3], PredRNN++ [11], and PredRNN-V2 [12] have been developed, introducing novel recurrent neural network [13] (RNN) cells designed to comprehensively address both long-term and short-term dependencies in time series data, thus generating more reliable forecasting results. Moreover, MIM [14] innovatively substitutes the traditional gating mechanisms in LSTMs with two recurrent modules, enhancing the extraction of both non-stationary and approximately stationary features during spatiotemporal evolution.

Some methods have been developed to extract temporal and spatial features either in parallel or sequentially, followed by their integration and correlation. STConvS2S [15] employs a fully convolutional architecture to distinctly implement time and space blocks. Furthermore, several research groups have introduced models predicated on an encoder-decoder framework with a core temporal module, such as SimVP [4], SIMVP-V2 [5], and TAU [6], demonstrating robust performance in spatiotemporal prediction tasks. Based on this, Earthformer [16] utilizes a space-time transformer with cuboid attention to achieve performance enhancement. Additionally, Rainformer [17] leverages a dual-branch structure to simultaneously address local and global features comprehensively.

The above single-modal spatiotemporal forecasting models rely on the statistical law of the predicted target itself, and usually only focus on spatiotemporal correlation mining of a single variable with simple design. However, these approaches ignore the influence of other physical factors on the predicted target, thus affecting the accuracy of the prediction.

2.2 Multi-modal Spatiotemporal Forecasting

Compared with single-modal approaches, multi-modal spatiotemporal forecasting adds multi-source data as inputs, introducing additional physical information to enhance the robustness and accuracy of prediction results. Some methods adopt the early-fusion mechanism to process multi-modal data, including MetNet [18], FourCastNet [19], and UNet [8] (SEVIR's benchmark model). These models usually use interpolation and downsampling to align multi-modal data such as radar, spectral image, temperature and precipitation into the same format, and integrate them into a single tensor as input in the channel dimension. Besides, other methods adopt the intermediate-fusion mechanism, integrating modalities in the encoded feature space. For example, Hurricast [21] and Cross-ViViT [22] add multi-modal meteorological information such as solar irradiation and wind power to the input, and fuse modal information in the feature space to assist spatiotemporal prediction.

In order to make full use of the rich prior information in the multi-modal spatiotemporal data, ClimaX [23], STIN [24], AutoML [25] and other models adopt complex feature extraction and association strategies, and integrate advanced strategies such as ViT [26], Transformer [27], Multi-Attention or NAS [28] to adjust the degree of influence of other modalities on the target modality.

Although better information interaction is introduced, the heavy computation of the attention mechanism reduces the efficiency of the model.

In summary, multi-modal information can provide abundant physical information for spatiotemporal forecasting and can assist target prediction. However, the existing model has the problem of complex and inefficient modeling and lack of efficient information interaction mechanisms.

2.3   Operator Learning in Forecasting

Some methods pay attention to the prior knowledge [34,35] in dynamic systems, introduce mathematical mechanisms to describe evolutionary dynamics in data-driven models [42], and propose prediction methods based on operator learning. Inspired by PDE-Net [29], PhyDNet [30] uses partial differential operators to extract physical laws in the evolution of meteorological systems, and implements a recurrent alignment framework based on the Kalman filter principle. Similar partial differential operator methods also include PDE-Net2.0 [31], PDOeConvs [32], PhyCRNet [33], etc., which approximate nonlinear dynamic equations through convolution kernel, expose hidden dynamic information, and generate predictions aligned with real complex dynamic systems.

PastNet [36] and Earthfarseer [37] use a two-branch framework to capture the global time evolution dynamics using Fourier operators. Fourier operator learning methods include FNO [38] and AFNO [39], which pay more attention to the mapping of different function spaces. Similar operator learning methods also include general operator DeepONet [7] and graph operator PDE-GCN [40]. Based on a two-stage conditional potential diffusion model, PreDiff [41] proposes an explicit knowledge alignment mechanism to align predictions with domain-specific physical constraints.

The method based on operator learning is conducive to generating physically reliable predictions. However, current methods are limited in integrating these frameworks with predictive models, highlighting a need for further exploration in this area.

3   Methodology

In this section, We will introduce the proposed multi-modal forecasting model via cross-scale operator learning and spatial representation aggregation. We will first introduce the overall model in Sect. 3.1. Our cross-scale operator learner (COL) is then introduced in Sect. 3.2. The details of spatial representation aggregator (SRA) are described in detail in Sect. 3.3.

3.1   Overall Model

Previous studies have not adequately addressed the impact of various physical factors on predicting VIL, often relying on single-modal data or adopting simple fusion modules, which degrades performance. To solve this problem, we

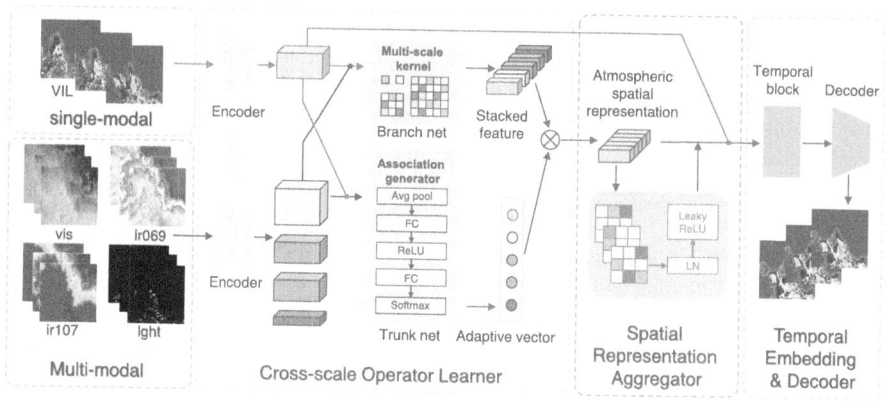

Fig. 2. The architecture of the proposed multi-modal spatiotemporal forecasting model with a cross-scale operator learner and a spatial representation aggregator.

developed a model suitable for the VIL prediction task that can accommodate multi-modal data input. The model's architecture, illustrated in Fig. 2, consists of a multi-modal input layer, a cross-scale operator learner, a spatial representation aggregator, a temporal embedding, and a decoder.

We use multi-modal data that are time-aligned with the VIL observations to enable a more comprehensive and systematic description of atmospheric evolution. We chose four kinds of data collected by GOES-16 satellites, including 0.6 µm visible satellite channel (vis), 6.9 µm and 10.7 µm infrared channels (ir069, ir107), and total lightning flashes (lght). They are well aligned in the SEVIR dataset [8], and more details are given in Sect. 4.1.

We redefine the VIL prediction task to take into account multi-modal inputs. Suppose that historical sequence of VIL is $x[1 : T]$, the historical sequences of other modes are combined as $y[1 : T]$, and the model predicts future K frames based on the historical T frames, that is, the prediction result is $x[T+1 : T+K]$. We regard the overall prediction model as F, and the entire prediction process can be expressed by the following formula:

$$x[T + 1 : T + K] = F(x[1 : T], y[1 : T]), \tag{1}$$

where $x[1 : T] \in \mathbb{R}^{T \times H \times W \times 1}$, $x[T + 1 : T + K] \in \mathbb{R}^{K \times H \times W \times 1}$, and $y[1 : T]$ contains a variety of modal data with different spatial scales, and each modal data has a T-frame. Therefore, the predictive model F is designed to model multi-scale historical sequences of VIL and other modalities well.

Specifically, through a parameter-shared encoder, VIL and other multi-modal data are transformed into feature maps of the feature space with different scales. Then, the multi-scale feature blocks are sent to the cross-scale operator learner (COL) with a branch net and a trunk net to realize the mapping from the input feature space to the hidden physical spatial space. The COL, inspired by the unstacked DeepONet [7], is designed using the principles of the universal approximation theorem for operators. It is capable of learning nonlinear operators from discrete multi-scale input data. Utilizing multi-modal features that conform to the co-evolution mapping relationship, COL is capable of learning a general nonlinear operator suited for capturing the atmospheric evolution process. This allows it to understand different nonlinear function representations associated with each modality, ultimately yielding a spatial representation of the atmospheric evolution. More details are available in Sect. 3.2.

The atmospheric spatial representation is subsequently input into the spatial representation aggregator (SRA), where it is combined with the VIL spatial representation produced by the encoder. This fusion results in an enhanced spatiotemporal representation that integrates VIL spatial details with the atmospheric physical background, thereby enriching the temporal embedding. It is fed into a temporal block to augment the temporal representation. This process employs Earthformer stack cuboid attention blocks with residual connections, enhancing the learning of spatiotemporal representations by capturing more comprehensive spatial details. Ultimately, this enriched spatiotemporal representation is utilized by the decoder to generate the final VIL prediction.

The entire end-to-end model adopts real future frame $x'[T+1:T+K]$ as the supervision, and constructs the loss function through the commonly used MSE. The formula is as follows:

$$MSE = \frac{1}{N}\Sigma_{i=1}^{N}(x[T+1:T+K]_i - x'[T+1:T+K]_i)^2, \qquad (2)$$

where $x[T+1:T+K] \in R^{K \times H \times W \times 1}$, $x'[T+1:T+K] \in R^{K \times H \times W \times 1}$ represent the prediction and real future frames respectively, and $N = K \times H \times W$ indicates the number of data pixels in all future frames.

In summary, through the above pipeline and end-to-end constraints, our model is able to take full advantage of the multi-modal information associated with VIL to extract a spatiotemporal representation that is more aligned with the real atmospheric physical background. Based on this, it achieves reliable and accurate predictions aligning with the overall atmospheric dynamics.

3.2   Cross-Scale Operator Learner

Following the network structure of unstacked DeepONet [7], we designed a cross-scale operator learner (COL), including a branch net and a trunk net, aiming at learning a mapping from input feature space to hidden physical space. We assume that the operator of the multi-modal input space u is expressed as $G(u)$ and uses v as the mark of the different modalities. Then the output of the operator can be regarded as $G(u)(v)$. This means that the framework can learn different representations of functions with discrete $[u(VIL), u(vis), u(ir069), u(ir107), u(lght)]$ in the input space.

Based on the generalized universal approximation theorem of operators, which has been proven in DeepONet's work, we can write the following formula:

$$\left| G(u)(v) - \left\langle \underbrace{g(u(VIL), u(vis), u(ir069), u(ir107), u(lght))}_{\text{branch}}, \underbrace{f(v)}_{\text{trunk}} \right\rangle \right| < \varepsilon. \quad (3)$$

For any $\varepsilon > 0$, there exist functions g and f to make the formula valid. As stated in [7], the functions g and f can be implemented using various network structures such as fully connected neural networks, residual neural networks, convolutional neural networks, or other arbitrary architectures. Based on this, we designed a Branch net based on a multi-scale kernel and a trunk net based on an association generator to generate the stacked feature and the adaptive vector respectively.

Specifically, the branch net employs a parallel configuration of multi-scale convolution kernels: 1×1, 1×1, 3×3, and 5×5. These kernels act on the features of each modality and use spatial interpolation to produce spatially aligned multi-modal stacked features. This configuration accommodates the heterogeneity of spatial scales and facilitates scale-invariant feature extraction. Concurrently, the features of each modality are fed into the trunk net, where they sequentially pass through a pooling layer, a fully connected (FC) layer, a ReLU activation layer, another FC layer, and a Softmax layer, culminating in the generation of mode-specific associations. These associations adaptively change with the input, forming an adaptive vector. Ultimately, the atmospheric spatial representation is produced through the dot product of the stacked feature and the adaptive vector.

3.3   Spatial Representation Aggregator

Spatial representation aggregator (SRA) plays a key role in the processing and integration of multi-modal data, combining different spatial representations into one spatio-temporal representation space to enhance overall model prediction. Specifically, we use the atmospheric spatial representation generated by COL and the spatial representation of VIL generated by the encoder to achieve further fusion. The two representations are simultaneously entered into a 3×3 convolution layer and connected to the layer normalization (LN) unit. The Leaky ReLU activation layer then ensures that even small changes in the input can still affect model learning, which is crucial for capturing subtle atmospheric dynamics.

Through these components, the SRA effectively combines detailed VIL spatial data with broader atmospheric spatial information, thereby enhancing spatiotemporal representations. This fusion not only blends the detailed spatial aspects of VIL with the atmospheric physics background, but also enriches the temporal embeddings of the model. Enhanced temporal embedding is crucial to improve the accuracy of temporal dynamics captured by the model, thus improving the reliability and accuracy of the system's weather forecasting capability.

Table 1. Detailed description of each modality in the SEVIR dataset.

Sensor	Data	Spatial resolution	Patch size	Time step
GOES-16 C02 0.64 μm	vis	0.5 km	768×768	5 min
GOES-16 C09 6.9 μm	ir069	2 km	192×192	5 min
GOES-16 C13 10.7 μm	ir107	2 km	192×192	5 min
NEXRAD radar mosaic of VIL	VIL	1 km	384×384	5 min
GOES-16 GLM flashes	lght	8 km	N/A	Continuous

4   Experiments

In this Section, we will evaluate the proposed model on commonly used meteorological datasets. We will first describe the experimental setup in Sect. 4.1 and detail our reconstructed modal alignment dataset, along with evaluation metrics and Implementation details. After that, we will present the fair experimental results and compare them with other advanced models in Sect. 4.2. Validation experiments for the validity of each component of our model are presented in Sect. 4.3.

4.1   Experimental Setting

Dataset. We use the SEVIR dataset [8] for our experiments, which contains a wealth of cross-scale and multi-modal meteorological data. The dataset contains more than 10,000 meteorological events, sampled across the continental United States from January 2017 to December 2019, with each event consisting of a four-hour sequence of images sampled five minutes apart. The spatiotemporal resolution of the individual data is shown in Table 1.

Except for lght, other modalities are in the format of image sequences. To unify the inputs, we organized the lght data into 48×48 image sequences, where each pixel represents the number of times lightning occurred in that area. It is worth noting that there is only the VIL modality in samples captured in 2017, which accounts for a large percentage of all the data, and there are a few missing modalities in the samples in 2018 and 2019. We refined the SEVIR dataset to ensure complete and aligned modalities, called SEVIR-MM (Multi-Modal).

We choose data from before Jan 2019 as training sets, data between Jan 2019 and June 2019 as validation sets, and data after June 2019 as test sets. We also choose several sequences from one sample, each containing 13 frames as historical data to forecast the next 12 frames in the future. The amount of sequences in the original dataset SEVIR and the new dataset SEVIR-MM is shown in Table 2. The aligned dataset SEVIR-MM removes some sequences that are modally missing, resulting in higher-quality data. We use accepted normalization methods to process data.

Table 2. Comparison of the number of sequences in the original dataset SEVIR and the new aligned dataset SEVIR-MM.

	SEVIR-MM	SEVIR
Training set	17754	35718
Validation set	7218	9060
Test set	9267	12159
Total	34239	56937

Table 3. Binary metrics for VIL prediction.

Abbr	Metrics	Definitions
CSI	Critical Success Index	$\#Hits/(\#Hits + \#Misses + \#F.Alarms)$
SUCR	Success Ratio	$\#Hits/(\#Hits + \#F.Alarms)$
POD	Probability of Detection	$\#Hits/(\#Hits + \#Misses)$
BIAS	Bias	$(\#Hits + \#F.Alarms)/(\#Hits + \#Misses)$

Evaluation Metrics. The evaluation metrics on the SEVIR dataset [8] are mainly divided into two parts: the metrics for pixel similarity, and the binary metrics for precipitation events. We use MSE and MAE as our metrics to evaluate pixel-wise similarity, which are widely used in spatiotemporal prediction. And for event-wise prediction, we first binarize the truth and prediction at a series of thresholds [16, 74, 133, 160, 181, 219]. The binary value is 1 if VIL is greater than or equal to a certain threshold, otherwise is 0. The binary values are scored as "Hits" if $prediction = truth = 1$, "False Alarms" if $prediction = 1, truth = 0$, "Misses" if $prediction = 0, truth = 1$, and "Correct Rejection" otherwise. The binary metrics are calculated by summing the counts of pixels over the test set, as shown in Table 3.

Implementation Details. Experiments are conducted on 4 NVIDIA A100-PCIE-40GB GPUs. We utilize PyTorch Lightning as our deep learning framework. The maximum number of training epochs is set to 100, with a batch size of 4, and each experiment takes approximately 1–1.5 days for training. We employ AdamW as our optimizer and utilize Warming-up & Cosine-Annealing as our learning rate scheduling strategy. Early stopping is implemented to monitor the mean CSI on the validation set during training, and the best model is selected based on its performance on the validation set for testing.

4.2 Comparison to State-of-the-Art

We validated our model on the aligned dataset SEVIR-MM and conducted fair experiments using state-of-the-art methods with both recurrent-based and recurrent-free state-of-the-art methods. The recurrent-based methods included

Table 4. Performance Comparison on the SEVIR-MM dataset. We retrained all models in the same experimental setting.

Category	Method	Conference/Journal	Metrics	
			mCSI ↑	MSE ↓
Recurrent-based	ConvLSTM [1]	NeurIPS 2015	0.4034	3.549
	E3D-LSTM [2]	ICLR 2019	0.3895	4.068
	PredRNN [3]	NeurIPS 2017	0.4217	3.707
	PredRNN++ [11]	ICML 2018	0.4276	3.649
	PredRNN-v2 [12]	PAMI 2022	0.4132	3.541
	MIM [14]	CVPR 2019	0.4105	**3.396**
Recurrent-free	Earthformer [16]	NeurIPS 2022	0.4198	3.830
	SimVP [4]	CVPR 2022	0.4127	4.137
	TAU [6]	CVPR 2023	0.4104	3.980
	Ours	–	**0.4289**	3.960

ConvLSTM, E3DLSTM, PredRNN, PredRNN++, PreDRNN-V2, and MIM, while the recurrent-free methods comprised SimVP, TAU, and Earthformer. The experimental results are shown in Table 4.

As we all know, compared with MSE metrics, mCSI metrics can better reflect the difference between prediction results and real situations for VIL forecasting tasks. Compared to other recurrent-free methods reproduced in Table 4, our model achieves the best results on the mCSI metrics, showing a 2.17% improvement over the second-best method Earthformer [16]. It also maintains favorable results in terms of the MSE metrics. The above results show that our model can fully utilize and integrate multi-modal information to align the model results with the real physical evolution process, so as to improve the accuracy of the model results. In addition, we also show a visualization of our model's predictions in Fig. 3.

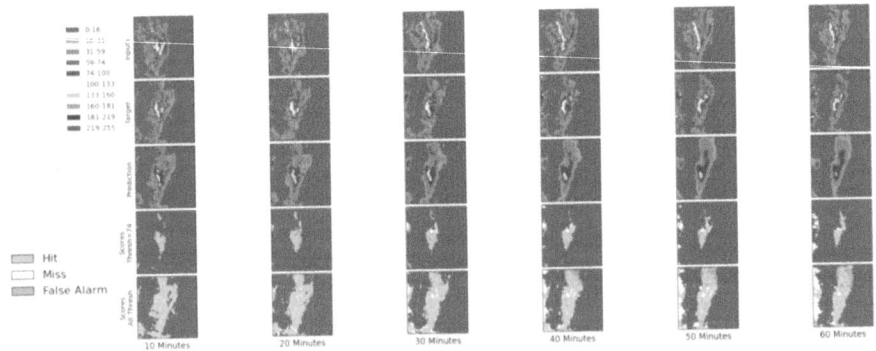

Fig. 3. Visualizations of the predicted frames on the SEVIR-MM dataset.

Table 5. Effects of the cross-scale operator learner (COL) and the spatial representation aggregator (SRA) on the SEVIR-MM dataset.

COL	SRA	Metrics	
		mCSI ↑	MSE ↓
○	○	**0.4289**	3.960
×	○	0.4176	3.916
○	×	0.4166	3.860
×	×	0.4198	**3.830**

4.3 Ablation Study

We designed ablation experiments on COL and SRA to prove their effectiveness, including the models without COL, without SRA, and without both COL and SRA, respectively. According to the experimental results in Table 5, COL and SRA can improve the model performance, with the mCSI increasing from 0.4198 to 0.4289. Furthermore, we observed that although COL was capable of modeling complex atmospheric evolution dynamics from multi-modal historical data, its sole incorporation into the baseline model did not enhance the mCSI metric. This may be attributed to the use of COL alone for extracting multi-modal information without adequate integration of these insights, leading to information redundancy and thus failing to improve model performance. Optimal results were obtained when both COL and SRA were utilized within the baseline model. This finding highlights the efficacy of COL and SRA in both extracting and integrating multi-modal information, demonstrating their complementary functions in enhancing model performance.

5 Conclusion

In this paper, we propose a novel multi-modal spatiotemporal forecasting model to achieve reliable and accurate predictions that align with real atmospheric dynamics, utilizing the physical spatiotemporal data obtained from satellites. The proposed framework consists of a Cross-scale Operator Learner (COL) and a Spatial Representation Aggregator (SRA), which extracts and integrates physical background information. As a result, The COL obtains an atmospheric spatial representation of atmospheric evolution processes and the SRA further integrates the atmospheric spatial representation and VIL's spatial representation, generating an enhanced spatiotemporal representation with both VIL spatial details and atmospheric physical background. Extensive experiments prove that this representation can realize temporal embedding better and improve the model's accuracy in predicting VIL.

Acknowledgments. This work is supported by grants No. KZ46009501.

Disclosure of Interests. Authors declare that the research was conducted in the absence of any commercial or financial relationships that could be construed as potential conflict of interest.

References

1. Shi, X., et al.: Convolutional LSTM network: a machine learning approach for precipitation nowcasting. In: Advances in Neural Information Processing Systems, vol. 28 (2015)
2. Wang, Y., et al.: Eidetic 3D LSTM: a model for video prediction and beyond. In: International Conference on Learning Representations (2018)
3. Wang, Y., et al.: PredRNN: recurrent neural networks for predictive learning using spatiotemporal LSTMs. In: Advances in Neural Information Processing Systems, vol. 30 (2017)
4. Gao, Z., et al.: SimVP: simpler yet better video prediction. In: Proceedings of the IEEE/CVF Conference on Computer Vision and Pattern Recognition (2022)
5. Tan, C., et al. SimVP: towards simple yet powerful spatiotemporal predictive learning. arXiv preprint, arXiv:2211.12509 (2022)
6. Tan, C., et al.: Temporal attention unit: towards efficient spatiotemporal predictive learning. In: Proceedings of the IEEE/CVF Conference on Computer Vision and Pattern Recognition, pp. 18770–18782 (2023)
7. Lu, L., Jin, P., Karniadakis, G.E.: DeepONet: learning nonlinear operators for identifying differential equations based on the universal approximation theorem of operators. arXiv preprint, arXiv:1910.03193 (2019)
8. Veillette, M., Samsi, S., Mattioli, C.: SEVIR: a storm event imagery dataset for deep learning applications in radar and satellite meteorology. In: Advances in Neural Information Processing Systems, vol. 33, pp. 22009–22019 (2020)
9. LeCun, Y., Bottou, L., Bengio, Y., et al.: Gradient-based learning applied to document recognition. Proc. IEEE **86**(11), 2278–2324 (1998)
10. Hochreiter, S., Schmidhuber, J.: Long short-term memory. Neural Comput. **9**(8), 1735–1780 (1997)
11. Wang, Y., Gao, Z., Long, M., et al.: PredRNN++: towards a resolution of the deep-in-time dilemma in spatiotemporal predictive learning. In: International Conference on Machine Learning, pp. 5123–5132 (2018)
12. Wang, Y., Wu, H., Zhang, J., et al.: PredRNN: a recurrent neural network for spatiotemporal predictive learning. IEEE Trans. Pattern Anal. Mach. Intell. **45**(2), 2208–2225 (2022)
13. Jordan, M.I.: Serial order: a parallel distributed processing approach. Adv. Psychol. **121**, 471–495 (1997)
14. Wang, Y., Zhang, J., Zhu, H., et al.: Memory in memory: a predictive neural network for learning higher-order non-stationarity from spatiotemporal dynamics. In: Proceedings of the IEEE/CVF Conference on Computer Vision and Pattern Recognition, pp. 9154–9162 (2019)
15. Castro, R., Souto, Y.M., Ogasawara, E., et al.: STConvS2S: spatiotemporal convolutional sequence to sequence network for weather forecasting. Neurocomputing **426**, 285–298 (2021)
16. Gao, Z., Shi, X., Wang, H., et al.: EarthFormer: exploring space-time transformers for earth system forecasting. In: Advances in Neural Information Processing Systems, vol. 35, pp. 25390–25403 (2022)

17. Bai, C., Sun, F., Zhang, J., et al.: RainFormer: features extraction balanced network for radar-based precipitation nowcasting. IEEE Geosci. Remote Sens. Lett. **19**, 1–5 (2022)

18. Sønderby, C.K., Espeholt, L., Heek, J., et al.: MetNet: a neural weather model for precipitation forecasting. arXiv preprint, arXiv:2003.12140 (2020)

19. Pathak, J., Subramanian, S., Harrington, P., et al.: FourCastNet: a global data-driven high-resolution weather model using adaptive Fourier neural operators. arXiv preprint, arXiv:2202.11214 (2022)

20. Ronneberger, O., Fischer, P., Brox, T.: U-Net: convolutional networks for biomedical image segmentation. In: Navab, N., Hornegger, J., Wells, W.M., Frangi, A.F. (eds.) MICCAI 2015. LNCS, vol. 9351, pp. 234–241. Springer, Cham (2015). https://doi.org/10.1007/978-3-319-24574-4_28

21. Boussioux, L., Zeng, C., Guénais, T., et al.: Hurricane forecasting: a novel multi-modal machine learning framework. Weather Forecasting **37**(6), 817–831 (2022)

22. Boussif, O., Boukachab, G., Assouline, D., et al.: Improving day-ahead solar irradiance time series forecasting by leveraging spatiotemporal context. In: Advances in Neural Information Processing Systems, vol. 36 (2024)

23. Nguyen, T., Brandstetter, J., Kapoor, A., et al.: Climax: a foundation model for weather and climate. arXiv preprint, arXiv:2301.10343 (2023)

24. Jin, Q., Zhang, X., Xiao, X., et al.: SpatioTemporal inference network for precipitation nowcasting with multi-modal fusion. IEEE J. Sel. Top. Appl. Earth Obs. Remote Sens. (2023)

25. Zhang, X., Jin, Q., Yu, T., et al.: Multi-modal spatiotemporal meteorological forecasting with deep neural network. ISPRS J. Photogramm. Remote. Sens. **188**, 380–393 (2022)

26. Dosovitskiy, A., Beyer, L., Kolesnikov, A., et al.: An image is worth 16×16 words: transformers for image recognition at scale. arXiv preprint, arXiv:2010.11929 (2020)

27. Vaswani, A., Shazeer, N., Parmar, N., et al.: Attention is all you need. In: Advances in Neural Information Processing Systems, vol. 30 (2017)

28. Ghiasi, G., Lin, T.Y., Le, Q.V.: NAS-FPN: learning scalable feature pyramid architecture for object detection. In: Proceedings of the IEEE/CVF Conference on Computer Vision and Pattern Recognition, pp. 7036–7045 (2019)

29. Long, Z., et al.: PDE-Net: Learning PDEs from data. In: International Conference on Machine Learning, pp. 3208–3216 (2018)

30. Guen, V.L., Thome, N.: Disentangling physical dynamics from unknown factors for unsupervised video prediction. In: Proceedings of the IEEE/CVF Conference on Computer Vision and Pattern Recognition, pp. 11474–11484 (2020)

31. Long, Z., Lu, Y., Dong, B.: PDE-Net 2.0: learning PDEs from data with a numeric-symbolic hybrid deep network. J. Comput. Phys. **399**, 108925 (2019)

32. Shen, Z., He, L., Lin, Z., et al.: PDO-eConvs: partial differential operator based equivariant convolutions. In: International Conference on Machine Learning, pp. 8697–8706 (2020)

33. Ren, P., Rao, C., Liu, Y., et al.: PhyCRNet: physics-informed convolutional-recurrent network for solving spatiotemporal PDEs. Comput. Methods Appl. Mech. Eng. **389**, 114399 (2022)

34. Ma, Y., et al.: Transductive relation-propagation network for few-shot learning. In: IJCAI, pp. 804–810 (2020)

35. Ma, Y., et al.: Transductive relation-propagation with decoupling training for few-shot learning. IEEE Trans. Neural Netw. Learn. Syst. **33**(11) (2021)

36. Wu, H., Xion, W., Xu, F., et al.: PastNet: introducing physical inductive biases for spatiotemporal video prediction. arXiv preprint, arXiv:2305.11421 (2023)

37. Wu, H., Liang, Y., Xiong, W., et al.: Earthfarsser: versatile spatiotemporal dynamical systems modeling in one model. In: Proceedings of the AAAI Conference on Artificial Intelligence, vol. 38, no. 14, pp. 15906–15914 (2024)

38. Li, Z., Kovachki, N., Azizzadenesheli, K., et al.: Fourier neural operator for parametric partial differential equations. arXiv preprint, arXiv:2010.08895 (2020)

39. Guibas, J., Mardani, M., Li, Z., et al.: Adaptive Fourier neural operators: efficient token mixers for transformers. arXiv preprint, arXiv:2111.13587 (2021)

40. Eliasof, M., Haber, E., Treister, E.: PDE-GCN: novel architectures for graph neural networks motivated by partial differential equations. In: Advances in Neural Information Processing Systems, vol. 34, pp. 3836–3849 (2021)

41. Gao, Z., Shi, X., Han, B., et al.: PreDiff: precipitation nowcasting with latent diffusion models. In: Advances in Neural Information Processing Systems, vol. 36 (2024)

42. Liu, X., et al.: A meaningful learning method for zero-shot semantic segmentation. Sci. China Inf. Sci. **66**(11) (2023)

Improved VLN-BERT with Reinforcing Endpoint Alignment for Vision-and-Language Navigation

Chuan Jin[1] , Boyuan Yang[2]([✉]) , and Ruonan Liu[3]

[1] College of Artificial Intelligence, Nankai University, Tianjin, China
2120230519@mail.nankai.edu.cn
[2] Center for Advanced Control and Smart Operations, Nanjing University, Suzhou, China
yby@nju.edu.cn
[3] Department of Automation, Shanghai Jiao Tong University, Shanghai, China

Abstract. Vision-and-Language Navigation (VLN) refers to an agent navigating a real-world environment by understanding natural language instructions and utilizing visual information from the surroundings. Currently, many pre-trained models and pre-training tasks have been proposed to assist agents in navigating unfamiliar environments using visual and linguistic information. However, ensuring that the agent stops near the endpoint is a challenging problem. Building on the existing VLN-BERT model, we propose an improved VLN-BERT model with a new pre-training task called Reinforcing Endpoint Alignment (REA-VLN-BERT). Through this pre-training task, the model can more effectively align the endpoint in the path with the corresponding instruction without requiring any additional data. Further experiments show that the reinforcing endpoint alignment task leads to improvements of 0.78% and 2.51% in Success Rate (SR) on the seen and unseen validation sets of the R2R dataset, respectively. Furthermore, inspired by Airbert, we combine shuffling loss with the reinforcing endpoint alignment task, resulting in a new model named SREA-VLN-BERT. SREA-VLN-BERT achieves improvements of 3.53% and 0.94% in SR on the seen and unseen validation sets of the R2R dataset, respectively, further enhancing the model's average performance in VLN.

Keywords: vision-and-language navigation · pre-training tasks · reinforcing endpoint alignment

1 Introduction

A long-term goal of artificial intelligence is to create an intelligent agent that can perceive the environment through visual information, communicate with humans using natural language, move freely in real-world environments and execute complex tasks. Vision-and-Language Navigation (VLN) [2] is a fundamental and interdisciplinary research topic to achieve this goal. As various

J. Guo et al. (Eds.): IJCAI 2024, CCIS 2160, pp. 119–133, 2024.
https://doi.org/10.1007/978-981-97-6125-8_10

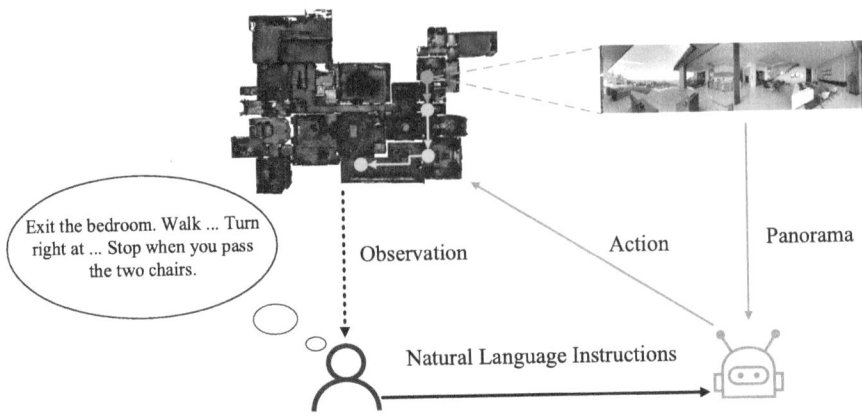

Fig. 1. The principle of VLN. The agent receives natural language instructions from humans and gathers visual information by interacting with the environment. It then processes both visual and linguistic information simultaneously to navigate in the real-world environment. Some elements in the figure are sourced from [3,16].

datasets [2,5,14,19,21,36,44] on VLN are proposed, more and more researchers are focusing on this field. Figure 1 illustrates the principle of VLN. Given the natural language instruction, *'Exit the bedroom. Walk in the opposite direction of the picture hanging on the wall through the kitchen. Turn right at the long white countertop. Stop when you pass the two chairs.'*, the agent must first recognize that it is in the bedroom and exit. Then, it needs to identify the picture on the wall and walk through the kitchen in the opposite direction. Next, it must find the long white countertop and turn right. Finally, it should locate the two chairs and stop at an appropriate position. To successfully complete the VLN task, the agent must effectively fuse visual and linguistic information, making decisions at each step until the navigation ends.

As an emerging research field, VLN faces numerous challenges [13,47]. Firstly, the agent needs to align and fuse information from the distinct modalities of vision and language. Secondly, the agent must make decisions and navigate complex environments using multimodal information. Thirdly, due to the high costs associated with 3D environment rendering and data annotation, datasets for VLN are relatively scarce. Fourthly, VLN models are trained in simulated environments with limited types of observations, while real-world navigation is dynamic and continuous. Improving the generalization capability of models in complex and variable real-world environments remains a significant challenge.

To address these challenges, many models [2,5,6,11,16,24,25,31,46,48] and pre-training tasks [4,5,14,15,17,32,34,35] have been proposed to enhance the performance of agents in VLN tasks. However, existing models do not consider the alignment weight of each viewpoint along the path with the corresponding instruction. In the actual navigation process, humans prefer that the agent correctly reaches the endpoint. Typically, humans can tolerate the agent taking some incorrect intermediate viewpoints as long as it reaches the endpoint correctly. Conversely, they cannot accept an agent failing to reach the endpoint correctly. Thus, we propose a new pre-training task called reinforcing endpoint alignment. Through this pre-training task, the improved VLN-BERT with Reinforcing Endpoint Alignment (REA-VLN-BERT) can more effectively align the endpoint in the path with the corresponding instruction without requiring any additional data. We extend the three-stage pre-training process of VLN-BERT into a four-stage pre-training process and fine-tune it through path selection [31]. Further experiments show that the reinforcing endpoint alignment task leads to improvements of 0.78% and 2.51% in Success Rate (SR) on the seen and unseen validation sets of the R2R dataset [2,3], respectively. Furthermore, we combine shuffling loss proposed by Airbert [14] with the reinforcing endpoint alignment task, resulting in a new model named SREA-VLN-BERT. SREA-VLN-BERT achieves improvements of 3.53% and 0.94% in SR on the seen and unseen validation sets of the R2R dataset, respectively, further enhancing the model's average performance in VLN.

We summarize our contributions as follows: (1) We propose the reinforcing endpoint alignment task, aimed at strengthening the visual-linguistic alignment of the model with the endpoint of the path. The new model is called REA-VLN-BERT. (2) We extend the three-stage pre-training process of VLN-BERT to a four-stage pre-training process, leading to improvements of 0.78% and 2.51% in SR on the seen and unseen validation sets of the R2R dataset, respectively. (3) We combine the shuffling loss, used to enhance the model's temporal reasoning ability, with our reinforcing endpoint alignment task, resulting in a new model named SREA-VLN-BERT, which achieves improvements of 3.53% and 0.94% in SR on the seen and unseen validation sets of the R2R dataset, respectively.

2   Related Work

Vision-and-Language Pre-training with Transformers. In recent years, significant progress has been made in Vision-and-Language Pre-training (VLP) models [7,22,23,26,30,37,42] based on the Transformer architectures [9,10,45]. ViLBERT [30] extends BERT [9] into a dual-stream model for vision and language processing. It first uses the Transformer encoder [10,45] to process visual and linguistic information separately, and then employs Co-attentional Transformer Layers (Co-TRM) to facilitate interaction between the two modalities. Additionally, many pre-training tasks have been proposed to enhance the alignment and fusion of visual and linguistic information, such as masked multi-modal modelling [30], multi-modal alignment prediction [30], word-region alignment [7], image question answering [42] and so on. CLIP [37] introduces contrastive learning [33,40] into VLP and is trained on large-scale Internet image and text datasets, significantly improving the model's generalization capability and performance across different tasks. Applying pre-trained VLP models to VLN tasks can more effectively align and fuse visual information from the environment with natural language instructions provided by humans, thereby improving navigation performance.

Pre-training Tasks in VLN. Unlike other vision-language tasks [12,18,28,41], VLN data consists of sequences of panoramic images and corresponding natural language instructions, which include actions such as *'turn left'*, *'turn right'*, *'stop'*, and so on. To adapt VLP models for VLN tasks, many pre-training tasks have been proposed. Instruction trajectory matching [5,14,31] is used to improve the model's ability to align sequences of panoramic images with natural language instructions. Action prediction [5,15] is utilized to assist the model in predicting actions based on current information. Shuffling loss [14] is used to improve the model's temporal reasoning ability. Some methods [1,5] are proposed to enhance the model's spatial awareness. Unlike the above methods, our reinforcing endpoint alignment task is designed to enhance the model's visual-linguistic alignment with the path's endpoint. Besides, We combine the shuffling loss with our reinforcing endpoint alignment task, resulting in better average performance.

Data Augmentation. Due to the high costs associated with 3D environment rendering and data annotation, datasets for VLN are relatively scarce. Synthesizing new data [11,29,43,49] based on existing environments and datasets is an effective way to improve the performance of VLN models. Airbert utilizes image-caption pairs from online rental marketplaces to construct the BnB dataset [14]. The GEL-R2R dataset [8] incorporates grounded entity-landmark human annotations into the R2R dataset [2]. Lily [27] uses numerous house tour videos from YouTube to build a new VLN dataset. Rich and diverse datasets are crucial for improving the generalization capability of VLN models. In this work, we create different paths for the reinforcing endpoint alignment task based on the R2R dataset.

3 Method

Problem Definition. In VLN [2], the agent is situated in a 3D environment represented by a navigation graph. The nodes of the graph denote viewpoints, while the edges represent paths. At the start of navigation, the agent is positioned at the initial viewpoint and given a natural language instruction $X = [x_1, x_2, \ldots, x_L]$ consisting of L words. At each step i, the agent is positioned at viewpoint $view_i$ and can observe the panoramic image P_i from the environment. The agent needs to choose an action a_i based on the current panoramic image P_i and the natural language instruction X simultaneously. When the agent chooses the *'stop'* action, the navigation ends. The final navigation path is denoted as $T = [P_1, P_2, \ldots, P_M]$.

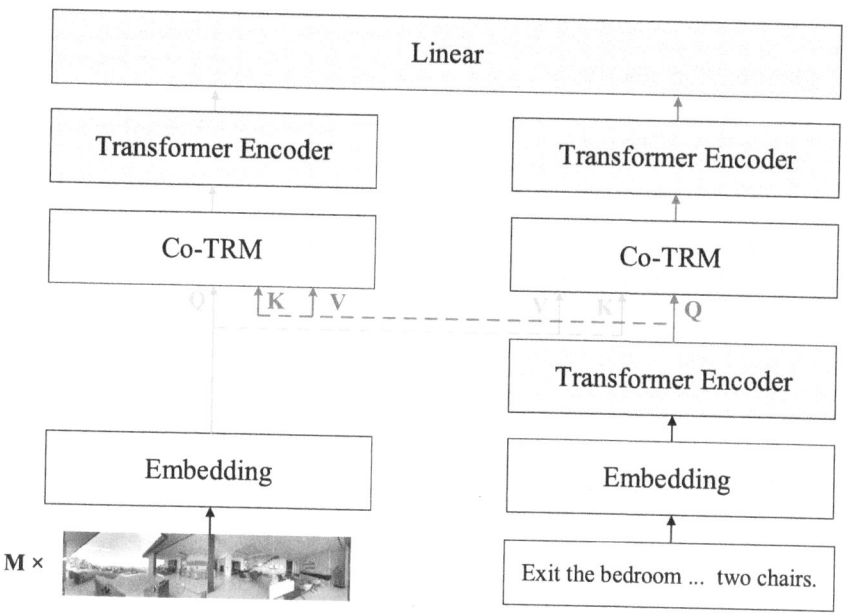

Fig. 2. The processing of each path-instruction pair in VLN-BERT. Some elements in the figure are sourced from [3,16].

3.1 VLN-BERT Architecture

VLN-BERT [31]uses a ViLBERT-like [30] architecture as model backbone. Given a natural language instruction, VLN-BERT first uses beam search with an instruction-following model [43] to generate N paths { T_1, T_2, ..., T_N }. For each path-instruction pair (T_j, X), VLN-BERT separately embeds the panoramic images sequence and the corresponding instruction. It then uses Co-Attentional Transformer Layers [30] to interact visual information with linguistic information. Similarity scores are calculated for each path-instruction pair. Finally, the path with the highest score is selected as the navigation path. Figure 2 illustrates VLN-BERT's processing of each path-instruction pair.

Visual Information Processing. Each path $T = [P_1, P_2, ..., P_M]$ contains M panoramic images. VLN-BERT [31] first uses a pre-trained Faster R-CNN [38] to extract region features $R_i = [r_1, r_2, ..., r_k]$ from each panorama. Then, for each panorama, VLN-BERT embeds the panorama index and the spatial information corresponding to each region. Finally, these embeddings are combined to obtain the final visual information:

$$v_k^{(i)} = r_k^{(i)} + W_P^{(i)} + W_S S_k^{(i)} \tag{1}$$

where $W_P^{(i)}$ denotes the embedded panorama index, $S_k^{(i)}$ denotes the region's spatial information, and W_S is used to map the region's spatial information to a high-dimensional space. A special token [IMG] is added to the features of each panorama to extract global visual information. The processed visual information is as follows:

$$F = [\,[\text{IMG}],\ v_1^{(1)},\ v_2^{(1)},\ \ldots, v_k^{(1)},\ \ldots, [\text{IMG}],\ v_1^{(M)},\ v_2^{(M)},\ \ldots, v_k^{(M)}\,] \quad (2)$$

Linguistic Information Processing. The instruction $X = [\,x_1,\ x_2,\ \ldots,\ x_L\,]$ is first converted into an embedding vector $\Omega = [\,[\text{CLS}],\ \omega_1,\ \omega_2,\ \ldots,\ \omega_L,\ [\text{SEP}]\,]$ through word embedding and position embedding [9]. [CLS] and [SEP] are two special tokens used to represent global information and to separate different sentences, respectively. Then, the embedding vector is input into the Transformer encoder [45] for attention calculation.

Co-attentional Transformer Layers. Co-Attentional Transformer Layers (Co-TRM) [30] uses two Transformer encoders [45] to process visual and linguistic information separately. Unlike the standard Transformer encoder, Co-TRM facilitates the interaction of visual and linguistic information by exchanging the key and value vectors between the visual and linguistic encoders. The calculation process is as follows:

$$\text{Visual-Attention}(Q_v, K_l, V_l) = \text{softmax}\left(\frac{Q_v K_l^T}{\sqrt{d_{K_l}}}\right) V_l \quad (3)$$

$$\text{Linguistic-Attention}(Q_l, K_v, V_v) = \text{softmax}\left(\frac{Q_l K_v^T}{\sqrt{d_{K_v}}}\right) V_v \quad (4)$$

where Q, K, and V denote the query vector, key vector, and value vector, respectively. And d_K is the dimension of the key vector.

Co-TRM takes the outputs h_{IMG} and h_{CLS}, corresponding to visual stream input [IMG] and linguistic stream input [CLS], as the global information of the outputs. VLN-BERT performs a matrix dot product on the outputs of the visual stream and the linguistic stream, and then calculates the similarity score through the linear mapping layer:

$$\text{Score} = \text{Linear}(h_{\text{IMG}} \odot h_{\text{CLS}}) \quad (5)$$

3.2   Pre-training and Fine-Tuning in VLN-BERT

Three-Stage Pre-training Process. VLN-BERT [31] utilizes image-text pairs from the Internet to pre-train the model, enabling it to acquire a comprehensive foundation in vision-language understanding. The three-stage pre-training process proposed by VLN-BERT is as follows: (1) Utilize Wikipedia and BooksCorpus [50] to pre-train the linguistic model through masked language model and next sentence prediction tasks [9], enabling the model to possess a general linguistic foundation. (2) Utilize the Conceptual Captions [39] to pre-train the model

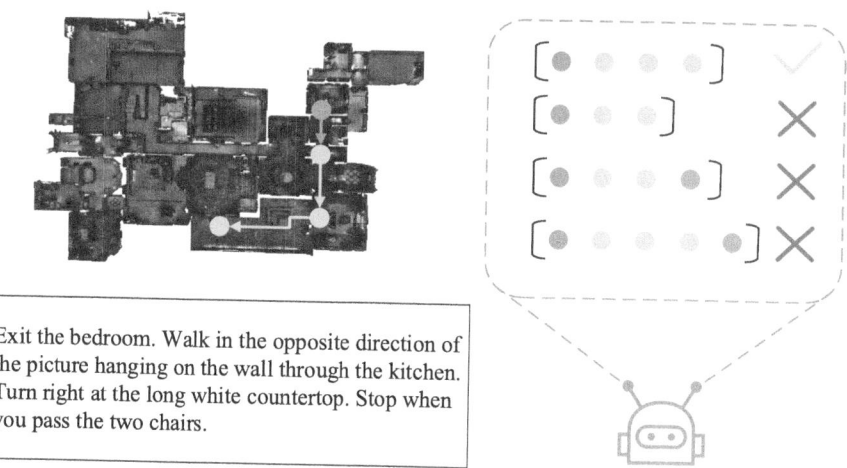

Exit the bedroom. Walk in the opposite direction of the picture hanging on the wall through the kitchen. Turn right at the long white countertop. Stop when you pass the two chairs.

Fig. 3. The principle of our reinforcing endpoint alignment task. Some elements in the figure are sourced from [3].

through masked multi-modal modelling and multi-modal alignment prediction tasks [30], enabling it to learn a general visual foundation. (3) Utilize R2R [2] to pre-train the model through masked multi-modal modelling, enabling it to learn an action foundation in VLN.

Path Selection. After a three-stage pre-training process, the model is fine-tuned to acquire the ability to perform path selection. VLN-BERT samples one correct path and three incorrect paths from paths generated by beam search. Then VLN-BERT trains the model to select the correct path from these paths through cross-entropy loss. It is implemented as follows:

$$D_{\text{sample}} = \{\, T_1^+,\ T_2^-,\ T_3^-,\ T_4^-\, \} \tag{6}$$

$$\mathbf{p} = \text{softmax}(\, \text{Score}_{T_1^+},\ \text{Score}_{T_2^-},\ \text{Score}_{T_3^-},\ \text{Score}_{T_4^-}\,) \tag{7}$$

$$\mathcal{L}_{PS} = -\log \mathbf{p}[0] \tag{8}$$

where T denotes navigation path, similarity scores in Eq. (7) are calculated by Eq. (5), $\mathbf{p}$ is a vector, and $\mathcal{L}_{PS}$ denotes the path selection loss function.

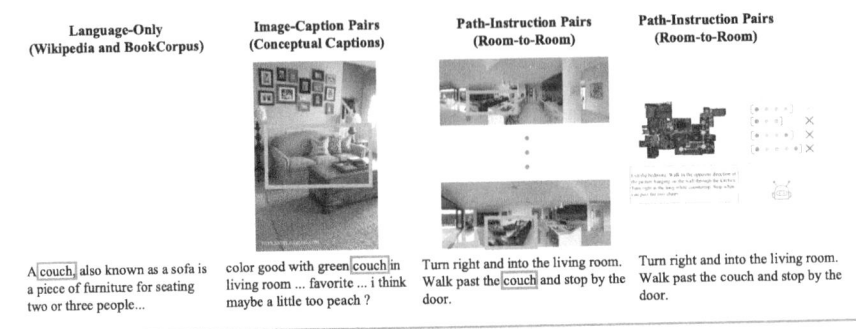

Language-Only
(Wikipedia and BookCorpus)   **Image-Caption Pairs**
(Conceptual Captions)   **Path-Instruction Pairs**
(Room-to-Room)   **Path-Instruction Pairs**
(Room-to-Room)

A couch, also known as a sofa is a piece of furniture for seating two or three people...   color good with green couch in living room ... favorite ... i think maybe a little too peach ?   Turn right and into the living room. Walk past the couch and stop by the door.   Turn right and into the living room. Walk past the couch and stop by the door.

Four-Stage Pretraining Process

Fig. 4. The four-stage pre-training process. Following the three-stage pre-training process, we train the model using our reinforcing endpoint alignment task, extending the three-stage pre-training process of VLN-BERT [31] to a four-stage pre-training process. Some elements in the figure are sourced from [3, 16, 39, 50].

3.3   Reinforcing Endpoint Alignment Task

In VLN, the primary concern for humans is navigation accuracy. The natural language instructions in VLN describe how the agent should move from the starting point to the endpoint step by step in detail. If the agent cannot reach the endpoint accurately, its previous navigation process will be meaningless, even if the earlier navigation path is consistent with the correct path. Therefore, the model should assign greater weight to aligning the endpoint with its corresponding instruction than to aligning other viewpoints with their respective instructions. In other words, the model should impose a greater penalty on an agent that fails to reach the endpoint correctly than on one that takes incorrect intermediate viewpoints but ultimately reaches the endpoint.

However, th pre-training and fine-tuning in VLN-BERT [31] do not pay attention to this. VLN-BERT first selects N candidate paths that best match the natural language instruction using beam search. Then VLN-BERT calculates similarity scores for these paths based on the given natural language instruction. Finally, it selects the path with the highest score as the navigation path. Throughout the entire process, VLN-BERT assigns equal weight to aligning each viewpoint in the path with its corresponding texts in the natural language instruction. To align the endpoint in the path with the corresponding texts in the natural language instruction, we propose a new pre-training task called reinforcing endpoint alignment.

Figure 3 shows our reinforcing endpoint alignment task in detail. Inspired by the path selection in VLN-BERT, we manually build three incorrect paths for each path-instruction pair in R2R [2]. We build the first incorrect path by removing the endpoint of the correct path. The endpoint of the second incorrect path is randomly replaced by other viewpoints. We build the third incorrect path by randomly adding a viewpoint after the endpoint of the correct path.

We calculate the similarity scores between the natural language instruction and each of these paths. Finally we use cross-entropy loss to strengthen the visual-linguistic alignment of the model with the endpoint of the path. The reinforcing endpoint alignment task is implemented as follows:

$$T_1^+ = [\, P_1, \, P_2, \, \ldots, \, P_{M-1}, \, P_M \,] \tag{9}$$

$$T_2^- = [\, P_1, \, P_2, \, \ldots, \, P_{M-1} \,] \tag{10}$$

$$T_3^- = [\, P_1, \, P_2, \, \ldots, \, P_{M-1}, \, P_{\mathrm{random}} \,] \tag{11}$$

$$T_4^- = [\, P_1, \, P_2, \, \ldots, \, P_{M-1}, \, P_M, \, P_{\mathrm{random}} \,] \tag{12}$$

$$\mathcal{L}_{REA} = - \log \mathbf{p}[0] \tag{13}$$

where T denotes navigation path, P denotes panoramic images, $\mathbf{p}$ is calculated by Eq. (7), and $\mathcal{L}_{REA}$ denotes the reinforcing endpoint alignment loss function. Besides, we extend the three-stage pre-training process of VLN-BERT to a four-stage pre-training process, as illustrated in Fig. 4.

4   Experiments

We first introduce R2R dataset [2] in Sect. 4.1. In Sect. 4.2, we list the evaluation metrics commonly used in VLN. Then we show the experimental results of REA-VLN-BERT in Sect. 4.3. Finally, we show the experimental results of SREA-VLN-BERT and ablation study in Sect. 4.4.

4.1   R2R Dataset

The R2R dataset contains a total of 7,189 paths and 21,567 natural language instructions. Each path corresponds to three natural language instructions that convey the same meaning but are described differently. The natural language instructions in R2R dataset include approximately 3,100 unique words. The average length of each instruction is about 29 words.

The R2R dataset is divided into training, validation, and test sets. The validation set is further divided into a seen validation set (Val Seen) and an unseen validation set (Val Unseen). The training set consists of 61 scenes, including 4,675 paths and 14,025 natural language instructions. The seen validation set contains 61 scenes, the same as the training set. It includes 340 paths and 1,020 natural language instructions. The unseen validation set contains 11 scenes, 783 paths, and 2,349 natural language instructions. The test set contains 18 scenes, 1,391 paths, and 4,173 natural language instructions.

Table 1. Performance comparison of VLN-BERT [31] and REA-VLN-BERT on Val Seen and Val Unseen sets. PL and NE represent the averages of all test samples.

Model	Validation Set	PL	NE↓	OSR↑	SR↑	SPL↑
VLN-BERT [31]	Val Seen	10.28	3.73	76.47	70.20	66.27
REA-VLN-BERT	Val Seen	10.28	**3.65**	**77.06**	**70.98**	**67.00**
VLN-BERT [31]	Val Unseen	9.60	4.10	69.22	59.26	55.00
REA-VLN-BERT	Val Unseen	9.63	**3.93**	**71.09**	**61.77**	**57.28**

4.2 Evaluation Metrics

We use Path Length (PL), Navigation Error (NE), Oracle Success Rate (OSR), Success Rate (SR), and Success weighted by Path Length (SPL) as the evaluation metrics in VLN. PL refers to the length of the agent's navigation trajectory. NE refers to the distance between the endpoint of the agent's navigation path and goal position. OSR is defined as the percentage of navigations where the agent passes within 3 m of the goal position. SR represents the percentage of successful navigations, while SPL takes both SR and PL into account.

4.3 REA-VLN-BERT

After the three-stage pre-training process, we train the model using our reinforcing endpoint alignment task. In this task, we use the Adam optimizer [20] with a learning rate of 4e-5 and a batch size of 32, training for a total of 10 epochs. Finally, we fine-tune the model through path selection. Since the test set is not public, we train the model using the training set and evaluate it using the Val Seen and Val Unseen sets.

The results presented in Table 1 demonstrate the improvement achieved by our reinforcing endpoint alignment task. In the Val Seen set, REA-VLN-BERT has the same PL as VLN-BERT. And its NE, OSR, SR, and SPL have all improved compared to VLN-BERT, with NE decreasing by 0.08, OSR increasing by 0.59%, SR increasing by 0.78%, and SPL increasing by 0.73%. In the Val Unseen set, the PL of REA-VLN-BERT is 0.03 higher than that of VLN-BERT, while NE decreases by 0.17. Additionally, OSR, SR, and SPL increase by 1.87%, 2.51%, and 2.28%, respectively. Through comparison, we find that the reinforcing endpoint alignment task is more effective in improving the performance of VLN-BERT in unseen environments. The task plays an important role in enhancing the generalization performance of VLN-BERT in VLN tasks. In fact, enhancing performance in unfamiliar environments is crucial for the agent, as it frequently undertakes VLN tasks in previously unseen settings.

4.4 SREA-VLN-BERT and Ablation Study

Furthermore, we combine shuffling loss in AirBERT [14] with our reinforcing endpoint alignment task. The new model is named SREA-VLN-BERT. Shuffling

Table 2. Performance comparison of different models on Val Seen and Val Unseen sets. S-VLN-BERT denotes VLN-BERT with shuffling loss. REAS-VLN-BERT denotes VLN-BERT with the reinforcing endpoint alignment task first, followed by shuffling loss.

Model	Validation Set	PL	NE↓	OSR↑	SR↑	SPL↑
VLN-BERT [31]	Val Seen	10.28	3.73	76.47	70.20	66.27
S-VLN-BERT	Val Seen	10.41	3.66	78.43	70.49	66.23
REA-VLN-BERT	Val Seen	10.28	3.65	77.06	70.98	67.00
REAS-VLN-BERT	Val Seen	10.28	3.51	**79.12**	71.86	67.84
SREA-VLN-BERT	Val Seen	10.32	**3.47**	**79.12**	**73.73**	**69.41**
VLN-BERT [31]	Val Unseen	9.60	4.10	69.22	59.26	55.00
S-VLN-BERT	Val Unseen	9.88	4.15	**71.35**	60.20	55.68
REA-VLN-BERT	Val Unseen	9.63	**3.93**	71.09	**61.77**	**57.28**
REAS-VLN-BERT	Val Unseen	9.66	4.13	69.82	60.20	55.58
SREA-VLN-BERT	Val Unseen	9.87	4.17	**71.35**	60.20	55.99

Table 3. Performance comparison of our models with previous models in SR on the Val Seen and Val Unseen sets.

Model	SR on Val Seen	SR on Val Unseen
Seq-2-Seq [2]	39	22
Speaker-Follower [11]	70	55
PRESS [25]	71	59
PREVALENT [15]	67	60
RCM + SIL [46]	73	61
VLN-BERT [31]	70	59
REA-VLN-BERT	71	**62**
SREA-VLN-BERT	**74**	60

loss first randomly shuffles the viewpoints in the correct path to generate three incorrect paths. It then uses the same cross-entropy loss as path selection in VLN-BERT to supervise the model's learning of temporal reasoning ability. The training parameters for shuffling loss are the same as those for the reinforcing endpoint alignment task.

Table 2 shows the experimental results of SREA-VLN-BERT and ablation study. Through comparative experiments, we find that both shuffling loss and the reinforcing endpoint alignment task can improve the performance of the VLN-BERT. Additionally, the training order impacts the extent of performance improvement. Training the model with shuffling loss first, followed by the reinforcing endpoint alignment task, produced the best average results. This makes intuitive sense, as a model with temporal reasoning ability is better able to align path endpoint with the corresponding instruction. SREA-VLN-BERT achieves

73.73% SR on the Val Seen set and 60.20% SR on the Val Unseen set, which are 3.53% and 0.94% higher than VLN-BERT, respectively, resulting in better average performance in VLN. However, we find that the SR of SREA-VLN-BERT on Val Unseen set is lower than that of REA-VLN-BERT. It may be due to overfitting during the pre-training process of SREA-VLN-BERT, which reduces its generalization performance in unseen environments. In addition, we compare the performance of our model with previous models in Table 3.

5   Conclusion

In this paper, we propose an improved VLN-BERT [31] model with a new pre-training task called reinforcing endpoint alignment. Experiments show that this task significantly enhances the model's generalization capability in unseen environments. Furthermore, we find that adding the shuffling loss in Airbert [14] before the reinforcing endpoint alignment task further improves the model's average performance in VLN.

References

1. An, D., et al.: BevBERT: multimodal map pre-training for language-guided navigation. In: Proceedings of the IEEE/CVF International Conference on Computer Vision, pp. 2737–2748 (2023)
2. Anderson, P., et al.: Vision-and-language navigation: interpreting visually-grounded navigation instructions in real environments. In: Proceedings of the IEEE Conference on Computer Vision and Pattern Recognition (CVPR) (2018)
3. Chang, A., et al.: Matterport3D: learning from RGB-D data in indoor environments. arXiv preprint arXiv:1709.06158 (2017)
4. Chen, K., Chen, J.K., Chuang, J., Vázquez, M., Savarese, S.: Topological planning with transformers for vision-and-language navigation. In: Proceedings of the IEEE/CVF Conference on Computer Vision and Pattern Recognition, pp. 11276–11286 (2021)
5. Chen, S., Guhur, P.L., Schmid, C., Laptev, I.: History aware multimodal transformer for vision-and-language navigation. In: Ranzato, M., Beygelzimer, A., Dauphin, Y., Liang, P., Vaughan, J.W. (eds.) Advances in Neural Information Processing Systems, vol. 34, pp. 5834–5847. Curran Associates, Inc. (2021). https://proceedings.neurips.cc/paper_files/paper/2021/file/2e5c2cb8d13e8fba78d95211440ba326-Paper.pdf
6. Chen, S., Guhur, P.L., Tapaswi, M., Schmid, C., Laptev, I.: Think global, act local: dual-scale graph transformer for vision-and-language navigation. In: Proceedings of the IEEE/CVF Conference on Computer Vision and Pattern Recognition, pp. 16537–16547 (2022)
7. Chen, Y.-C., et al.: UNITER: UNiversal Image-TExt representation learning. In: Vedaldi, A., Bischof, H., Brox, T., Frahm, J.-M. (eds.) ECCV 2020. LNCS, vol. 12375, pp. 104–120. Springer, Cham (2020). https://doi.org/10.1007/978-3-030-58577-8_7
8. Cui, Y., Xie, L., Zhang, Y., Zhang, M., Yan, Y., Yin, E.: Grounded entity-landmark adaptive pre-training for vision-and-language navigation. In: Proceedings of the IEEE/CVF International Conference on Computer Vision, pp. 12043–12053 (2023)

9. Devlin, J., Chang, M.W., Lee, K., Toutanova, K.: BERT: pre-training of deep bidirectional transformers for language understanding. arXiv preprint arXiv:1810.04805 (2018)
10. Dosovitskiy, A., et al.: An image is worth 16×16 words: transformers for image recognition at scale. arXiv preprint arXiv:2010.11929 (2020)
11. Fried, D., et al.: Speaker-follower models for vision-and-language navigation. In: Advances in Neural Information Processing Systems, vol. 31 (2018)
12. Goyal, Y., Khot, T., Summers-Stay, D., Batra, D., Parikh, D.: Making the V in VQA matter: elevating the role of image understanding in visual question answering. In: Proceedings of the IEEE Conference on Computer Vision and Pattern Recognition, pp. 6904–6913 (2017)
13. Gu, J., Stefani, E., Wu, Q., Thomason, J., Wang, X.: Vision-and-language navigation: a survey of tasks, methods, and future directions. In: Muresan, S., Nakov, P., Villavicencio, A. (eds.) Proceedings of the 60th Annual Meeting of the Association for Computational Linguistics (Volume 1: Long Papers), pp. 7606–7623. Association for Computational Linguistics, Dublin, Ireland (2022). https://doi.org/10.18653/v1/2022.acl-long.524. https://aclanthology.org/2022.acl-long.524
14. Guhur, P.L., Tapaswi, M., Chen, S., Laptev, I., Schmid, C.: AirBERT: in-domain pretraining for vision-and-language navigation. In: Proceedings of the IEEE/CVF International Conference on Computer Vision (ICCV), pp. 1634–1643 (2021)
15. Hao, W., Li, C., Li, X., Carin, L., Gao, J.: Towards learning a generic agent for vision-and-language navigation via pre-training. In: Proceedings of the IEEE/CVF Conference on Computer Vision and Pattern Recognition, pp. 13137–13146 (2020)
16. Hong, Y., Wu, Q., Qi, Y., Rodriguez-Opazo, C., Gould, S.: VLN BERT: a recurrent vision-and-language BERT for navigation. In: Proceedings of the IEEE/CVF Conference on Computer Vision and Pattern Recognition, pp. 1643–1653 (2021)
17. Huang, H., Jain, V., Mehta, H., Baldridge, J., Ie, E.: Multi-modal discriminative model for vision-and-language navigation. arXiv preprint arXiv:1905.13358 (2019)
18. Hudson, D.A., Manning, C.D.: GQA: a new dataset for real-world visual reasoning and compositional question answering. In: Proceedings of the IEEE/CVF Conference on Computer Vision and Pattern Recognition, pp. 6700–6709 (2019)
19. Jain, V., Magalhaes, G., Ku, A., Vaswani, A., Ie, E., Baldridge, J.: Stay on the path: Instruction fidelity in vision-and-language navigation. In: Korhonen, A., Traum, D., Màrquez, L. (eds.) Proceedings of the 57th Annual Meeting of the Association for Computational Linguistics, pp. 1862–1872. Association for Computational Linguistics, Florence, Italy (2019). https://doi.org/10.18653/v1/P19-1181. https://aclanthology.org/P19-1181
20. Kingma, D.P., Ba, J.: Adam: a method for stochastic optimization. arXiv preprint arXiv:1412.6980 (2014)
21. Ku, A., Anderson, P., Patel, R., Ie, E., Baldridge, J.: Room-across-room: multilingual vision-and-language navigation with dense spatiotemporal grounding (2020)
22. Li, J., Li, D., Savarese, S., Hoi, S.: Blip-2: bootstrapping language-image pre-training with frozen image encoders and large language models. In: International Conference on Machine Learning, pp. 19730–19742. PMLR (2023)
23. Li, J., Li, D., Xiong, C., Hoi, S.: Blip: bootstrapping language-image pre-training for unified vision-language understanding and generation. In: International Conference on Machine Learning, pp. 12888–12900. PMLR (2022)
24. Li, X., Wang, Z., Yang, J., Wang, Y., Jiang, S.: KERM: knowledge enhanced reasoning for vision-and-language navigation. In: Proceedings of the IEEE/CVF Conference on Computer Vision and Pattern Recognition, pp. 2583–2592 (2023)

25. Li, X., et al.: Robust navigation with language pretraining and stochastic sampling. arXiv preprint arXiv:1909.02244 (2019)

26. Li, X., et al.: OSCAR: object-semantics aligned pre-training for vision-language tasks. In: Vedaldi, A., Bischof, H., Brox, T., Frahm, J.-M. (eds.) ECCV 2020. LNCS, vol. 12375, pp. 121–137. Springer, Cham (2020). https://doi.org/10.1007/978-3-030-58577-8_8

27. Lin, K., Chen, P., Huang, D., Li, T.H., Tan, M., Gan, C.: Learning vision-and-language navigation from YouTube videos. In: Proceedings of the IEEE/CVF International Conference on Computer Vision, pp. 8317–8326 (2023)

28. Lin, T.-Y., et al.: Microsoft COCO: common objects in context. In: Fleet, D., Pajdla, T., Schiele, B., Tuytelaars, T. (eds.) ECCV 2014. LNCS, vol. 8693, pp. 740–755. Springer, Cham (2014). https://doi.org/10.1007/978-3-319-10602-1_48

29. Liu, C., Zhu, F., Chang, X., Liang, X., Ge, Z., Shen, Y.D.: Vision-language navigation with random environmental mixup. In: Proceedings of the IEEE/CVF International Conference on Computer Vision, pp. 1644–1654 (2021)

30. Lu, J., Batra, D., Parikh, D., Lee, S.: ViLBERT: pretraining task-agnostic visiolinguistic representations for vision-and-language tasks. In: Advances in Neural Information Processing Systems, vol. 32 (2019)

31. Majumdar, A., Shrivastava, A., Lee, S., Anderson, P., Parikh, D., Batra, D.: Improving vision-and-language navigation with image-text pairs from the web. In: Vedaldi, A., Bischof, H., Brox, T., Frahm, J.-M. (eds.) ECCV 2020. LNCS, vol. 12351, pp. 259–274. Springer, Cham (2020). https://doi.org/10.1007/978-3-030-58539-6_16

32. Moudgil, A., Majumdar, A., Agrawal, H., Lee, S., Batra, D.: SOAT: a scene-and object-aware transformer for vision-and-language navigation. In: Advances in Neural Information Processing Systems, vol. 34, pp. 7357–7367 (2021)

33. van den Oord, A., Li, Y., Vinyals, O.: Representation learning with contrastive predictive coding. arXiv preprint arXiv:1807.03748 (2018)

34. Pashevich, A., Schmid, C., Sun, C.: Episodic transformer for vision-and-language navigation. In: 2021 IEEE CVF International Conference on Computer Vision (ICCV), pp. 15922–15932 (2021)

35. Qi, Y., Pan, Z., Hong, Y., Yang, M.H., Van Den Hengel, A., Wu, Q.: The road to know-where: an object-and-room informed sequential BERT for indoor vision-language navigation. In: Proceedings of the IEEE/CVF International Conference on Computer Vision, pp. 1655–1664 (2021)

36. Qi, Y., et al.: Reverie: remote embodied visual referring expression in real indoor environments. In: Proceedings of the IEEE/CVF Conference on Computer Vision and Pattern Recognition (CVPR) (2020)

37. Radford, A., et al.: Learning transferable visual models from natural language supervision. In: International Conference on Machine Learning, pp. 8748–8763. PMLR (2021)

38. Ren, S., He, K., Girshick, R., Sun, J.: Faster R-CNN: towards real-time object detection with region proposal networks. In: Advances in Neural Information Processing Systems, vol. 28 (2015)

39. Sharma, P., Ding, N., Goodman, S., Soricut, R.: Conceptual captions: a cleaned, hypernymed, image alt-text dataset for automatic image captioning. In: Proceedings of the 56th Annual Meeting of the Association for Computational Linguistics (Volume 1: Long Papers), pp. 2556–2565 (2018)

40. Sohn, K.: Improved deep metric learning with multi-class N-pair loss objective. In: Advances in Neural Information Processing Systems, vol. 29 (2016)

41. Suhr, A., Zhou, S., Zhang, A., Zhang, I., Bai, H., Artzi, Y.: A corpus for reasoning about natural language grounded in photographs. arXiv preprint arXiv:1811.00491 (2018)

42. Tan, H., Bansal, M.: LXMERT: learning cross-modality encoder representations from transformers. arXiv preprint arXiv:1908.07490 (2019)

43. Tan, H., Yu, L., Bansal, M.: Learning to navigate unseen environments: back translation with environmental dropout. In: Burstein, J., Doran, C., Solorio, T. (eds.) Proceedings of the 2019 Conference of the North American Chapter of the Association for Computational Linguistics: Human Language Technologies, Volume 1 (Long and Short Papers), pp. 2610–2621. Association for Computational Linguistics, Minneapolis, Minnesota (2019). https://doi.org/10.18653/v1/N19-1268. https://aclanthology.org/N19-1268

44. Thomason, J., Murray, M., Cakmak, M., Zettlemoyer, L.: Vision-and-dialog navigation. In: Kaelbling, L.P., Kragic, D., Sugiura, K. (eds.) Proceedings of the Conference on Robot Learning. Proceedings of Machine Learning Research, vol. 100, pp. 394–406. PMLR (2020). https://proceedings.mlr.press/v100/thomason20a.html

45. Vaswani, A., et al.: Attention is all you need. In: Advances in Neural Information Processing Systems, vol. 30 (2017)

46. Wang, X., et al.: Reinforced cross-modal matching and self-supervised imitation learning for vision-language navigation. In: Proceedings of the IEEE/CVF Conference on Computer Vision and Pattern Recognition, pp. 6629–6638 (2019)

47. Wu, W., Chang, T., Li, X., Yin, Q., Hu, Y.: Vision-language navigation: a survey and taxonomy. Neural Comput. Appl. **36**(7), 3291–3316 (2024)

48. Zhang, W., Ma, C., Wu, Q., Yang, X.: Language-guided navigation via cross-modal grounding and alternate adversarial learning. IEEE Trans. Circuits Syst. Video Technol. **31**(9), 3469–3481 (2020)

49. Zhu, W., et al.: Multimodal text style transfer for outdoor vision-and-language navigation. arXiv preprint arXiv:2007.00229 (2020)

50. Zhu, Y., et al.: Aligning books and movies: towards story-like visual explanations by watching movies and reading books. In: Proceedings of the IEEE International Conference on Computer Vision, pp. 19–27 (2015)

Bridging the Language Gap: Domain-Specific Dataset Construction for Medical LLMs

Chae Yeon Kim, Song Yeon Kim, Seung Hwan Cho, and Young-Min Kim[✉] 🄳

Department of Industrial Data Engineering, Hanyang University, Seoul 04763,
Republic of Korea
{cyeon97,olik72,shcho95,yngmnkim}@hanyang.ac.kr

Abstract. The advent of large language models (LLMs) has transformed the field of natural language processing (NLP), demonstrating impressive capabilities across a variety of tasks such as text generation, translation, and question answering. However, their effectiveness in specialized domains is constrained by the lack of domain-specific data. This paper presents an effective methodology for constructing domain-specific datasets using domain-specific corpora, thus overcoming the challenges posed by linguistic and cultural differences in non-English-speaking regions. By leveraging mining techniques, this methodology facilitates the construction of datasets tailored to local languages and cultures. A Korean medical corpus served as the foundation for dataset construction, leading to the development of a medical language model that demonstrated high performance and versatility across various NLP tasks. A bidirectional encoder representation from transformer-based comparative analysis revealed comparable performance. The objective is to streamline LLM applications across diverse domains, thereby enhancing language model efficiency. In the future, our efforts will be directed towards implementing the proposed methodology across diverse domains and investigating strategies for extracting domain-specific tasks and vocabulary to enhance the quality of domain datasets.

Keywords: Large Language Model · Mining · Domain Dataset

1 Introduction

Large language models (LLMs) have emerged as a significant advancement in natural language processing (NLP), demonstrating remarkable comprehension and reasoning abilities as generative language models. This ability enables them to solve complex problems and achieve outstanding performance across a variety of NLP tasks [1, 2].

Open-source LLMs such as Llama [3] and Alpaca [4] demonstrate innovative potential and facilitate the integration of artificial intelligence into specialized domains, such as medicine and law. This necessitates the development of domain-specific models, leading to the emergence of domain-specific LLMs [5–7].

J. Guo et al. (Eds.): IJCAI 2024, CCIS 2160, pp. 134–146, 2024.
https://doi.org/10.1007/978-981-97-6125-8_11

However, the application of LLMs in specific domains poses several challenges, with the primary one being the lack of domain-specific datasets. This challenge is exacerbated by complexities in data labeling and limitations in data accessibility. Previous studies [8, 9] have attempted to address this challenge; however, most have used English-language data, which has encountered significant challenges when applied in non-English-speaking countries due to linguistic and cultural differences. These challenges manifest in various adverse effects, including a decline in model performance and an increase in learning errors, posing a significant obstacle to the effective deployment of LLMs in specialized domains within non-English-speaking countries. To overcome these challenges, it is essential to develop a methodology for constructing datasets that considers both linguistic attributes and domain-specific characteristics.

We propose a methodology for constructing domain-specific data that utilizes raw domain corpora to improve the performance of LLMs for a variety of tasks. We constructed datasets based on raw domain corpora using mining techniques to enhance the model's comprehension and maintain prompt performance. This methodology addresses domain-specific data challenges in non-English-speaking countries, such as South Korea, by considering the cultural and linguistic characteristics of localities during the data construction process.

The proposed methodology was evaluated using LLM and bidirectional encoder representations from transformers (BERT) [10], trained on a dataset constructed from medical domain literature. The model achieved an accuracy of over 87%. However, the benchmark evaluation revealed that its performance was lower compared to Korean LLMs. This is attributed to the limited domain-specific dataset, resulting in relatively insufficient Korean training data compared to Korean LLM datasets.

The contributions can be summarized as follows:

- We propose a methodology for constructing training data using mining techniques within constrained domain datasets.
- We address data acquisition challenges in non-English-speaking countries by constructing culturally and linguistically tailored datasets.
- We apply this methodology to the medical domain to develop a specialized LLM for medical purposes.

2   Related Works

2.1   Medical Domain Language Models

Large Language Model (LLM). LLMs, such as generative LLMs like GPT-4 and Gemini, have demonstrated exceptional performance across a range of NLP tasks, including text summarization, question-answering, and translation. Moreover, the flourishing open-source movement has facilitated the development of numerous high-performance LLM models, including Llama 2 [11], Vicuna [12], and Mistral [13]. Considering the availability of open-source models, researchers are actively exploring their applications in various specialized domains, particularly in healthcare, law, and finance.

Domain Language Model (LM). The application of language models to specialized domains has led to the development of models that can encode and utilize domain-specific knowledge. These models are often adaptations of pretrained models from general domains. Examples include BERT [10] and T5 [14], which are encoder-based and encoder-decoder models, respectively, and have been applied across various domains [15, 16]. However, difficulties arise when these models are applied to tasks beyond their original training scope. Recently, generative LLMs such as BioGPT [17] based on GPT-2 [18], Llama 2 [11], and adapted BioMedGPT [19], utilizing decoder-only architectures, have been developed in the medical domain.

2.2 Instruction Tuning

LLMs excel in contextual understanding and generate context-aware responses, often through next-word prediction, trained on massive datasets. However, this inherent focus on statistical predictions within a learned distribution may not always align with user expectations. Instruction tuning [20] has emerged as a promising approach to bridge this gap between LLM training objectives and user goals.

Instruction tuning involves leveraging pairs of instructions and outputs. The instruction component represents user directives, guiding the model's output towards desired responses, while the output signifies the ideal response of the LLM to the provided instructions. This approach empowers users to exert control over the model's response generation by aligning it with human instructions.

The flexibility of instruction tuning enables LLM adaptation to specific domains without requiring architectural modifications, thus enhancing user-centric performance.

3 Methods

LLMs are often trained on extensive corpora, but their learning objectives may not always align with user expectations. To address this misalignment, researchers have investigated data augmentation techniques to refine the training data for LLMs. This method, introduced by Van de Kar et al. (2022) [21], involves mining the original pre-training corpus to enhance the language model's comprehension and responsiveness to user instructions. The proposed approach aims to enhance the LLM's responsiveness, particularly in question-answering tasks, by augmenting the model's ability to generate informative prompts. This strategy, even with a limited dataset, fosters diversity in both input and output. Consequently, enhancing the model's zero-shot performance and domain-specific knowledge [20].

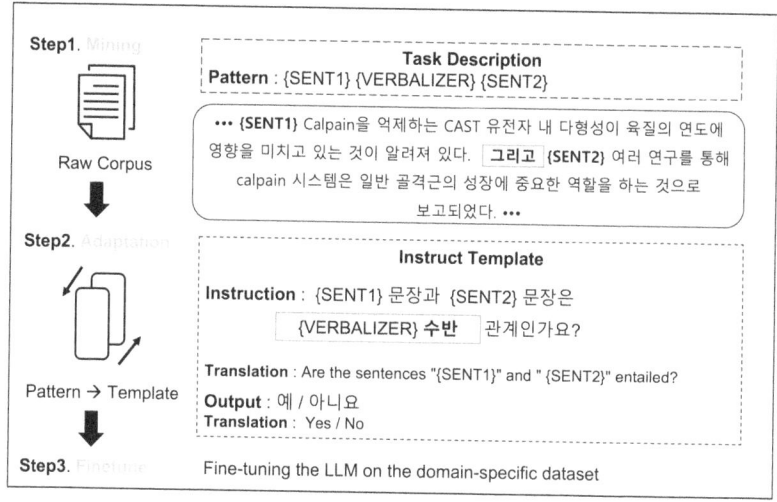

Fig. 1. Task patterns and verbalizers employed in this study, as presented in Table 1.

3.1 Mining

We define patterns and verbalizers to construct task-specific training data from a raw corpus. This process involves effectively extracting sentences that match the raw corpus using the patterns and verbalizers listed in Table 1. Patterns are defined by analyzing the structure of the raw corpus to create regular expression-based patterns suitable for extracting tasks and their corresponding data. Verbalizers encompass verbs, nouns, adverbs, and other elements used within these patterns, aiming to differentiate tasks and labels within the extracted data. Given the inherent variations in writing systems, grammatical rules, and data formats across languages, it is necessary to customize the patterns and verbalizer definitions to suit the specific characteristics of each language or domain. This ensures the effective extraction of relevant sentences from diverse sources, as the extracted data serves as a resource for training models to acquire domain knowledge and adapt to instructions.

3.2 Adaptation

The extracted textual data are transformed into task-specific templates. This approach facilitates the acquisition of domain knowledge and guided learning based on user instructions. Two distinct templates are defined for each task to ensure template diversity. This diversity in templates enables the model to learn from various prompts, ultimately enhancing its comprehension and zero-shot performance.

Summary. We generate a concise abstract or key sentence from the given document by applying the principles of summary writing outlined in the text, "What is a summary?" This provides a concise overview of the document. The matching sentences, as identified through the regular expressions in Table 1, were then assembled into input-output templates. The summary sentence was then used as the target, and the model was instructed on how to summarize the content of the raw corpus. Moreover, summary sentences were employed as input data to generate articles pertinent to the domain.

Table 1. Pattern and instruction template. Pattern and verbalizer vary for each task and corpus. The symbol "{WORD}" denotes a single word, while "{SENT}" signifies a single sentence. The instruction template provides diversity in prompts/

Task Type	Pattern	Instruction Template	Verbalizer
Summary	{VERBALIZER} {TITLE / PURPOSE}	What is a summary? {TITLE} What is the purpose of {TITLE}? {PURPOSE}	Title 목적(Purpose)
Keyword	{VERBALIZER} ⊆ {SENT} and |VERBALIZER| ≥ 3	Generate a sentence about these {DOMAIN} keywords [{WORD1}, {WORD2}, {WORD3}]: {SENT} What is {domain} keyword about {SENT}: [{WORD1}, {WORD2}, {WORD3}]	초음파, 대조군, 세포의, 증후군, 뇌졸중, 임플란트를, 양상을, 에탄올, 임상적으로, ... Translate: ultrasound, control group, cellular, syndrome, stroke, implant, modality, ethanol, clinically,...
Natural Language Inference	{SENT1} {VERBALIZER} {SENT2}	Are the sentences {SENT1} and {SENT2} {VERBALIZER}?: {Yes/No} What is the cause of {SENT1}? {SENT2}	그리고,그래서,그리하여,그러면서,그러면,또한,그러나,하지만,다만,그렇지만,그런데,오히려,또는,따라서,그러니까 Translate: and, so, hence, while, then, also, but, however, just, nevertheless, by the way, or, therefore, thus

Keyword. We address the challenge of enhancing the model's comprehension of domain-specific vocabulary by prompting it to generate sentences containing these keywords. Domain-specific vocabulary was extracted from the raw corpus for the target domain using SentencePiece [22] to construct a general vocabulary for the languages involved, which can then be used in conjunction with domain vocabulary extraction. While general language models can be employed for vocabulary construction, this approach presents difficulties in non-English languages. In response, we constructed a general vocabulary for each language while also extracting domain-specific vocabulary. Subsequently, the constructed domain vocabulary is compared with the general vocabulary to identify domain-specific terms. The terms were further filtered to include only nouns, forming the final domain vocabulary set. For each sentence, the number of domain-specific words was counted, and sentences containing at least three words were extracted. In order to guide the model in generating domain-relevant sentences, we utilize prompts in the form of "Generate a sentence about {domain} related keywords [{WORD1}, {WORD2}, {WORD3}]." Alternatively, we provided prompts that specify whether a sentence should contain the domain-specific vocabulary set, thus facilitating the model's learning of domain-specific vocabulary. Domain represents the target domain of the study, and the list of domain words extracted from the sentence is denoted by [{WORD1}, {WORD2}, {WORD3}]. The model was trained to generate domain-specific sentences using regular expression patterns and instruction templates listed in Table 1, leveraging the domain-specific vocabulary dictionary.

Natural Language Inference (NLI). NLI is a task that determines the relationship between two given sentences. As illustrated in Fig. 1, verbalizers are conjunction words that express entailment relationships. The preceding and following sentences were extracted using the verbalizer and used as input templates. The output template is a classification task of "yes" or "no." Since there is considerable variation between languages in their criteria for conjunctions, our approach involved not only examining the linguistic characteristics of each language in question but also identifying the most frequently used conjunctions in a specific corpus of texts. For Korean, we selected the most frequently occurring conjunctions based on the findings of Han and Han (2016), published in the Korean Semantics journal. We defined four types of relationships based on conjunctions and extracted the preceding and following sentences accordingly. By establishing the relationship between each extracted sentence and the defined conjunction, we instruct the model with the command, "Are the sentences {SENT1} and {SENT2} entailed?" This helps the model comprehend the relationships between sentences. In addition, we transformed the classification task into a generation task to diversify the prompts provided by the model.

3.3 Fine-Tuning

The language model was fine-tuned using instructional tuning on the constructed dataset. This approach enables the model to learn responses to the user's intent, effectively conveying information. Despite the implementation of various patterns and prompts aimed at enhancing model performance, it is not feasible to completely solve complex real-world problems. Nevertheless, this methodology facilitates the model's capacity to learn domain knowledge in various ways.

4 Experiments

We employed Method 3 to train the language models and compared their performance with those of both the LLM and BERT models. To evaluate their performance in the medical domain, experiments were conducted using benchmark datasets.

4.1 Experiment Setting

Dataset. We selected a dataset consisting of approximately 18,000 medical domain papers from the domestic literature text dataset provided by the Korea Institute of Science and Technology Information (KISTI)[1]. The translated Alpaca dataset[2] was incorporated into our corpus to augment the limited Korean training data, thereby enhancing its suitability for Korean-language tasks.

Training Details. We employed the AdamW [23] scheduler. We minimized the memory requirements by applying the BitsandBytes [24] quantization technique while setting the input context length to 2,048 tokens. For optimization, we set the learning rate to 2×10^{-4}, weight decay to 0.01, gradient accumulation to 2, and batch size to 4 on an NVIDIA A100 80GB GPU, conducting training over three epochs.

4.2 Experimental Results

Model Comparison

Table 2. Results of evaluation using BERTScore [25], where the input context length for each model is indicated.

Model	Precision	Recall	F1
Llama-2-7B_2048	0.83	0.83	0.83
Llama-2-7B_4096	0.84	0.84	0.84
Mistral-2_2048	0.86	0.86	0.86
Mistral-2_4096	0.86	0.86	0.86
Solar-10.7B_2048	0.76	0.75	0.75
Solar-10.7B_4096	0.86	0.86	0.86

Table 2 presents the results of the model evaluation using BERTScore, indicating the input context length for each model. The dataset was constructed using the proposed methodology and divided into training and testing sets in an 8:2 ratio. All models were

---

[1] KISTI (2021) https://doi.org/10.23057/38.
[2] KoAlpaca (2023) https://huggingface.co/datasets/beomi/KoAlpaca-v1.1a.

trained using the same procedure and evaluated using BERTScore. The results demonstrated that the models exhibited comparable overall performance, with Mistral achieving the highest performance. As presented in Table 2, even with an input context length of 4096, Mistral exhibited the highest performance, maintaining its lead.

Comparison to Korean-Specialized BERT (KR-BERT)

Table 3. Binary classification evaluation results for KR-BERT [26] and Mistral models with varying input context lengths.

Model	Accuracy
KR-BERT	0.91
Mistral-7B_2048	0.87
Mistral-7B_4096	0.87

We applied the BERT model to the constructed dataset to compare its performance with that of LLM. The objective was to assess the practical applicability, relative strengths, and weaknesses of both datasets and models. We extracted 5,083 data instances corresponding to the binary classification task from the constructed dataset and divided them into training and testing sets in an 8:2 ratio. Subsequently, KR-BERT was fine-tuned for this task (Table 3).

The evaluation results demonstrated that KR-BERT outperformed Mistral in the binary classification task, achieving an accuracy of 91% compared to Mistral's 87%. This performance disparity suggests the effectiveness of the constructed dataset for fine-tuning both models. However, it is crucial to acknowledge that KR-BERT is designed for single-task learning, while Mistral, as an LLM, possesses flexibility for multitask learning through domain adaptation. This difference in task specificity is likely to have contributed to KR-BERT's advantage over other models in this specific domain. These findings highlight the dataset's capability to acquire domain knowledge and instructions. The constructed dataset facilitated the performance enhancement of both the Mistral and KR-BERT models through domain-specific learning. The diverse range of prompts contributed to enhancing performance, demonstrating the effectiveness of the system in accommodating various model architectures and improving overall performance. Furthermore, domain-specific model training has the potential to enhance performance in specific domains.

KorMedMCQA

Table 4. Evaluation results for KorMedMCQA [27]. KorMedMCQA is a medical qualification examination conducted in South Korea for physicians, nurses, and pharmacists.

Model	Doctor	Nurse	Pharm	Avg.
beomi/KoAlpaca-Polyglot-12.8B	0.1474	0.1533	0.1482	0.1496
beomi/Yi-Ko-6B	0.2386	0.4191	0.3339	0.3305
Mistral-7B_2048	0.1333	0.1499	0.1645	0.1492
Mistral-7B_4096	0.1228	0.2283	0.2313	0.1941

The performance of our model was evaluated using the KorMedMCQA dataset, which comprises medical qualification examinations conducted in South Korea that require specialized knowledge in the medical field. Compared with other general Korean LLMs, our trained model exhibited superior performance, particularly when benchmarked against KoAlpaca. However, its performance was inferior to that of Yi-Ko-6B (Table 4).

The suboptimal performance of this model can be attributed to several factors. However, the primary factor appears to be the insufficient training data for Koreans. Despite the potential for constructing domain-specific datasets using this methodology, it has been demonstrated that the proficiency of the Korean language lags behind that of other large Korean language models. This highlights the necessity of having comprehensive datasets that are specific to each language when training language-specific domain models. Moreover, beyond specialized corpora, such as research papers, the significance of corpora containing knowledge spanning various domains is underscored.

5 Discussion and Conclusion

We addressed the challenge of data scarcity for training language models in non-English-speaking countries by proposing a novel methodology that utilizes data mining techniques within a restricted domain dataset to construct training data. This methodology effectively overcomes the limitations of traditional data collection methods and enables the development of language models.

The application of our proposed methodology to the medical domain resulted in the development of a specialized medical model. Additionally, we observed minor performance differences between LLM and BERT. The constructed dataset demonstrated its ability to acquire domain knowledge and satisfy instructions, thereby validating its usefulness in assisting LLMs in various NLP tasks.

The extraction of domain-specific operations and the construction of domain-specific dictionaries will be important future tasks. However, their study focused on general NLP tasks and did not address domain-specific tasks. Real-world challenges require the identification of specific tasks and the creation of tailored datasets. Furthermore, integrating domain-specific dictionaries into models can improve comprehension of other languages. Consequently, the development of higher-quality datasets is expected to enhance both the efficacy and capacity of the model for comprehending specific domains.

The results of this study indicate that there is considerable potential for the adaptation of LLMs to a wide range of domains and for enhancing their effectiveness in a variety of downstream tasks in specialized fields.

Acknowledgments. This work was supported by the Artificial Intelligence Industrial Convergence Cluster Development project, funded by the Ministry of Science and ICT (MSIT, Korea) and Gwangju Metropolitan City.

Appendix

(See Table 5).

Table 5. Examples of task-specific data.

Task Type	Instruction	Output
Summary	다음 글을 요약하시오 '비골에 발생한 원발성 골 종양'의 목적은?	장관골에 발생한 Stage IIB 골육종의 치료결과 본 연구에서는 골 종양의 발생 부위 중 비교적 드문 부위인 비골에서 원발하는 골 종양의 종류와 그 치료 후 경과에 대하여 연구하고자 하였다.
Keyword	아래 문장에서 의료 관련 키워드는 무엇인가? 골 종양에 2차적으로 발생한 소아 대퇴골의 병적 골절은 그 치료가 어려우나 원발 골 종양의 종류 및 그 특성에 따른 적절한 치료 방법을 선택하면 우수한 결과를 얻을 수 있을 것으로 생각된다. 의료 관련 키워드 ['영상의', '소견 ','임상적']에 관련된 문장을 생성하시오.	'우수한', '종양의', '치료가' 이에 신경 초종의 자기 공명 영상의 특징적 소견 찾아 조직 학적 소견과 비교, 분석하고 임상적 특징 및 수술적 치료의 결과를 알아보기 위해 본 연구를 시행하였다.
Natural Lan-guage Inference	다음 두 문장 간의 관계를 파악하시오. "굴 효소 가수분해물을 처리한 실험군에서는 아무런 처리를 하지 않은 실험군에 비하여 높은 세포 생존율을 확인할 수 있었다" 문장과 "GOT와 LDH 역시 감소하는 것을 알 수 있었다." 문장은 수반 관계 인가요?	예
	아래 문장의 원인을 생성하시오 그 원인을 진단하고 적절한 치료를 시행하여 이러한 문제들을 해결하도록 해야 한다.	환자들에게 의치를 사용하는 동안 겪었던 문제들에 대해 질문하고 구강조직과 의치를 철저히 검사해야 하며, 검사 과정 동안에 조직 손상 등을 발견할 수도 있다

References

1. Zhao, Z., Wallace, E., Feng, S., Klein, D., Singh, S.: Calibrate before use: improving few-shot performance of language models. In: Meila, M., Zhang, T. (eds.) 38th International Conference on Machine Learning, ICML, 2021, 18–24 July 2021, Virtual Event, vol. 139 of Proceedings of Machine Learning Research, pp. 12697–12706. PMLR (2021)
2. Zhou, C., et al.: LIMA: less is more for alignment. In: Oh, A., Naumann, T., Globerson, A., Saenko, K., Hardt, M., Levine, S. (eds.) Advances in Neural Information Processing Systems 36: Annual Conference on Neural Information Processing Systems 2023, NeurIPS 2023, New Orleans, LA, USA, December 10–16, 2023 (2023)
3. Touvron, H., et al.: Llama: open and efficient foundation language models. CoRR, abs/2302.13971 arXiv:2302.13971 (2023)
4. Taori, R., et al.: Stanford alpaca: an instruction-following Llama model (2023). https://github.com/tatsulab/stanfordalpaca
5. Labrak, Y., Bazoge, A., Morin, E., Gourraud, P.-A., Rouvier, M., Dufour, R.: Biomistral: a collection of open-source pretrained large language models for medical domains. CoRR, abs/2402.10373 arXiv:2402.10373 (2024)
6. Li, Y., Li, Z., Zhang, K., Dan, R., Zhang, Y.: Chatdoctor: A medical chat model fine-tuned on Llama model using medical domain knowledge. CoRR, abs/2303.14070 arXiv:2303.14070 (2023)
7. Yang, H., Liu, X.-Y., Wang, C.D.: Fingpt: open-source financial large language models. CoRR, abs/2306.06031 arXiv:2306.06031 (2023)
8. Gururangan, S., et al.: Don't stop pretraining: adapt language models to domains and tasks. In: Jurafsky, D., Chai, J., Schluter, N., Tetreault, J.R. (eds.) Proceedings of the 58th Annual Meeting of the Association for Computational Linguistics, ACL 2020, Online, July 5–10, 2020, pp. 8342–8360. Association for Computational Linguistics (2020)
9. Cheng, D., Huang, S., Wei, F.: Adapting large language models via reading comprehension. CoRR, abs/2309.09530 arXiv:2309.09530 (2023)
10. Devlin, J., Chang, M.-W., Lee, K., Toutanova, K.: BERT: pre-training of deep bidirectional transformers for language understanding. In: Burstein, J., Doran, C., Solorio, T. (eds.) Proceedings of the 2019 Conference of the North American Chapter of the Association for Computational Linguistics: Human Language Technologies, NAACL-HLT 2019, Minneapolis, MN, USA, June 2–7, 2019, Volume 1 (Long and Short Papers), pp. 4171–4186. Association for Computational Linguistics (2019)
11. Touvron, H., et al.: Llama 2: open foundation and fine-tuned chat models. CoRR, abs/2307.09288 arXiv:2307.09288 (2023)
12. Chiang, W.-L., et al.: Vicuna: an open-source chatbot impressing gpt-4 with 90%* chatgpt quality, March 2023 (2023)
13. Jiang, A.Q., et al.: Mistral 7B. CoRR, abs/2310.06825 arXiv:2310.06825 (2023)
14. Raffel, C., et al.: Exploring the limits of transfer learning with a unified text-to-text transformer. J. Mach. Learn. Res. **21**, 1–67 (2020)
15. Kim, Y., et al.: A pre-trained BERT for Korean medical natural language processing. Sci. Rep. **12**(1), 13847 (2022)
16. Singhal, S., Singh, S., Yadav, S., Parihar, A.S.: LTSum: legal text summarizer. In: 2023 14th International Conference on Computing Communication and Networking Technologies (ICCCNT), pp. 1–6. IEEE (2023)
17. Luo, R., et al.: BioGPT: generative pre-trained transformer for biomedical text generation and mining. Briefings Bioinform. **23**(6), bbac409 (2022)
18. Radford, A., Wu, J., Child, R., Luan, D., Amodei, D., Sutskever, I.: Language models are unsupervised multitask learners. OpenAI blog **1**(8), 9 (2019)

19. Zhang, K., et al.: BiomedGPT: a unified and generalist biomedical generative pre-trained transformer for vision, language, and multimodal tasks. CoRR, abs/2305.17100 arXiv:2305.17100 (2023)
20. Wei, J., et al.: Finetuned language models are zero-shot learners. In: The Tenth International Conference on Learning Representations, ICLR 2022, Virtual Event, April 25–29, 2022. OpenReview.net (2022)
21. van de Kar, M., Xia, M., Chen, D., Artetxe, M.: Don't prompt, search! mining-based zero-shot learning with language models. In: Goldberg, Y., Kozareva, Z., Zhang, Y. (eds.) Proceedings of the 2022 Conference on Empirical Methods in Natural Language Processing, EMNLP 2022, AbuDhabi, United Arab Emirates, December 7–11, 2022, pp. 7508–7520. Association for Computational Linguistics (2022)
22. Kudo, T., Richardson, J.: Sentencepiece: a simple and language independent subword tokenizer and detokenizer for neural text processing. In: Blanco, E., Lu, W. (eds.) Proceedings of the 2018 Conference on Empirical Methods in Natural Language Processing, EMNLP 2018: System Demonstrations, Brussels, Belgium, October 31–November 4, 2018, pp. 66–71. Association for Computational Linguistics (2018)
23. Loshchilov, I., Hutter, F.: Decoupled weight decay regularization. In: 7th International Conference on Learning Representations, ICLR 2019, New Orleans, LA, USA, May 6–9, 2019. OpenReview.net (2019)
24. Dettmers, T., Lewis, M., Shleifer, S., Zettlemoyer, L.: 8-bit optimizers via block-wise quantization. In: The Tenth International Conference on Learning Representations, ICLR 2022, Virtual Event, April 25–29, 2022. OpenReview.net (2022)
25. Zhang, T., Kishore, V., Wu, F., Weinberger, K.Q., Artzi, Y.: Bertscore: evaluating text generation with BERT. In: 8th International Conference on Learning Representations, ICLR 2020, Addis Ababa, Ethiopia, April 26–30, 2020. OpenReview.net (2020)
26. Lee, S., Jang, H., Baik, Y., Park, S., Shin, H.: KR-BERT: a small-scale Korean-specific language model. CoRR, abs/2008.03979 arXiv:2008.03979 (2020)
27. Kweon, S., Choi, B., Kim, M., Park, R.W., Choi, E.: KorMedMCQA: multi-choice question answering benchmark for Korean healthcare professional licensing examinations. CoRR, abs/2403.01469 arXiv:2403.01469 (2024)

Integrating Text-to-Image and Vision Language Models for Synergistic Dataset Generation: The Creation of Synergy-General-Multimodal Pairs

Mao Xun Huang[1] and Hen-Hsen Huang[2](✉)

[1] Department of Management Information Systems, National Chengchi University, Taipei, Taiwan
110306019@g.nccu.edu.tw
[2] Institute of Information Science, Academia Sinica, Taipei, Taiwan
hhhuang@iis.sinica.edu.tw

Abstract. This study presents the creation of the Synergy-General-Multimodal Pairs dataset through an innovative integration of vision language models (VLMs) and text-to-image (T2I) technologies. The code and dataset used in this research are publicly available for replication and further research. The code can be accessed at GitHub Repository and the dataset at Dataset Link. We developed a cyclical generation process that begins with generating initial narratives using either VLMs or large language models (LLMs), which are then visualized by a T2I model. This initiates a feedback loop where each generated image inspires a new narrative, creating a rich sequence of text-image pairs. This iterative approach enhances the diversity and complexity of the dataset, fostering advancements in multimodal research by providing a voluminous and varied resource. Key experimental results show significant improvements: the mean BERTScore increased by 15% (from 0.54 to 0.625), BLEU score by 20% (from 0.026 to 0.032), and ROUGE-L score by 18% (from 0.20 to 0.235). These results demonstrate substantial enhancements in the multimodal model's performance. The dataset is specifically designed to support the development and fine-tuning of models for enhanced performance and generalization in tasks requiring deep multimodal understanding and generation.

Keywords: Multimodal generalization · Dataset construction · Vision language models

1 Introduction

The development of vision large language models (VLMs) [15] like GPT-4 [9] and LLaVA [6–8] and advanced text-to-image (T2I) models such as Stable Diffusion [13] highlights the need for datasets that fully leverage these technologies.

The original version of the chapter has been revised. Affiliation 1 has been modified. A correction to this chapter can be found at
https://doi.org/10.1007/978-981-97-6125-8_16

J. Guo et al. (Eds.): IJCAI 2024, CCIS 2160, pp. 147–161, 2024.
https://doi.org/10.1007/978-981-97-6125-8_12

Existing datasets often lack the necessary diversity and complexity for effective training and evaluation of multimodal tasks. To address this, our research introduces the Synergy-General-Multimodal Pairs dataset, a self-generated collection characterized by its diversity and complexity, surpassing existing datasets like MS COCO [5] and Flickr30k [11].

Our dataset is uniquely created through a cyclical process utilizing VLMs and T2I technologies. Unlike traditional static datasets, Synergy-General-Multimodal Pairs is dynamically generated, allowing for iterative refinement of multimodal pairs. This method ensures a high level of diversity and complexity, with each text-image pair inspiring the next. The dataset supports a wide array of multimodal tasks and extends current dataset capabilities in volume, variety, and domain specificity.

The aim is to fine-tune multimodal models to enhance their descriptive capabilities for images. We hypothesize that using a sophisticated generation model for dataset creation will improve the trained model's ability to generate detailed image descriptions. Our unique generative cycle involves fixed prompts for narrative creation, visualization through T2I models, and narrative variation based on generated images, repeated across multiple iterations. The contributions of this work are fourfold:

- **Advancing Dataset Generality:** By introducing a dataset created through a feedback loop between VLMs and T2I models, we significantly increase the complexity and diversity of multimodal pairs available for research. This generality is crucial for developing more sophisticated AI models capable of understanding and generating content across a wider range of contexts and nuances.
- **Improving Model Generalization:** The iterative generation process ensures that the dataset includes a broad spectrum of variations on a theme, which can help AI models to better generalize across different but related scenarios. This is particularly beneficial for tasks that require deep multimodal understanding and creativity, such as automatic storytelling, visual question answering, or advanced image captioning.
- **Facilitating Innovative Research:** With its unique generation process and structure, the dataset opens new avenues for research, including the study of how AI models can inspire each other in a cyclical creative process. This can lead to breakthroughs in generative AI, where models not only learn from static datasets but also dynamically generate and learn from new content they help create.
- **Enabling Fine-Tuning and Evaluation:** The dataset provides a resource for fine-tuning and evaluating multimodal models, with a particular focus on their ability to generate detailed and accurate image descriptions. This is an essential step towards building AI systems that can understand and generate human-like descriptions of complex visual content.

2   Related Work

The Synergy-General-Multimodal Pairs dataset advances multimodal dataset generation. Key related works include DataComp, InternVid, and MMSum.

DataComp provides 12.8 billion image-text pairs from the public internet, focusing on refining static datasets. In contrast, our dataset employs an iterative feedback loop between vision language models (VLMs) and text-to-image (T2I) models, creating a continuously evolving and diverse dataset [1]. InternVid introduces a large-scale video-centric multimodal dataset with over 7 million videos for video-text representation learning. Unlike InternVid's static video-text pairs, our dataset dynamically generates text-image pairs, increasing both volume and diversity through iterative feedback, enhancing training data quality [14]. MMSum focuses on multimodal summarization and thumbnail generation with 5,100 human-annotated videos. While MMSum ensures high-quality annotations, our approach uses an automated iterative method to generate diverse text-image pairs, supporting various multimodal tasks beyond summarization [2].

Our dataset's iterative feedback loop enhances diversity and complexity, ensuring continuous evolution and relevance, which is not addressed by the static approaches of DataComp and InternVid. This dynamic approach positions Synergy-General-Multimodal Pairs as a valuable resource for advancing multimodal AI research (Fig. 1).

3   Dataset Creation

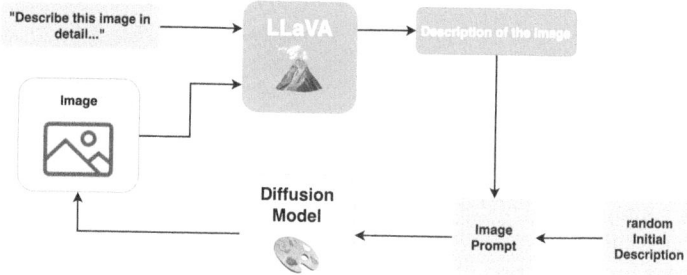

Fig. 1. Illustration of the dataset generation process using cyclical feedback loops between Vision or Large Language Models and Text-to-Image technologies

Our dataset generation process employs a novel strategy where different initial descriptions are used to create variable data rows, each serving as a unique starting point for generating text-image pairs. This technique is akin to data augmentation in natural language processing but adapted for multimodal scenarios. The process of creating our self-generated dataset involves several key steps:

1. **Initial Narrative Generation**: We utilize a Vision or Large Language Model (VLM or LLM, denoted as H) with a fixed prompt (P) to create a simple initial narrative D^{init} (i.e., D_0). These narratives are deliberately varied to encompass a wide range of themes and scenarios.

2. **Image Generation**: We feed D^{init} into a Text-to-Image model (G) to produce a corresponding image (M):

$$G(D^{init}) = M_1$$

This image acts as a new stimulus for generating a variant narrative, thus introducing variation and complexity into the dataset.

3. **Variant Narrative Creation**: In this step, we use the generated image, along with a fixed instruction (I), to prompt the VLM (F) to create a variant narrative $(D^{variant})$:

$$F(I, M_1) = D_1^{variant}$$

The purpose of creating variant narratives is to introduce diversity and complexity into the dataset. This process simulates real-world scenarios where interpretations and representations can vary widely. By generating variant narratives based on the initial image, we ensure that the dataset captures a broad spectrum of themes and nuances. This iterative refinement helps in training models to better understand and generate detailed image descriptions, improving their generalization capabilities.

4. **Iterative Process**: Then, we repeat the image generation with the variant narrative, creating multiple text-image data pairs through an iterative loop:

$$G(D_i) = M_{i+1},$$
$$F(I, M_i) = D_i^{variant},$$
$$\forall i = 1, 2, \ldots, n$$

This iterative refinement not only diversifies the dataset but also simulates a real-world scenario where interpretations and representations can vary widely, thereby enhancing the dataset's utility for training AI models capable of robust generalization.

5. **Dataset Compilation**: Different initial narratives (D_i^{init}) lead to datasets of text-image pairs $S = (D_{i,j}, M_{i,j})$. Generating m initial narratives and iterating each through n variation cycles results in a final dataset $S_{m \times n}$.

6. **Maximum Iterations**: The process concludes after reaching a pre-set maximum number of iterations (i.e., $m \times n$).

7. **Batch Generation**: Experiments indicate that generating too many initial narratives simultaneously is inefficient. Therefore, narratives are produced in multiple batches, forming the final dataset $S_{b \times m \times n}$, where b represents the batch count.

8. **Multiple Rounds**: The entire process is repeated for r rounds, resulting in a dataset $r \times S_{b \times m \times n}$. Each text-image pair is thus categorized by its round, row, and column within this structure.

Our method ensures a dataset that is diverse and complex, relying on the quality of the initial narrative and the performance of the text-to-image and image-to-text models. In our methodology, we utilize a cyclical feedback loop mechanism that iteratively refines the multimodal pairs to enhance the dataset's diversity and applicability in real-world scenarios.

The specifics of this process are detailed in Algorithm 1, which presents the systematic approach used to dynamically generate and refine data. This algorithm is pivotal in enabling our dataset to adapt and evolve continually, thus supporting the development of AI models that can generalize effectively from limited data.

The term *'refined_round'* refers to the number of iterations each initial narrative undergoes to generate variant narratives and corresponding images. In each round, the generated image serves as a new input to create a refined narrative, enhancing the dataset's complexity and variation. This iterative process ensures that the dataset evolves with each cycle, providing a rich and diverse set of multimodal pairs.

Algorithm 1. Synergistic Feedback Loop for Dataset Generation with Batching

Require: D_init_count: number of initial descriptions per batch
Require: $refined\_round$: number of refinement rounds
Require: $fixed\_instruction$: instruction for generating refined descriptions
Require: $batch\_count$: number of batches
Ensure: res_output: Cumulative list of tuples containing text-image pairs
1: Initialize an empty list res_output to store the cumulative dataset
2: **for** i from 0 to $batch\_count - 1$ **do**
3:     Initialize an empty list S to store the dataset for the current batch
4:     Generate initial descriptions D_inits of length D_init_count
5:     **for** each D_init in D_inits **do**
6:         Initialize an empty list row to store multimodal pairs for D_init
7:         Append D_init to row
8:         Set $D\_current = D\_init$
9:         **for** j from 0 to $refined\_round - 1$ **do**
10:             Generate an image M from $D\_current$ using a T2I model
11:             Generate a refined description $D\_refined$ based on M using VLM with $fixed\_instruction$
12:             Append the tuple $(M, D\_refined)$ to row
13:             Set $D\_current = D\_refined$
14:         **end for**
15:         Append row to S
16:     **end for**
17:     Append S to res_output
18: **end for**
19: **return** res_output

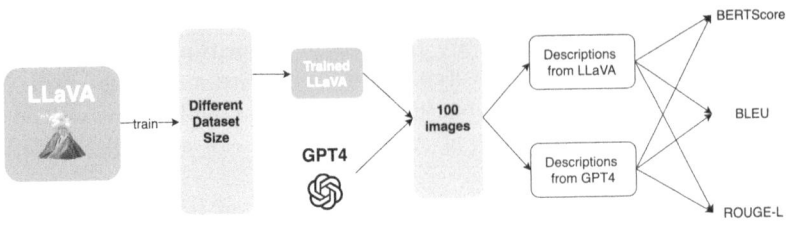

Fig. 2. Overview of the dataset evaluation process, detailing the steps for training models and assessing their performance in generating image descriptions

4   Experiments

This dataset predominantly comprises a collection of images accompanied by their respective descriptions, encapsulating a broad spectrum of scenarios. We aim to assess the model's performance in describing images, both before and after training, to determine the dataset's effectiveness in augmenting the model's capability to generate detailed and accurate image descriptions. Through this comparative analysis, we seek to understand the impact of the dataset on enhancing the VLM's proficiency in capturing and articulating the nuances of visual content. We adopt the vision large language model LLaVA as the subject to train [6–8]. The focus will be on fine-tuning the LoRA layers [3] of this models using the entirety of our dataset.

Upon completion of the training phase, we evaluate the models' enhanced abilities by examining the level of detail they provide in image descriptions. Additionally, to quantitatively measure their performance, we will compute the mean and the standard deviation of BERTScores [16], BLEU [10], and ROUGE-L [4] scores over descriptions of 100 images. GPT-4 serves as a benchmark for comparison. This comprehensive approach allows us to gauge the models' improved capabilities in generating precise and contextually rich descriptions post-training, providing a holistic performance evaluation across different dataset sizes.

The generation of the dataset involves the utilization of several advanced models. These models are pivotal in processing the data, ensuring high-quality dataset creation. See Tables 1 and 2 which summarizes the models and dataset settings used in this dataset generation process. Users can also change the factors in this process to generate their own dataset. This iterative refinement process not only enhances model performance but also underscores the importance of dataset size in improving the descriptive abilities of multimodal language models.

Table 1. Settings of models used in dataset generation

Model Type	Model Name	Version/Size
VLM	LLaVA	v1.3-13b
LLM	Vicuna	v.15-7b
T2I Model	SDXL	1.0(base)

Table 2. Overview of Settings Used in Dataset Generation

Name	Value
Round (r)	7
Batch Count (b)	20
Initial Description Count (m)	10
Variant Count (n)	5
Total Data Count ($r \times b \times m \times n$)	7000

4.1 Detailed Rationale for the Choice of Models

Our selection of Vision Language Models (VLMs) and Text-to-Image (T2I) models is based on their superior performance and alignment with our research goals. We chose LLaVA due to its state-of-the-art capabilities in visual instruction tuning, advanced reasoning, OCR, and extensive world knowledge integration [6]. LLaVA's ability to generate highly accurate and contextually rich descriptions makes it ideal for creating and refining narratives iteratively. For the T2I model, we selected Stable Diffusion (SDXL), known for its high-resolution image synthesis and ability to generate diverse and detailed visual content [12]. Stable Diffusion ensures that visual outputs are realistic and detailed, which is crucial for producing high-quality text-image pairs. This combination exploits LLaVA's language understanding and generation strengths and Stable Diffusion's image synthesis capabilities, ensuring diverse, complex, and realistic multimodal pairs, thereby advancing multimodal research.

4.2 Evaluation Metrics

We employ the following metrics to evaluate the linguistic quality and relevance of the text generated by our models:

– **BERTScore** calculates the cosine similarity between the BERT embeddings of the predicted and reference texts. It is particularly useful for capturing semantic similarity. We compute the mean and standard deviation of BERTScore across the dataset as follows:

$$\text{Mean BERTScore} = \frac{1}{N} \sum_{i=1}^{N} \text{BERTScore}(\text{reference}_i, \text{candidate}_i) \quad (1)$$

Std. Deviation of BERTScore $=$

$$\sqrt{\frac{1}{N-1}\sum_{i=1}^{N}(\text{BERTScore}_i - \text{Mean BERTScore})^2} \quad (2)$$

where:

- reference$_i$ are descriptions by GPT-4,
- candidate$_i$ are those generated by LLaVA,
- N is the total number of description pairs evaluated.

- **BLEU (Bilingual Evaluation Understudy)**: This metric is used to measure the syntactic consistency between machine-generated descriptions and a set of predefined ideal descriptions (represented here by GPT-4 generated descriptions). The BLEU score is calculated using the following formula:

$$\text{Mean BLEU} = \frac{1}{N}\sum_{i=1}^{N} b(p)_i \cdot \exp\left(\sum_{n=1}^{4} w_n \log p_{n,i}\right) \quad (3)$$

where:
- $p_{n,i}$ is the n-gram precision for the nth n-gram in the ith pair of descriptions (reference and candidate),
- w_n are the weights assigned to each n-gram size,
- $b(p)_i$ is the brevity penalty for the ith pair,
- Smoothing is applied to $p_{n,i}$ to handle zero counts in n-gram comparisons.

reference$_i$ and candidate$_i$ are as defined above.

- **ROUGE-L (Recall-Oriented Understudy for Gisting Evaluation)**: This metric focuses on the longest common subsequence (LCS) to assess how much of the content in the generated description matches with the reference. The mean ROUGE-L score is given by:

$$\text{Mean ROUGE-L} = \frac{1}{N}\sum_{i=1}^{N} \text{ROUGE-L}(\text{reference}_i, \text{candidate}_i) \quad (4)$$

where ROUGE-L$(reference, candidate)$ is computed as:

$$F1 = 2 \times \frac{\text{precision} \times \text{recall}}{\text{precision} + \text{recall}} \quad (5)$$

reference$_i$ and candidate$_i$ are as defined above. The ROUGE-L score considers the ratios of the longest common subsequence, calculated both as a precision and recall between each pair of texts, and combines them into an F1 score.

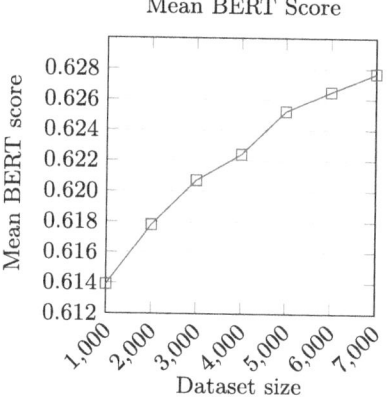

Fig. 3. The progression of mean BERT scores as the dataset size increases.

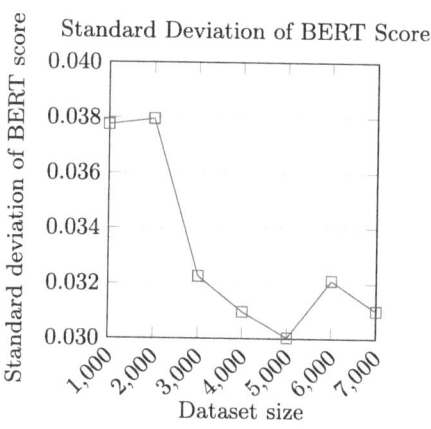

Fig. 4. The progression of standard deviation of BERT scores as the dataset size increases.

4.3   Result

We trained LLaVA-v1.3-vicuna-7b (a lower-parameter multimodal LLMs compared to the generation model) on our dataset, which varies in size from 1,000 to 7,000 instances. We employed an evaluation method using the mean BERTScore (focusing on recall), based on the descriptions of 100 images with the output of GPT-4 to assess the performance post-training on our dataset. We also use BLEU and ROUGE-L score to get more insights. Figures 3, 4, 5, 6 and 7 show the experimental results.

Our findings of the increase in mean BERT Score, BLEU, and ROUGE-L scores with larger dataset sizes indicates a positive correlation between dataset size and the descriptive capabilities of the models. Additionally, the decrease

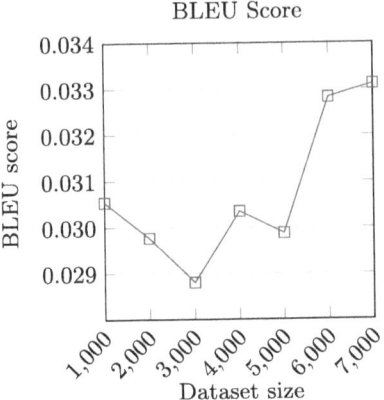

Fig. 5. The progression of BLEU score as the dataset size increases.

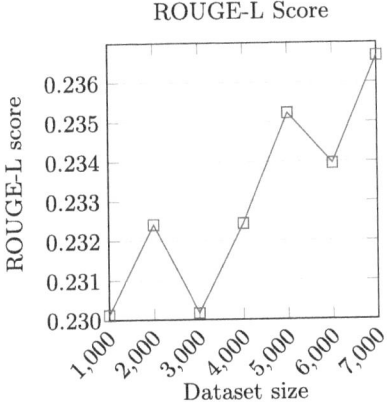

Fig. 6. The progression of ROUGE-L score as the dataset size increases.

in the standard deviation of the BERT Score suggests improved consistency in model performance across different dataset sizes.

This trend suggests that the method employed for dataset generation has the potential to incrementally improve the image description capabilities of VLMs. Table 3 illustrates the output of the LLaVa model trained on the different dataset sizes describing Fig. 8.

Refer to Fig. 9 for a visual representation of the initial row of images within the dataset and an overview of the dataset's structural composition, respectively. The variant description provides a narrative that corresponds to the image indicated by the image path.[1]

---

[1] The source code and the dataset will be publicly available in the final version.

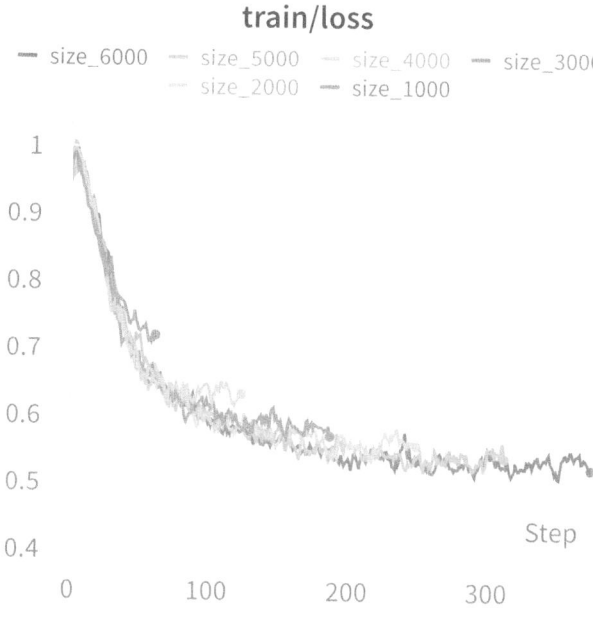

Fig. 7. Loss of different training dataset sizes

4.4 Comparative Analysis with Existing Datasets in the Context of AI Model Generalization

AI models must generalize effectively from limited resources in open-world settings, necessitating rich, diverse datasets. Traditional datasets like MS COCO and Flickr30k, while foundational, are often static and limited in real-world scenario representation, impeding generalization across diverse situations.

MS COCO offers extensive annotations but lacks contextual variability necessary for sophisticated generalization. Similarly, Flickr30k, despite its natural language descriptions, confines models to a narrow slice of visual and textual contexts. In contrast, the Synergy-General-Multimodal Pairs dataset employs a dynamic generation process through a feedback loop between vision-language models (VLMs) and text-to-image (T2I) technologies. This enhances diversity and adaptability, making it an excellent resource for training AI models requiring robust generalization. By continuously refining and expanding through iterative feedback, the dataset fosters AI models that efficiently learn from sparse samples and adapt to new, unseen scenarios, essential for open-world environments. Table 4 simply compare these datasets.

This comparative analysis demonstrates that the Synergy-General-Multimodal Pairs dataset is particularly well-suited to address the challenges discussed at this workshop. Its design and methodology directly contribute to

Fig. 8. The reference image described by Table 3

Fig. 9. First 3 rows of images in the real dataset

Table 3. Comparison of the descriptions generated by the LLaVa model trained on different dataset sizes

Dataset Size	Result
1000	The image features a narrow cobblestone street lined with tall, red brick buildings on either side. The street is lined with tall, red brick buildings on either side, creating a charming and historic atmosphere. The street is lined with tall, red brick buildings on either side, creating a charming and historic atmosphere. The street is lined with tall, red brick buildings on either side, creating a charming and historic atmosphere. The street is lined with tall, red brick buildings on either side, creating a charming and historic atmosphere. The street is lined with tall, red brick buildings on either side
2000	The image features a narrow, cobblestone street lined with buildings on either side. The street is lined with tall, narrow buildings, and the buildings are made of stone. The street is lined with cobblestone, which is a type of stone that is commonly used for paving roads and sidewalks. The street appears to be in a city or town, as there are buildings on either side of the street, and the street is lined with cobblestones. The street is also narrow, which suggests that it is a small, residential street. The buildings on either side of the street are tall and narrow, and they are made of stone, which suggests that they are old and historic
7000	The image features a narrow, cobblestone street with a brick wall on one side and a building on the other side. The street is lined with trees, and there is a sidewalk running along the length of the street. The scene is set in a city, as evidenced by the presence of buildings and the presence of a sidewalk. The cobblestone street adds a sense of old-world charm and character to the scene, while the presence of trees and the sidewalk suggest that the area is well-maintained and pedestrian-friendly. The overall atmosphere of the image is peaceful and serene, with the narrow street providing a sense of intimacy and the presence of trees adding

Table 4. Comparison of dataset characteristics important for AI model generalization.

Feature	MS COCO	Flickr30k	Synergy-General-Multimodal Pairs
Contextual Diversity	Limited	Moderate	High
Real-World Applicability	Low	Moderate	High
Dynamic Data Generation	No	No	Yes
Support for Sparse Sample Learning	Poor	Moderate	Excellent
Adaptation to Unpredictable Scenarios	Low	Moderate	High

overcoming the limitations of existing datasets, paving the way for more robust and effective AI model generalization in real-world applications. Through this innovative approach, our dataset not only advances the field of multimodal research but also aligns closely with the workshop's goal of fostering advancements in real-world AI applications.

5   Conclusions and Limitations

Our study presents innovative methodologies for generating datasets using Vision Language Models (VLMs) and Text-to-Image (T2I) models, enhancing AI systems' generalization in complex scenarios. However, the reliance on advanced technologies introduces potential biases and demands substantial computational resources, limiting practical deployment in resource-constrained environments. Continuous updates are necessary to keep pace with technological advancements.

While our dataset captures diverse real-world scenarios, it may not cover the full spectrum needed for true open-world generalization. Conventional metrics like BERTScores may not fully capture model performance complexities in practical applications.

Future research will focus on enhancing the robustness and adaptability of these methodologies, reducing computational demands through model sparsification and compact model design. We will also develop methods for effective operation under limited data conditions, including few-shot learning and domain adaptation, bridging current AI capability gaps towards flexible and efficient generalization.

6   Ethic Policy

This research adheres to strict ethical standards, ensuring that all data are independently generated without using external sources or any personally identifiable information (PII). We do not involve human subjects in our research, thereby eliminating ethical concerns related to consent, confidentiality, and potential impacts on individuals. The manuscript was written by the authors. ChatGPT was only applied to refinement and grammatical error correction.

References

1. Anonymous: DataComp: in search of the next generation of multimodal datasets. arXiv preprint arXiv:2304.14108 (2023)
2. Anonymous: MMSum: a dataset for multimodal summarization and thumbnail generation of videos. arXiv preprint arXiv:2306.04216 (2023)
3. Hu, E., Shen, Y., Wallis, P., et al.: LoRA: low-rank adaptation of large language models. arXiv preprint arXiv:2106.09685 (2021)
4. Lin, C.Y.: Rouge: a package for automatic evaluation of summaries. In: Text Summarization Branches Out, pp. 74–81. Association for Computational Linguistics (2004)

5. Lin, T.Y., et al.: Microsoft COCO: common objects in context. In: Fleet, David, Pajdla, Tomas, Schiele, Bernt, Tuytelaars, Tinne (eds.) ECCV 2014. LNCS, vol. 8693, pp. 740–755. Springer, Cham (2014). https://doi.org/10.1007/978-3-319-10602-1_48

6. Liu, H., et al.: LLaVA-next: Improved reasoning, OCR, and world knowledge (2024). https://llava-vl.github.io/blog/2024-01-30-llava-next/

7. Liu, H., Li, C., Li, Y., Lee, Y.J.: Improved baselines with visual instruction tuning. arXiv:2310.03744 (2023)

8. Liu, H., Li, C., Wu, Q., Lee, Y.J.: Visual instruction tuning. In: NeurIPS (2023)

9. Achiam, J., et al.: Gpt-4 technical report. arXiv preprint arXiv:2303.08774 (2023)

10. Papineni, K., Roukos, S., Ward, T., Zhu, W.J.: BLEU: a method for automatic evaluation of machine translation. In: Isabelle, P., Charniak, E., Lin, D. (eds.) Proceedings of the 40th Annual Meeting of the Association for Computational Linguistics, pp. 311–318. Association for Computational Linguistics, Philadelphia, Pennsylvania, USA (2002). https://doi.org/10.3115/1073083.1073135, https://aclanthology.org/P02-1040

11. Plummer, B.A., et al.: Flickr30k entities: collecting region-to-phrase correspondences for richer image-to-sentence models. In: Proceedings of the IEEE International Conference on Computer Vision, pp. 2641–2649 (2015)

12. Podell, D., et al.: SDXL: improving latent diffusion models for high-resolution image synthesis. arXiv preprint arXiv:2307.01952 (2023)

13. Rombach, R., et al.: High-resolution image synthesis with latent diffusion models. In: Proceedings of the IEEE/CVF Conference on Computer Vision and Pattern Recognition, pp. 10684–10695 (2022)

14. Wang, Y., et al.: InternVid: a large-scale video-text dataset for multimodal understanding and generation. In: ICLR 2024 (2024)

15. Yin, S., et al.: A survey on multimodal large language models. arXiv preprint arXiv:2306.13549 (2023)

16. Zhang, T., Kishore, V., Wu, F., Weinberger, K.Q., Artzi, Y.: Bertscore: evaluating text generation with bert. In: International Conference on Learning Representations (2020). https://openreview.net/forum?id=SkeHuCVFDr

Recognition and Reasoning in the Open World

Semantic-Degrade Learning Framework for Open World Object Detection

Siqi He[1] , Cancan Yu[2] , and Hainan Li[3]([✉])

[1] School of Computer Science, Peking University, Beijing 100871, China
hesq47@foxmail.com
[2] Northking Information Technology Co., Ltd., Beijing 100080, China
cancan@buaa.edu.cn
[3] Institute of Dataspace, Hefei 230031, Anhui, China
lihainan@idata.ah.cn

Abstract. Open World Object Detection (OWOD) challenges the conventional closed-world assumption of traditional object detection models, addressing the dynamic nature of real-world scenarios where systems encounter unknown objects. Unlike existing OWOD approaches which often rely on manually selected unknown proposals, we introduce an Adaptive Semantic-Degrade Learning framework. This framework, inspired by cognitive development theory, guides the model to capture more low-level semantic features by naturally degrading the learned feature patterns, thereby enabling the discovery of unknown targets that share these features with different known classes. We implement this framework based on the closed-set object detector Deformable DETR, constructing a reusable open world architecture of two branches for known class detection and unknown object detection. Extensive experiments on the common-used benchmark validate the progressiveness of our framework. The experimental results show that compared with other state-of-the-art methods, our model achieves nearly 50% improvement in unknown mAP and even higher known detection performance, demonstrating excellent detection performance.

Keywords: Adaptive semantic-degrade learning framework · Open world object detection · Artificial intelligence

1 Introduction

Traditional object detection [7,17,38,39] typically relies on a closed and predefined set of detected classes, where the classes are pre-labeled during the training process. However, this paradigm falls short in addressing the detection of unknown objects that are frequently encountered in the real world. To address this challenge, Open World Object Detection (OWOD) has been proposed in [15], compelling the detection models to detect unknown objects not present in the training set and incrementally learn about these unknown classes

J. Guo et al. (Eds.): IJCAI 2024, CCIS 2160, pp. 165–179, 2024.
https://doi.org/10.1007/978-981-97-6125-8_13

once their annotations are available. OWOD aims to leverage the model's inherent knowledge to tackle the challenges of openness and uncertainty in the real world, while generally imposing strict constraints on semantic leakage.

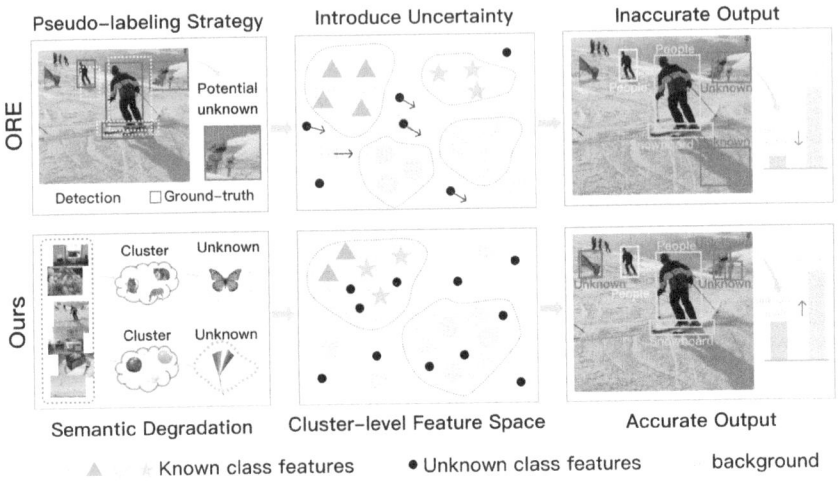

Fig. 1. Previous works are unable to address the knowledge coupling during the learning process of known and unknown classes and commonly suffer uncertainty by means of selecting some known proposals or background regions as unknowns.

To accomplish the detection of unknown classes, as shown in Fig. 1, previous OWOD methods [11,15,24,26] have mainly employed various pseudo-labeling strategies to select potential unknown object regions. For example, ORE [15] utilizes an auto-labeling strategy, considering the top-k background region proposals sorted by objectness as potential unknown targets. OW-DETR [11] designs an attention-based pseudo-labeling approach, selecting background regions with high attention scores from the query as potential unknown objects. CAT [24] further integrates attention-driven and input-driven pseudo-label generation methods, introducing an adaptive selection mechanism to choose higher-quality pseudo-labels for unknown classes. However, these pseudo-labeling methods for unknown classes often misclassify numerous background regions as unknown objects, introducing significant uncertainty. Consequently, these methods frequently show high Recall performance of unknown classes but generally perform sub-optimally in terms of unknown mAP. Additionally, the method ALLOW [26] explores the object-level feature entanglement phenomenon in object detection models and proposes a label-transfer learning method to decouple features of known and unknown classes. Nonetheless, ALLOW struggles to precisely control the feature decoupling process, limiting the improvement of unknown class detection performance.

Unlike previous approaches, our motivation is to facilitate the learning of unknown classes by utilizing stable features, aiming to minimize uncertainty due to the inclusion of background information. In object detection, a widely accepted inference is that there may exist shared low-level semantic features among various classes [18,41], including both known and potential unknown classes, often located nearby in the feature space. Thus, these shared low-level features can help detection models discover potential unknown objects with less uncertainty. However, traditional object detection models learn class-level semantic features during training, acquiring relatively fewer shared low-level semantic features that cannot be fully exploited for unknown detection.

Drawing inspiration from cognitive development theory, which suggests that humans guide the learning of new knowledge by abstracting general rules from specific instances, we propose an Adaptive Semantic-Degrade Learning framework. This framework, simulating the human ability to abstract and generalize, guides the model to capture more low-level semantic features by naturally degrading the learned feature patterns. This approach facilitates the discovery of unknown targets by identifying shared features with various known classes. Our framework is realized by fine-tuning additional parameters in a closed set detection model.

Specifically, the Semantic-Degrade Learning method guides the model in learning lower-level common features. We degrade the semantic feature space of the detection model from "class level" to "cluster level". At this level, each cluster encompasses multiple known classes and potential unknown classes, all sharing common low-level semantic features. The degradation process preserves the original feature distribution of known classes as much as possible to mitigate the adverse effects of feature recombination on cluster-level semantic extraction. By extracting shared cluster-level semantics from stable features of known classes, our model accomplishes unknown class detection, avoiding the introduction of background information and uncertainty associated with pseudo-labels.

In summary, our contributions are:

- We propose a novel Adaptive Semantic-Degrade Learning Framework for OWOD, which leverages the degradation of feature space granularity to enhance the detection of unknown objects.
- We introduce the Semantic-Degrade Learning method to guide the model to acquire generalized information shared between adjacent classes in the feature space to advance the unknown learning.
- Experiments on commonly used datasets demonstrate that our framework achieves precise OWOD performance, with nearly 50% unknown mAP improvement compared to the even higher known detection performance.

2   Related Work

The development of deep learning [3,5,9,10,12,20–22,25,27–29,49,52] has significantly advanced the research in object detection, which involves the recognition and localization of multiple objects within an image. Traditional object detection models operate under the ideal closed-world assumption, where it is required that all classes to be detected are labeled and provided during the training phase. Nevertheless, there is a high likelihood that an object detection system will encounter unknown objects that were not present during the training phase. To address this issue, previous approaches have explored open-set and open-world settings.

Open Set Classification and Detection. In the open set setting, the knowledge obtained from the training set is incomplete, and as a result, the classifier during inference may encounter categories that do not appear in the training set. To address this challenge, several studies [8,13,16,33,37,40] have explored this task under various assumptions. The open set classification problem was initially defined in [36] as a constrained minimization problem and later extended to a multi-class classifier by subsequent works [14,35].

Bendale and Boult [2] proposed a method to identify the unknowns in the feature space of the model and used the OpenMax classifier to estimate the ensemble risk. Liu et al. [23] developed a metric learning framework that identifies invisible classes as unknown classes through a long-tail recognition setting for category coexistence. PROSER [51] encouraged discrimination between known and unknown classes, neglecting the dynamic balance between the known and unknown instances. Additionally, self-supervised learning [32] and unsupervised learning with reconstruction [47] methods have been employed in the recognition problem of open sets. Dhamija et al. [4] conducted a study on the open set object detection task and introduced the open set object detection protocol.

Open World Classification and Detection. Unlike open set tasks that only focus on the identification of unknown classes, open world tasks also involve incremental learning based on newly obtained category data. Bendale et al. [1] proposed the first open world image recognition model and introduced a protocol for evaluating open world recognition systems. Some recent works [30,43] have attempted to address open world classification in the context of long-tail distribution [48], few-shot learning [42], and zero-shot learning [45], respectively, in order to tackle more complex scenarios.

For open world detection, Joseph et al. [15] introduced the ORE method, featuring an unknown object-aware RPN designed to equip the model with the capability to detect unknown objects. The work SA [46] utilizes semantic topology to define a semantic centroid in feature space for each category, guiding object instances closer to their respective centroids during the learning process. OW-DETR [11] proposed an end-to-end framework incorporating pseudo-labeling, novelty classification, and object scoring. Wu et al. [44] addressed the Unknown-Classified OWOD problem and developed a two-stage detector based on similarity and clustering to differentiate between multiple distinct unknown classes. Ma et al. [24] proposed the cascade decoupled decoding method, which effectively separates the decoding process through a shared decoder to improve the retrieval of unknown objects. Zhao et al. [50] put forward an auxiliary proposal advisor and a class-specific expelling classifier to enhance the performance of unknown detection. Ma et al. [26] introduced Label-Transfer Learning to disentangle meaningful unknown traits from all known proposals, thereby alleviating uncertainties in the detection process.

Previous methods [11,15,44,46,50] usually adopted complex unknown-discover strategies to deal with the unknown detection, and cannot always accurately select unknown proposals and thus introduce too many uncertainties, harming the learning of unknown objects and influencing the known classification as well. In contrast, our method only explores the unknown information from the known proposals through a reasonable disentanglement process, which improves the detection performance of the unknown objects while maintaining that of the known objects.

3   Method

Our Adaptive Semantic-Degrade Learning Framework guides the model to learn "cluster-level" generalized information through the natural degradation of semantic space to enhance the model's capability for precise detection of unknown classes in OWOD. This section provides a comprehensive overview of the structure of our proposed framework. Initially, we elucidate the formulation of the OWOD problem, laying the groundwork for our approach. Subsequently, we reveal the reusable open world architecture for our framework, and provide a detailed introduction to the Semantic-Degrade Learning method for acquiring generalized semantics. Finally, we introduce the training and inference process of our framework.

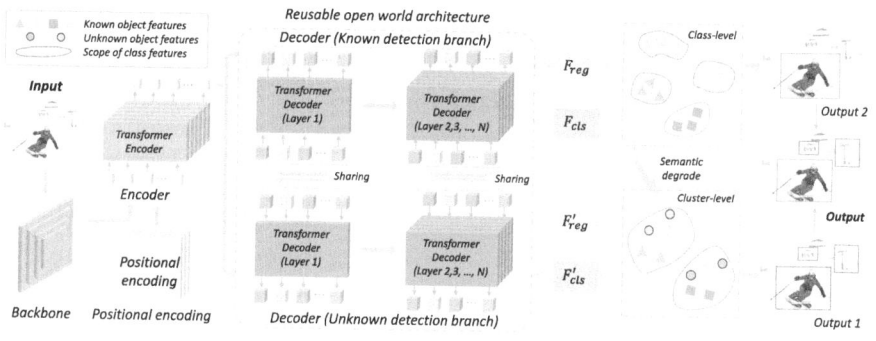

Fig. 2. Overview of our adaptive semantic degradation learning framework. By degrading the semantic feature from "class-level" to "cluster-level", the proposed framework can accomplish unknown learning with less uncertainty.

3.1   Problem Formulation

In the context of open-world object detection, the entire training process is divided into T tasks. At each task $t \in \{1, ..., T\}$, we denote the set of known classes as $\mathcal{K}^t$ and the set of unknown classes as $\mathcal{U}^t$, where $\mathcal{K}^t \cap \mathcal{U}^t = \varnothing$. During the training phase at Task t, the annotations for the known classes $\mathcal{K}^t$ are available to ensure that the model is capable of accurately classifying instances belonging to these known classes. Specifically, each instance i_k of class $c \in \mathcal{K}^t$ is annotated as $y_k = [l_k, b_k]$, where $l_k = c \in \mathcal{K}^t$ represents the corresponding label, and $b_k = [x_k, y_k, w_k, h_k]$ represents the coordinates of the corresponding bounding box. In contrast, the instances of the unknown classes $\mathcal{U}^t$ appear during the training phase without annotations but are required to be classified as "unknown", denoted by the label $l_k = 0$ during inference.

For incremental learning, a subset of the unknown classes $\bar{\mathcal{U}}^t \in \mathcal{U}^t$ are labeled, and the known classes are updated as $\mathcal{K}^{t+1} = \mathcal{K}^t \cup \bar{\mathcal{U}}^t$, while the unknown classes are updated as $\mathcal{U}^{t+1} = \mathcal{U}^t - \bar{\mathcal{U}}^t$ at Task $t+1$. The model adapts itself by incorporating new knowledge and accurately identifies the current known classes $\mathcal{K}^{t+1}$ while classifying the current unknown classes $\mathcal{U}^{t+1}$. This cycle continues throughout the lifespan of the object detector.

3.2   Adaptive Semantic-Degrade Learning Framework

The architecture of our Adaptive Semantic-Degrade Learning Framework is shown in Fig. 2. The Semantic-Degrade Learning method could guide the model to acquire generalized semantic information shared between adjacent classes in the feature space to advance the unknown learning.

Reusable Open World Detector Architecture. Our framework is built on a closed-set object detector Deformable DETR [52]. Given an image instance i_k, we processed it through a pyramid feature extractor to derive multi-scale image features, which are then encoded to obtain rich semantic features $M \in \mathbb{R}^{N_s \times D}$. N_s denotes the length of the semantic features and D is the dimension of the transformer.

The framework behind the encoder is divided into two branches for known class detection and unknown object detection respectively. These two branches are built on a reusable open world detector architecture. In the known detection branch, we keep the original architecture of the closed-set detector. The decoder of the unknown detection branch shares most of the parameters with the decoder of the known class branch, in which only some additional parameters are fine-tuned to give the model the unknown class detection ability.

To accomplish accurate detection of unknown classes, we propose Semantic-Degrade learning in the unknown detection branch. The semantic features M from the encoder are sent to the shared decoder together with a set of N queries $Q \in \mathbb{R}^{N \times D}$. The shared decoder transforms the queries Q to a set of N query embeddings $E \in \mathbb{R}^{N \times D}$. Under the proposed framework, these query embeddings are capable of acquiring cluster-level generic semantics, while being able to roughly distinguish between known and unknown classes. The query embeddings E are sent into the unknown detection head to predict the labels and the bounding boxes of unknown objects. Based on our Semantic-Degrade learning, the unknown branch can effectively capture cluster-level semantic features and improve the unknown class detection ability of the model significantly.

Ultimately, the model combines the outputs from both branches. Predictions of generalized objects with an Intersection Over Union (IOU) exceeding a set threshold relative to known class predictions are discarded, ensuring distinct and accurate detection results.

Adaptive Semantic-Degrade Learning. In the training of closed-set detection models, the model tends to abstract class-level discriminative features to distinguish between different known classes. However, the shared low-level semantic features between different classes are often overlooked, and these low-level semantic features are crucial for detecting unknown classes. Therefore, we aim to degrade the semantic features of the model from class-level to cluster-level. The latter represents a set composed of multiple classes sharing common low-level semantics, guiding the model to focus more on those ignored generic features. These cluster-level semantics will assist the model in discovering unknown objects with similar generic features.

Additionally, for a closed-set detection model, a notable fact is that there are some false positives among the predicted results for known classes. These false positives result from sharing more generic features with certain known classes, causing them to have similar distributions in the feature space and leading to misjudgments by the detector. While these false positives interfere with the detection of known classes, they can help the model discover more cluster-level generic features.

Based on this, to achieve semantic degradation and facilitate the detection of unknown classes, we divide these classes into C clusters according to the distribution of each known class in the model's feature space. Subsequently, we assign cluster-level labels to all instances of known ground truth T^t and high-confidence false positives $\mathcal{P}^t$ of known classes, guiding the model to construct a semantic space at the cluster level. For true instances of known classes, we assign the cluster label corresponding to their true class. For false positives of known classes, we assign the cluster label corresponding to their predicted class. The process of semantic degradation can be represented as:

$$\widetilde{\mathbf{y}}' = \begin{cases} \mathbf{y}_i^C \mid \mathbf{y}_i^{truth}, & \text{if } i \in T \\ \mathbf{y}_i^C \mid \mathbf{y}_i^{Pred}, & \text{if } i \in \mathcal{P} \end{cases} \tag{1}$$

where $\mathbf{y}_i^C \mid \mathbf{y}_i^{truth}$ represents the cluster-level label after semantic degradation of the known ground truth, $\mathbf{y}_i^C \mid \mathbf{y}_i^{Pred}$ denotes the cluster-level label of the predicted false positive instances of known classes. The classification regularization of our Semantic-Degrade Learning can be denoted as follows:

$$\widetilde{\ell}_{unkown}^{cls} = -\sum_i \widetilde{\mathbf{y}}' \log \mathbf{x}^{(\mathcal{K}^t) \cup (\mathcal{P}^t)} \tag{2}$$

where $\mathbf{x}^{(\mathcal{K}^t) \cup (\mathcal{P}^t)}$ represents the union of known class truth instances and predicted high confidence vacation positive instances.

By implementing Class-Degrade Learning, our model refines its ability to discern generalized cluster-level features, enhancing the detection of unknown categories that share these generalized features.

3.3   Training and Inference

Our training framework comprises two distinct training phases: the Class-Level Feature Learning Phase and the Class-Degrade Learning Phase.

In the Class-Level Feature Learning Phase, we adopt traditional closed-set model training methods to learn class-level features. This phase focuses on recognizing and distinguishing known classes. During this stage, we exclusively train the existing structural parameters of the closed-set model, excluding the newly introduced parameters for unknown classes:

$$\underset{[\mathbf{W}/\mathbf{W}_u]}{\arg\min} \ell_{class} = \ell_{known}^{cls} + \ell_{known}^{reg} \tag{3}$$

where $\mathbf{W}/\mathbf{W}_u$ denotes the original full parameters of the model without our additional module.

In the subsequent phase, we implement Class-Degrade Learning to guide the model towards forming cluster-level semantic feature space. During this phase, we only train the additional parameters of the proposed module and keep the original parameters of the model frozen:

$$\underset{[\mathbf{W}_u]}{\arg\min} \ell_{cluster} = \widetilde{\ell}_{unknown}^{cls} + \ell_{unknown}^{reg} \tag{4}$$

During the inference phase, the model generates outputs from two branches, obtaining class-level results for known objects and cluster-level results for generalized objects. The latter encompasses a certain number of unknown targets. Subsequently, we straightforwardly filter out known targets from the cluster-level output, thereby obtaining the detection results for unknown classes.

4   Experiments

In this section, we conduct extensive experiments and thorough analyses to demonstrate the efficacy of the proposed framework for open-world object detection.

Datasets. Following the standard configuration of OWOD [15], we utilize the PascalVOC [6] and MS-COCO [19] datasets and split all classes from MS-COCO dataset into 4 incremental tasks. During the learning of the initial task, denoted as t_1, we consider classes and data from Pascal-VOC as the training set, treating the remaining 60 classes from MS-COCO as unknown. Subsequent tasks adhere to the same class division strategy as outlined in ORE. The Pascal-VOC test set and MS-COCO validation set are employed for evaluation.

Evaluation Metrics. Following most commonly used OWOD evaluation criteria, we employ metrics such as mean average precision (mAP), recall, Wilderness Impact (WI) [4], Absolute Open-Set Error (A-OSE) [31], UDP, and UDR to evaluate the model's detection performance for OWOD problem. We advocate for the incorporation of mAP for unknown classes in the evaluation to provide a more comprehensive assessment, as opposed to solely relying on recall.

Implementation Details. Our method is implemented based on an advanced closed-world detection model Deformable DETR [52]. To facilitate a fair comparison, following previous approaches [11], we employ the ResNet-50 pre-trained on ImageNet through self-supervised training as the feature extractor. The number of layers for both the encoder and decoder is set to 6. We set the number of queries $M = 100$, and the dimension of the embeddings $D = 256$. All experiments are performed on 4 V100 GPUs. During training, the SGD optimizer is employed and the batch size is set to 8.

Table 1. State-of-the-art Comparison for OWOD according to traditional detection metrics. "K-" indicates the known classes, and "U-" represents the unknown classes. Our model achieves state-of-the-art performance in terms of traditional evaluation metrics in unknown detection.

Task IDs ($\rightarrow$)	Task 1			Task 2			Task 3			Task 4
	K-mAP	U-mAP	U-Recall	K-mAP	U-mAP	U-Recall	K-mAP	U-mAP	U-Recall	K-mAP
	($\uparrow$)	($\uparrow$)	($\uparrow$)	($\uparrow$)	($\uparrow$)	($\uparrow$)	($\uparrow$)	($\uparrow$)	($\uparrow$)	($\uparrow$)
Faster RCNN [34]	56.94	0	0	41.56	0	0	32.41	0	0	27.03
ORE [15]	56.49	0.71	5.72	39.64	0.14	2.66	30.17	0.12	3.34	25.95
SA [46]	55.56	0.20	1.93	39.02	0.03	0.79	31.54	0.003	0.12	26.42
DETR [52]	59.75	0	0	46.08	0	0	38.28	0	0	30.60
OW-DETR [11]	58.78	0.07	7.65	44.11	0.04	5.83	35.96	0.03	5.97	27.94
CAT [24]	60.92	0.69	23.66	44.10	0.27	19.05	32.94	0.24	24.35	29.9
ALLOW-DETR [26]	60.00	0.56	13.56	45.58	0.06	10.04	37.97	0.03	14.30	30.60
Ours	59.52	**1.01**	16.71	44.19	0.24	17.13	35.65	0.20	22.97	**32.63**

4.1   State-of-the-Art Comparison

Table 1 shows the comparison of our framework respectively with the state-of-the-art methods according to traditional object detection metrics, such as mAP and Recall. Note that after completing incremental learning of Task 4, all our classes have become known, and there are no longer any unknown targets in the test set. As a result, metrics related to unknown targets, such as U-mAP, UDR, UDP WI, etc., are not included.

From Table 1, our method outperforms other state-of-the-art OWOD methods in most cases. Specifically, The mAP performance of our method for unknown classes surpasses that for the model CAT [24] with the better-known mAP performance by nearly 50%, while the unknown class recall of our method reaches 16.71 and is higher than most of the previous method. These phenomena clearly demonstrate the effectiveness of our Adaptive Semantic-Degrade Learning Framework. While our method may not exhibit Recall performance on unknown classes as strong as CAT, this is an inevitable outcome resulting from our emphasis on improving the mAP for unknown class detection. This is because our framework facilitates the learning of unknown classes by utilizing

Table 2. State-of-the-art comparison for OWOD according to the newly proposed detection metrics, including WI, A-OSE, UDR, and UDP. Our model achieves superior performance on the newly proposed evaluation metrics in most cases.

Task IDs ($\rightarrow$)	Task 1				Task 2				Task 3			
	WI-0.8	A-OSE	UDR	UDP	WI-0.8	A-OSE	UDR	UDP	WI-0.8	A-OSE	UDR	UDP
	($\downarrow$)	($\downarrow$)	($\uparrow$)	($\uparrow$)	($\downarrow$)	($\downarrow$)	($\uparrow$)	($\uparrow$)	($\downarrow$)	($\downarrow$)	($\uparrow$)	($\uparrow$)
Faster RCNN [34]	0.0645	**10502**	17.58	0	0.0273	**8653**	16.32	0	0.0164	7345	24.69	0
ORE [15]	0.0528	11998	18.58	31.28	0.0315	9744	17.30	15.37	0.0209	7769	23.67	14.95
SA [46]	0.0563	23320	8.51	22.73	0.0181	16768	5.74	13.83	**0.0136**	1428	9.12	1.30
DETR [52]	0.0600	57430	20.74	0	0.0245	27795	14.41	0	0.0187	17822	**34.48**	0
OW-DETR [11]	0.0599	42331	18.31	41.77	0.0319	25857	16.24	35.88	0.0220	18056	21.53	27.72
CAT [24]	0.66	22406	**24.21**	**97.93**		13633	**20.22**	**94.19**		7276	25.54	**95.37**
ALLOW-DETR [26]	0.0564	46589	18.47	73.42	0.0274	24709	13.92	72.15	0.0194	14952	18.53	77.19
Ours	**0.0306**	13214	21.79	84.26	**0.0155**	10736	15.35	84.08	0.0137	8570	20.92	86.22

stable features, preventing the common issue in pseudo-labeling methods where many background regions are incorrectly labeled as unknown objects. As a result, our framework can more accurately identify unknown objects, which significantly enhances the mAP for unknown classes. However, by avoiding the misclassification of background regions as unknown objects, the Recall of unknown classes will inevitably decrease.

As novel known classes are added in the subsequent tasks, the recognition ability of unknown classes decreases, which is consistent with the performance of other methods. However, the features of unknown objects are partially reconstructed in incremental learning, which further influences the performance of our framework. Despite this, our method still outperforms most comparison methods in U-mAP and unknown Recall metrics. Furthermore, it can be observed that our method outperforms the majority of approaches on known classes as well. This implies that our proposed framework, while achieving effective detection of unknown classes, incurs minimal degradation in performance for known classes. This once again substantiates the effectiveness of our method.

Table 2 further shows the comparison of our method respectively with the state-of-the-art methods according to common-used open-set evaluation metrics, such as WI, UDR, and UDP. From Table 2, it is evident that our method achieves similar WI scores to state-of-the-art methods while obtaining higher UDR and UDP scores. Specifically, our method achieves the lowest A-OSE under the DETR architecture, indicating that our approach minimizes the likelihood of misclassifying numerous unknown objects as known classes. Our framework approaches or outperforms existing methods comprehensively in UDR at each task, indicating that our framework helps discover more unknown objects. Moreover, our framework exhibits a significant improvement in UDP, suggesting that our framework has a more accurate classification capability for the discovered unknown objects.

Overall, our method has significantly improved its performance in unknown class detection, indicating that the proposed framework effectively addresses the performance penalty of introducing backgrounds with other methods.

4.2   Ablation Study

As shown in Table 3, we investigate different components in our proposed framework. "random split" indicates that the cluster division in our semantic degradation process is done randomly rather than through feature space clustering. "random train" signifies that no cluster division is performed, and training involves randomly assigning cluster-level labels to instances and false positives for each known class. "w/o ASDL" represents the results obtained by removing adaptive semantic degradation learning from our method.

The experimental results in the table indicate that our framework with random cluster division and our framework with random training severely impair the detection performance of unknown classes, especially the unknown class mAP. This underscores the effectiveness of our Adaptive Semantic-degrade Learning, highlighting the crucial role of clustering within the model's original feature space for the semantic degradation process. This approach enables the model to avoid substantial restructuring of the feature space during training, allowing it to discover more precise and shared cluster-level objects. Furthermore, the removal of Adaptive Semantic-Degrade Learning results in the model losing its ability to detect unknown classes. In conclusion, our full model achieves the best performance, and each module contributes to the proposed model.

Table 3. Ablation study. "random split" indicates that the framework with random cluster division in our semantic degradation process. "random train" signifies that training involves randomly assigning cluster-level labels to instances and false positives for each known class. "w/o ASDL" represents our framework without the Adaptive Semantic-Degrade learning. Our full model yields superior performance, and each module contributes to the proposed model.

	K-mAP	U-mAP	U-Recall	UDR	UDP
random split	59.80	0.49	15.83	19.85	79.76
random train	55.99	0.34	15.30	19.73	77.57
w/o ASDL	60.62	0	0	0	0
Ours	59.52	1.01	16.71	21.79	84.26

4.3   Visualization

Figure 3 shows the visualization results of our model in both Task 1 and Task 4, respectively. It can be seen that the model has the ability to recognize unfamiliar instances as unknown entities, and can correctly label these entities after progressively learning the semantic classes of all instances.

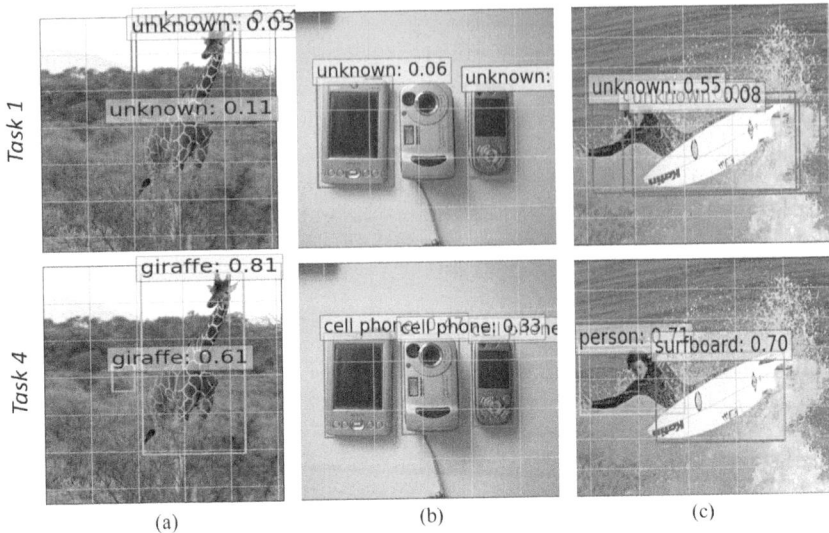

Fig. 3. Visualization result in both Task 1 and Task 4. The model can identify unfamiliar objects as unknown in Task 1, and label them correctly in Task 4.

5   Conclusion

In this work, we propose an effective Adaptive Semantic-Degrade Learning framework for open world object detection. This framework operates by degrading semantic features from the "class level" to the "cluster level". Through the Adaptive Semantic-Degrade Learning method, our framework addresses the uncertainty stemming from background interference in the learning of unknown classes. Rigorous experiments conducted on widely used benchmarks substantiate that our model demonstrates state-of-the-art performance in open-world object detection.

Disclosure of Interests. The authors declare no conflict of interest.

References

1. Bendale, A., Boult, T.: Towards open world recognition. In: 2015 IEEE Conference on Computer Vision and Pattern Recognition (CVPR), pp. 1893–1902 (2015)
2. Bendale, A., Boult, T.E.: Towards open set deep networks. In: 2016 IEEE Conference on Computer Vision and Pattern Recognition (CVPR), pp. 1563–1572 (2016). https://doi.org/10.1109/CVPR.2016.173
3. Carion, N., Massa, F., Synnaeve, G., Usunier, N., Kirillov, A., Zagoruyko, S.: End-to-end object detection with transformers. In: Vedaldi, A., Bischof, H., Brox, T., Frahm, J.-M. (eds.) ECCV 2020. LNCS, vol. 12346, pp. 213–229. Springer, Cham (2020). https://doi.org/10.1007/978-3-030-58452-8_13

4. Dhamija, A., Gunther, M., Ventura, J., Boult, T.: The overlooked elephant of object detection: open set. In: Proceedings of the IEEE/CVF Winter Conference on Applications of Computer Vision, pp. 1021–1030 (2020)
5. Dosovitskiy, A., et al.: An image is worth 16×16 words: transformers for image recognition at scale. arXiv preprint arXiv:2010.11929 (2020)
6. Everingham, M., Van Gool, L., Williams, C.K., Winn, J., Zisserman, A.: The pascal visual object classes (VOC) challenge. Int. J. Comput. Vision **88**, 303–338 (2010)
7. Fang, Y., et al.: You only look at one sequence: rethinking transformer in vision through object detection. Adv. Neural. Inf. Process. Syst. **34**, 26183–26197 (2021)
8. Fei, G., Liu, B.: Breaking the closed world assumption in text classification. In: Proceedings of the 2016 Conference of the North American Chapter of the Association for Computational Linguistics: Human Language Technologies, pp. 506–514 (2016)
9. Guo, J., Ouyang, W., Xu, D.: Channel pruning guided by classification loss and feature importance. In: Proceedings of the AAAI Conference on Artificial Intelligence, vol. 34, pp. 10885–10892 (2020)
10. Guo, J., Xu, D., Lu, G.: CBANet: toward complexity and bitrate adaptive deep image compression using a single network. IEEE Trans. Image Process. **32**, 2049–2062 (2023)
11. Gupta, A., Narayan, S., Joseph, K., Khan, S., Khan, F.S., Shah, M.: OW-DETR: open-world detection transformer. In: Proceedings of the IEEE/CVF Conference on Computer Vision and Pattern Recognition, pp. 9235–9244 (2022)
12. He, K., Zhang, X., Ren, S., Sun, J.: Deep residual learning for image recognition. In: Proceedings of the IEEE Conference on Computer Vision and Pattern Recognition, pp. 770–778 (2016)
13. Heflin, B., Scheirer, W., Boult, T.E.: Detecting and classifying scars, marks, and tattoos found in the wild. In: 2012 IEEE Fifth International Conference on Biometrics: Theory, Applications and Systems (BTAS), pp. 31–38. IEEE (2012)
14. Jain, L.P., Scheirer, W.J., Boult, T.E.: Multi-class open set recognition using probability of inclusion. In: Fleet, D., Pajdla, T., Schiele, B., Tuytelaars, T. (eds.) ECCV 2014, Part III. LNCS, vol. 8691, pp. 393–409. Springer, Cham (2014). https://doi.org/10.1007/978-3-319-10578-9_26
15. Joseph, K., Khan, S., Khan, F.S., Balasubramanian, V.N.: Towards open world object detection. In: Proceedings of the IEEE/CVF Conference on Computer Vision and Pattern Recognition, pp. 5830–5840 (2021)
16. Li, F., Wechsler, H.: Open set face recognition using transduction. IEEE Trans. Pattern Anal. Mach. Intell. **27**(11), 1686–1697 (2005). https://doi.org/10.1109/TPAMI.2005.224
17. Liang, T., et al.: CBNet: a composite backbone network architecture for object detection. IEEE Trans. Image Process. **31**, 6893–6906 (2022). https://doi.org/10.1109/TIP.2022.3216771
18. Liang, W., Xue, F., Liu, Y., Zhong, G., Ming, A.: Unknown sniffer for object detection: don't turn a blind eye to unknown objects. In: Proceedings of the IEEE/CVF Conference on Computer Vision and Pattern Recognition (2023)
19. Lin, T.-Y., et al.: Microsoft COCO: common objects in context. In: Fleet, D., Pajdla, T., Schiele, B., Tuytelaars, T. (eds.) ECCV 2014. LNCS, vol. 8693, pp. 740–755. Springer, Cham (2014). https://doi.org/10.1007/978-3-319-10602-1_48
20. Liu, A., et al.: Perceptual-sensitive GAN for generating adversarial patches. In: Proceedings of the AAAI Conference on Artificial Intelligence, vol. 33, pp. 1028–1035 (2019)

21. Liu, A., Liu, X., Yu, H., Zhang, C., Liu, Q., Tao, D.: Training robust deep neural networks via adversarial noise propagation. IEEE Trans. Image Process. **30**, 5769–5781 (2021)
22. Liu, X., et al.: A meaningful learning method for zero-shot semantic segmentation. Sci. China Inf. Sci. **66**(11), 210103 (2023)
23. Liu, Z., Miao, Z., Zhan, X., Wang, J., Gong, B., Yu, S.X.: Large-scale long-tailed recognition in an open world. In: Proceedings of the IEEE/CVF Conference on Computer Vision and Pattern Recognition, pp. 2537–2546 (2019)
24. Ma, S., et al.: CAT: localization and identification cascade detection transformer for open-world object detection. In: Proceedings of the IEEE/CVF Conference on Computer Vision and Pattern Recognition, pp. 19681–19690 (2023)
25. Ma, Y., et al.: Transductive relation-propagation network for few-shot learning. In: IJCAI, vol. 20, pp. 804–810 (2020)
26. Ma, Y., et al.: Annealing-based label-transfer learning for open world object detection. In: Proceedings of the IEEE/CVF Conference on Computer Vision and Pattern Recognition, pp. 11454–11463 (2023)
27. Ma, Y., et al.: Few-shot visual learning with contextual memory and fine-grained calibration. In: IJCAI, pp. 811–817 (2020)
28. Ma, Y., Liu, X., Bai, S., Wang, L., He, D., Liu, A.: Coarse-to-fine image inpainting via region-wise convolutions and non-local correlation. In: IJCAI, pp. 3123–3129 (2019)
29. Ma, Y., et al.: Regionwise generative adversarial image inpainting for large missing areas. IEEE Trans. Cybern. (2022)
30. Mancini, M., Naeem, M.F., Xian, Y., Akata, Z.: Open world compositional zero-shot learning. In: Proceedings of the IEEE/CVF Conference on Computer Vision and Pattern Recognition, pp. 5222–5230 (2021)
31. Miller, D., Nicholson, L., Dayoub, F., Sünderhauf, N.: Dropout sampling for robust object detection in open-set conditions. In: 2018 IEEE International Conference on Robotics and Automation (ICRA), pp. 3243–3249. IEEE (2018)
32. Perera, P., et al.: Generative-discriminative feature representations for open-set recognition. In: Proceedings of the IEEE/CVF Conference on Computer Vision and Pattern Recognition, pp. 11814–11823 (2020)
33. Pritsos, D.A., Stamatatos, E.: Open-set classification for automated genre identification. In: Serdyukov, P., et al. (eds.) ECIR 2013. LNCS, vol. 7814, pp. 207–217. Springer, Heidelberg (2013). https://doi.org/10.1007/978-3-642-36973-5_18
34. Ren, S., He, K., Girshick, R., Sun, J.: Faster R-CNN: towards real-time object detection with region proposal networks. Adv. Neural Inf. Process. Syst. **28** (2015)
35. Scheirer, W.J., Jain, L.P., Boult, T.E.: Probability models for open set recognition. IEEE Trans. Pattern Anal. Mach. Intell. **36**(11), 2317–2324 (2014)
36. Scheirer, W.J., de Rezende Rocha, A., Sapkota, A., Boult, T.E.: Toward open set recognition. IEEE Trans. Pattern Anal. Mach. Intell. **35**(7), 1757–1772 (2012)
37. Scherreik, M.D., Rigling, B.D.: Open set recognition for automatic target classification with rejection. IEEE Trans. Aerosp. Electron. Syst. **52**(2), 632–642 (2016)
38. Sun, P., et al.: Sparse R-CNN: end-to-end object detection with learnable proposals. In: Proceedings of the IEEE/CVF Conference on Computer Vision and Pattern Recognition, pp. 14454–14463 (2021)
39. Tao, R., et al.: Exploring endogenous shift for cross-domain detection: a large-scale benchmark and perturbation suppression network. In: 2022 IEEE/CVF Conference on Computer Vision and Pattern Recognition (CVPR), pp. 21157–21167. IEEE (2022)

40. Vareto, R., Silva, S., Costa, F., Schwartz, W.R.: Towards open-set face recognition using hashing functions. In: 2017 IEEE International Joint Conference on Biometrics (IJCB), pp. 634–641. IEEE (2017)
41. Wang, Y., Yue, Z., Hua, X.S., Zhang, H.: Random boxes are open-world object detectors. In: Proceedings of the IEEE/CVF International Conference on Computer Vision (ICCV), pp. 6233–6243 (2023)
42. Wang, Y., Yao, Q., Kwok, J.T., Ni, L.M.: Generalizing from a few examples: a survey on few-shot learning. ACM Comput. Surv. (CSUR) **53**(3), 1–34 (2020)
43. Willes, J., Harrison, J., Harakeh, A., Finn, C., Pavone, M., Waslander, S.: Bayesian embeddings for few-shot open world recognition. IEEE Trans. Pattern Anal. Mach. Intell. (2022)
44. Wu, Z., Lu, Y., Chen, X., Wu, Z., Kang, L., Yu, J.: UC-OWOD: unknown-classified open world object detection. In: Avidan, S., Brostow, G., Cissé, M., Farinella, G.M., Hassner, T. (eds.) ECCV 2022. LNCS, vol. 13670, pp. 193–210. Springer, Cham (2022). https://doi.org/10.1007/978-3-031-20080-9_12
45. Xian, Y., Schiele, B., Akata, Z.: Zero-shot learning-the good, the bad and the ugly. In: Proceedings of the IEEE Conference on Computer Vision and Pattern Recognition, pp. 4582–4591 (2017)
46. Yang, S., et al.: Objects in semantic topology. arXiv preprint arXiv:2110.02687 (2021)
47. Yoshihashi, R., Shao, W., Kawakami, R., You, S., Iida, M., Naemura, T.: Classification-reconstruction learning for open-set recognition. In: Proceedings of the IEEE/CVF Conference on Computer Vision and Pattern Recognition, pp. 4016–4025 (2019)
48. Zhang, S., Li, Z., Yan, S., He, X., Sun, J.: Distribution alignment: a unified framework for long-tail visual recognition. In: Proceedings of the IEEE/CVF Conference on Computer Vision and Pattern Recognition, pp. 2361–2370 (2021)
49. Zhao, X., et al.: Temporal speciation network for few-shot object detection. IEEE Trans. Multimed. (2023)
50. Zhao, X., Ma, Y., Wang, D., Shen, Y., Qiao, Y., Liu, X.: Revisiting open world object detection. IEEE Trans. Circuits Syst. Video Technol. (2023)
51. Zhou, D.W., Ye, H.J., Zhan, D.C.: Learning placeholders for open-set recognition. In: 2021 IEEE/CVF Conference on Computer Vision and Pattern Recognition (CVPR), pp. 4399–4408 (2021). https://doi.org/10.1109/CVPR46437.2021.00438
52. Zhu, X., Su, W., Lu, L., Li, B., Wang, X., Dai, J.: Deformable DETR: deformable transformers for end-to-end object detection. arXiv preprint arXiv:2010.04159 (2020)

Multi-modal Prompts with Feature Decoupling for Open-Vocabulary Object Detection

Duorui Wang and Xiaowei Zhao[✉]

State Key Laboratory of Complex and Critical Software Environment,
Beihang University, Beijing 100191, China
{wangduorui,xiaoweizhao}@buaa.edu.cn

Abstract. Open-vocabulary object detection aims to acquire the ability to recognize novel categories through text description using data of limited categories for training. The Prompt serves as a template to assist in the construction of textual descriptions for categories. With the development of open-vocabulary object detection, multi-modal prompts with better performance have emerged. However, existing multi-modal prompts fail to align the context and object components across different modalities during the construction. To address the issue, we propose an open-vocabulary object detection framework based on multi-modal prompts with feature decoupling. The framework consists of two modules, the construction of Multi-modal Prompts with Feature Decoupling (MPFD) and the visual Region Expansion (RE). During prompts constructing, the MPFD decouples the object and context components from the visual embeddings and then performs multi-modal fusion with the corresponding parts of the text embeddings respectively. The RE incorporates additional context information into the visual embeddings to enhance the discriminative ability of the prompts. Sufficient experiments have demonstrated that feature decoupling multi-modal prompts can effectively improve the performance of open-vocabulary object detection models.

Keywords: feature decoupling · multi-modal prompts · open-vocabulary object detection · region expansion

1 Introduction

With the development of computer vision [11,12,15,19,20], deep learning-based object detection [6,14,23,30] has made tremendous progress in recent years. However, traditional object detection methods are usually performed on closed sets, where the model can only encounter a limited number of object categories during the training phase. Whereas in the real open world [32], novel categories of objects are constantly appearing, and existing detection methods are unable to effectively identify categories that have not been seen in training. Labeling

J. Guo et al. (Eds.): IJCAI 2024, CCIS 2160, pp. 180–194, 2024.
https://doi.org/10.1007/978-981-97-6125-8_14

all unseen categories is not possible due to the limited availability of annotation resources [16–18] and privacy preservation, preventing researchers from including all possible categories in the training set. Open-Vocabulary Object Detection (OVD) tasks [28,31] are proposed to address the problem of recognizing categories unseen during training in the testing phase. It uses semantic embeddings of category names as classifiers to classify images into the appropriate categories. When novel categories appear during testing, they can be classified into unseen categories through the model's generalization capabilities with the assistance of text description.

OVR-CNN is the first to propose the task of OVD, which relies on a region-aware training detection model to establish correspondence between regions and related text content. To further enhance OVD performance, some methods increase the number of image-text pairs by generating pseudo labels using pre-trained Vision-Language Models (VLMs) or self-training techniques. Knowledge distillation (KD) based methods [2,5,24] are extensively studied and leverage the vast knowledge in pre-trained VLMs, such as CLIP [22], to improve generalization to novel categories. These KD-based methods align embeddings extracted by the VLM's visual encoder with region embeddings from the student model, and they replace the student's classifier weights with text embeddings from the VLM's text encoder. Initially, the text encoder input combines category names with text prompt templates [22]. Later, visual prompts [8] and multimodal prompts [9] are introduced. Multimodal prompts effectively utilize visual features and enhance category information with text prompts, thereby increasing the distinction between similar category cues and improving classification accuracy.

Despite the explosive development of OVD research [24,25], some challenges remain unresolved in the construction of multi-modal prompts for knowledge distillation-based methods. (1) There is a lack of alignment between the context and object components across different modalities during the construction of multi-modal prompts. Existing multi-modal prompts often integrate vision and text as two separate entities, neglecting the correspondence between the context and object. This results in the inability to effectively incorporate visual information into the prompt. (2) Insufficient context features in the visual modality of multi-modal prompt. Most methods directly utilize the boxes provided by Region Proposal Network (RPN) or Ground Truth (GT) to crop images and extract visual features. Such a strategy results in the absence of visual context information, leading to a decline in the classification ability of multi-modal prompts.

In order to address the above problems, this paper proposes a novel open-vocabulary object detection framework based on multi-modal prompts with feature decoupling. Multi-modal Prompts with Feature Decoupling (MPFD) solve the problem of misalignment between context and object across modalities. MPFD decouples the object and context components in both visual and text then performs fusion separately. Specifically, masks of objects and a visual encoder are employed to extract visual embeddings from the ground truth regions. Simultaneously, a text encoder is used to acquire text embeddings of categories. Object components in multi-modal prompts are then generated by fusing these two types of embeddings. Similarly, context visual embeddings extracted through a context mask and text prompts are integrated to construct multi-modal prompts, enabling the decoupling of object and context.

To further address the issue of insufficient context features contained in the visual modality of the multi-modal prompt, RE employs a series of expansion and correction strategies to enlarge the GT boxes, thereby enriching the context information encompassed within the visual modality. Specifically, we first resize the boxes into a square shape to minimize the distortion generated by the visual encoder during the preprocessing. Subsequently, we scale up the region proportionally to capture more of the surrounding background context. Finally, we correct any boxes that extend beyond the image boundary, ensuring that no additional meaningless empty pixels are introduced into the region.

The main contributions of this paper can be summarized as follows:

- We propose a multi-modal prompt construction method based on feature decoupling, which eliminates the mixture of context and object features in multi-modal prompts.
- We propose a new region expansion strategy, which not only alleviates the distortion but also makes the region contain complete objects and enough context information.
- We conduct sufficient experiments on two widely used general datasets OV-COCO to demonstrate the effectiveness of our proposed method.

2   Related Work

2.1   Open-Vocabulary Object Detection

Open-vocabulary object detection [5,28,33] aims to accurately identify all categories, both seen and unseen during the training process, with the assistance of text data. OVR-CNN [28] was the first to propose the setting of OVD, learning the vision-semantics correspondence through pre-training with image-caption pairs, and then using these pre-trained backbones and vision-to-language mapping layers to train an open-vocabulary detector. ViLD [5] first introduced knowledge distillation architecture into OVD. By aligning the regional embedding of the student with the image and text embeddings inferred by the teacher, it distilled the knowledge from the pre-trained open-vocabulary classification model into the detector. RegionCLIP [33] achieves fine-grained image-text alignment by generating pseudo labels at the region-level, thereby mitigating the domain shift caused by image-level captions. CORA [26] employs region prompts to alleviate the distribution gap between images and regions, and utilizes a region-aware matching mechanism to localize novel categories. BARON [25] embedded a bag of contextual regions into the text space and aligns these regions as a whole with their text embeddings. Compared with these methods, we propose an open-vocabulary detector based on knowledge distillation, which introduces more context information through multi-modal prompts to enhance the detection performance.

2.2 Prompt Tuning

Vision-language models are typically trained with image-text pairs, and the utilization of prompts in OVD tasks can enable them to obtain more effective features. Initially, some methods [5,13,33,36] only employed fixed text prompts to generate better text embeddings. With the introduction of learnable prompts in open-vocabulary classification tasks by CoOp [35], methods such as PromptDet [3] and DetPro [2] have also employed learnable prompts in OVD. PromptDet achieves offline learning of regional prompts to align regional visual features with text embeddings of categories. DetPro leverages both positive and negative samples to jointly constrain the learnable prompt. CoCoOp [34] indicated that the prompts learned by CoOp fail to effectively generalize to novel categories. Therefore, it proposed to fuse the mapped image feature with the learnable prompts, leveraging the multi-modal learnable prompts to enhance the generalization capability of the model. MaPLe [9] introduces a hierarchical prompt shared by vision and text to improve generalization. The multi-modal prompts with feature decoupling proposed in this paper differs from the aforementioned methods. We regard vision and text embeddings containing object and context components, decoupling them and aligning the corresponding parts to enhance the detection performance.

3 Method

3.1 Preliminaries

In the open-vocabulary object detection, we have the training set $\mathcal{D}^T = \{I_i, Y_i\}_{i=1}^{N}$, I_i is the image and $Y_i \in C^B$ is the annotation information. C^B denotes the base classes. In the test stage, we have the novel classes C^N in the test set $\mathcal{D}^V$, and $C^N \cap C^B = \varnothing$.

We construct a distillation-based open-vocabulary object detection model based on the Faster R-CNN [23] architecture. Faster R-CNN serves as the student model, and the Vision-Language Models CLIP [22] is adopted as the teacher. Given an input image $I \in \mathbb{R}^{H \times W \times 3}$, it undergoes the backbone (ResNet50) to extract image features F. Then the RPN generated proposals $P_r \in \mathbb{R}^4$ and obtain their region embeddings $\{e_p | p \in P_r\}$ through RoI Align. Text encoder E_t of the teacher is used to capture the text embeddings t_c of categories. The logits of proposals are calculated as follows:

$$l(p, c) = \frac{e_p \cdot t_c}{\|e_p\| \cdot \|t_c\|}. \tag{1}$$

The probabilities of the proposals p belonging to category c are predicted as:

$$P(p,c) = \frac{\exp(l(p,c))}{\sum\limits_{c' \in C^B \cup C^N} \exp(l(p,c'))}. \tag{2}$$

Then, the visual encoder of the teacher extracts $\hat{e}_p$ as distillation embedding of proposals. We use the L1 loss as the distillation loss:

$$L_{dis} = L_1(e_p, \hat{e}_p). \tag{3}$$

As the previous method ignores the alignment across different modalities, in this paper we employ a multi-modal prompt integrated with decoupled visual features to text embeddings, serving as the classifier head for the detector. Additionally, we introduce a novel form of region expansion to optimize the visual features for constructing multi-modal prompts, enabling it to encompass both the entire object and more effective context information. The overall architecture of the proposed method in this paper is illustrated in the Fig. 1.

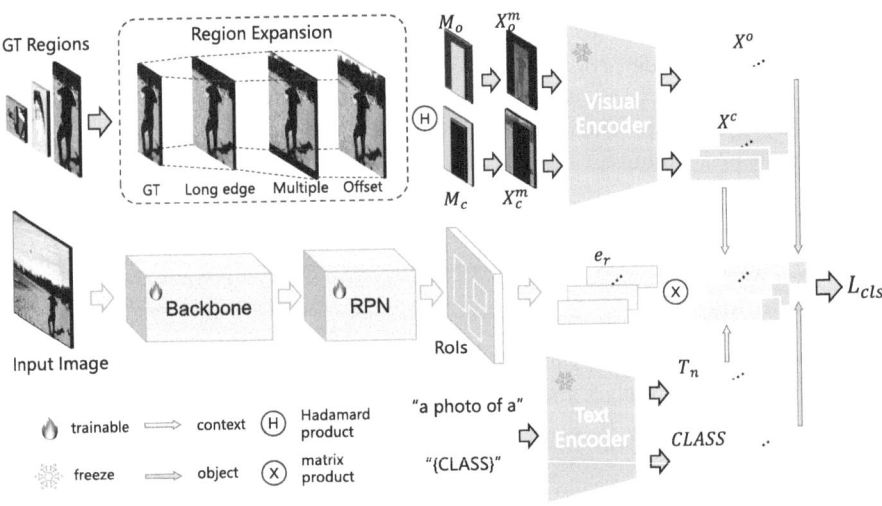

Fig. 1. Overall framework of multi-modal prompts with feature decoupling for open-vocabulary object detection.

3.2 Multi-modal Prompts with Feature Decoupling

In open-vocabulary object detection, the image input usually contains the object $\mathcal{V}^o$ and the environmental context $\mathcal{V}^c$. The text input similarly contains the category name $\mathcal{T}^o$ and the context description $\mathcal{T}^c$, which belong to the category-related and category-irrelevant parts respectively. However, the existing construction of multi-modal prompts ignores the correspondence between visual and textual inputs. Both vision and text are regarded as a whole and mixed with object and context features. In order to solve the problem above, we decouple the object and context from the regions. Then, we integrate these region embeddings with textual embeddings in a similar manner to word tokens respectively, resulting in feature-decoupled multi-modal prompts.

During the training phase, we utilize the ground-truth bounding boxes of the base categories to crop the image I. Subsequently, two distinct masks $M_c, M_o \in \mathbb{R}^{n \times w \times h}$ are employed for the cropped regions $R_{gt} \in \mathbb{R}^{n \times w \times h}$, where n is the number of ground-truth regions, w and h represents the width and height. Masks are leveraged for soft extraction of object features $X_o^m = R_{gt} \cdot M_o$ and context features $X_c^m = R_{gt} \cdot M_c$, where $\cdot$ denotes the Hadamard product. These features are then fed into a pre-trained visual encoder $E_v(\cdot)$ to obtain visual features $X_o, X_c \in \mathbb{R}^{n \times d}$, where d is the dimension of the features. The masks can be generated directly based on the ground-truth boxes, or methods such as attention mechanisms can be applied.

$$
\begin{aligned}
X^o &= E_v(X_o^m), \\
X^c &= E_v(X_c^m).
\end{aligned}
\tag{4}
$$

The textual prompts $\mathcal{T} = (T^c, T^o)$ are initialized using the format "a photo of a {CLASS}". The token embeddings $P^t = \{p_i^t \in \mathbb{R}^{k \times d} | i \in N\}$ of $\mathcal{T}$ is applied, where N represents the number of classes and k is a fixed value indicating the maximum length of the token sequence.

The visual context features $X^c = \{x_i^c | i \in n\}$ are repeated l_c times and inserted into the textual prompts corresponding to the respective class $p_i^t = \{[T_1], [T_2], ..., [T_Q], [CLASS]\}$, where $\{T_q | q \in Q\}$ denotes the token embeddings of context words and M is the total number of words in the context. The visual context features are positioned before the class name token, serving as part of the contextual tokens. The multi-modal prompts $P^m = \{p_i^m | i \in N\}$ can be represented as:

$$
p_i^m = \{[T_1], [T_2], ..., [T_Q], [x_i^c] \times l_c, [CLASS]\},
\tag{5}
$$

where l_c represents the context intensity, indicating the degree of participation of the visual context features within the multi-modal prompts. x_i^c denotes the visual context feature belonging to class i, and $[x_i^c] \times l_c$ indicates that x_i^c is repeated l_c times. Similarly, the visual object features are repeated l_o times and inserted into the prompt corresponding to the respective class, positioned after the class name token. In this case, l_o represents the object intensity, reflecting the level of involvement of the visual object features within the multi-modal prompts. And x_i^o represents i-th class object feature. At this point, the multi-modal prompts P^m transforms into:

$$
p_i^m = \{[T_1], [T_2], ..., [T_Q], [x_i^c] \times l_c, [CLASS], [x_i^o] \times l_o\}.
\tag{6}
$$

By feeding the multi-modal prompt P^m into a pre-trained text encoder $E_t(\cdot)$, we obtain classification weights for each category. The prediction probability of the open word detection model is calculated as follows.

$$P(y = i|e_r) = \frac{\exp(\cos(E_t(p_i^m), e_r))}{\sum_{j=1}^{N} \exp(\cos(E_t(p_j^m), e_r))}, \tag{7}$$

where e_r represents the proposal features of the detection model. We follow the training setup of OADP [24], the total loss contains the loss of Faster R-CNN as well as the distillation loss. RPN loss L_{rpn} as well as classification loss L_{cls} and regression loss L_{reg} are included in L_{frcnn}.

$$\begin{aligned} L &= L_{frcnn} + L_{dis}, \\ L_{frcnn} &= L_{rpn} + L_{cls} + L_{reg}. \end{aligned} \tag{8}$$

3.3   Region Expansion

The current region expansion methods are generally aimed at altering the shape of the region to minimize deformation during the extraction of regional features. Therefore, a single expansion strategy is often employed to minimize the proportion of background within the entire region. However, the reason for region expansion in this paper extends beyond minimizing the impact of regional deformation on the accuracy of feature extraction. It also necessitates the inclusion of sufficient environmental information within the region to describe the context of each category. When relying solely on the native ground-truth boxes from the dataset for cropping, the environmental information is not adequate for constructing multi-modal prompts effectively. A single expansion strategy has limited effectiveness, and it is essential to organically integrate several expansion strategies to maximize their impact.

Ground Truth Region   Long Edge Expansion   Multiple Expansion   Offset Expansion

Fig. 2. The specific operation process of region expansion.

The specific form of expansion is illustrated in the Fig. 2. The expansion process for a region in the form of $b = (w, h, x_c, y_c)$, where (w, h) represents the width and height, and (x_c, y_c) represents the center coordinates, is divided into three steps. To ensure that the entire object is encompassed within the region, we first adopt an expansion form with an unchanged region center. Keeping the original (x_c, y_c) unchanged, the area is expanded to a square with the longest edge as its side length:

$$l_l = \max(w, h). \tag{9}$$

We then enlarge this region proportionally by a parameter α to obtain a larger square region with side length l_m:

$$l_m = \sqrt{\alpha \times l_l^2}. \tag{10}$$

Finally, if the new region exceeds the boundary of the input image, we will offset the region to ensure that it is contained within the original input image. The width and height of the input image are represented as (w_{max}, h_{max}). And new center coordinates are calculated as follows:

$$\begin{cases} x_c' = x_c + |x_c - l_m/2|, & x_c - l_m/2 < 0 \\ x_c' = x_c - |x_c + l_m/2|, & x_c + l_m/2 > w_{max} \\ y_c' = y_c + |y_c - l_m/2|, & y_c - l_m/2 < 0 \\ y_c' = y_c - |y_c + l_m/2|, & y_c + l_m/2 > h_{max} \end{cases}. \tag{11}$$

4   Experiment

We detail our experimental setup in this section, including the data set information, the evaluation metrics, and the experimental detail Settings. Then we will compare with the existing SOTA results to demonstrate the effectiveness of our method.

4.1   Datasets

In this paper, two main experimental settings are as followed, open-vocabulary COCO (OV-COCO) [28].

OV-COCO. This dataset is derived from the MSCOCO dataset which contains 80 categories. According to the setup of [28], the categories in the COCO dataset are re-classified into 48 basic categories and 17 novel categories. The training set is the same as COCO, but only image samples containing at least one base class are used during training. There are three main metrics to evaluate the performance of the model, mAP_N, mAP_B, and mAP_{50}. Where mAP_N represents the mAP of the novel categories with an IoU threshold of 0.5, and mAP_B and mAP_{50} represent the base categories and the full categories, respectively.

4.2   Implementation Details

We train the model using 8 V-100 GPUs with a total batch size of 16. We follow the implementation details of [24] and use SGD as the optimizer with an initial learning rate of 0.01, momentum of 0.9, and weight decay of 0.0001. We use ViT-B/32 CLIP as our teacher model, and its text and visual encoders are used to generate multimodal prompts. Our student model uses the classic Faster RCNN and initializes its ResNet-50 backbone with SoCo. We trained on OV-COCO for a total of 40,000 iterations and reduced the learning rate to 0.0001 at 30,000 iters.

4.3 Main Results

For a fair comparison of experimental results, we reproduce the results of the SOTA method under the same conditions and compare them with our proposed method.

The experimental results on the OV-COCO dataset are presented in Table 1. By adopting multi-modal prompts, we effectively improve the performance on the base categories while maintaining its performance on the novel categories. We achieved a performance of 27.2% mAP on the novel categories, which is slightly lower than OADP and 4.4% higher than OVR-CNN. On the base categories, we achieved a result of 55.6%, which is 3.9% and 9.6% higher than OADP and OVR-CNN respectively. VLDet achieved the best result on the novel classes, but our performance surpasses it by 5.0% on the base classes and by 2.4% on the full classes. This can prove that the decoupled visual information added to the multi-modal prompts increases its discriminative ability for base categories and reduces misclassifications. Although we did not achieve the optimal results on the novel categories, we have struck a balance between the novel and the base categories to attain the best performance across all categories.

Table 1. Comparison results with other state-of-the-art methods on OV-COCO dataset. Methods with the symbol "†" indicate the method result that has been reproduced. "T(cat)" denotes using text prompts only, while "M" denotes multi-modal prompts. "✗" indicates the method does not utilize the CLIP text encoder.

Methods	Detector	Prompts	mAP_N	mAP_B	mAP_{50}
ZSD-YOLO [27]	YOLOv5x	✗	13.6	31.7	19.0
HierKD [21]	ATSS [29]	T(cat)	20.3	51.3	43.2
PB-OVD [4]	MRCNN	T(cat)	30.8	46.1	42.1
F-VLM [10]	MRCNN	T(cat)	28.0	–	39.6
OVR-CNN [28]	FRCNN	✗	22.8	46.0	39.9
LocOv [1]	FRCNN	✗	28.6	51.3	45.7
VLDet [13]	FRCNN	T(cat)	**32.0**	50.6	45.8
XPM [7]	FRCNN	✗	27.0	46.3	41.2
Detic [36]	FRCNN	T(cat)	27.8	47.1	45.0
OADP† [24]	FRCNN	T(cat)	29.9	51.7	46.0
Ours	FRCNN	M(cat)	27.2	**55.6**	**48.2**

4.4 Ablation Study

We conduct ablation experiments on the OV-COCO dataset to demonstrate the effectiveness of our proposed method.

Table 2. Ablation study of multi-modal prompts with feature decoupling on OV-COCO dataset.

Textual	Multi-modal	Decoupling	mAP_N	mAP_B	mAP_{50}
✓			**29.9**	51.7	46.0
	✓		1.7	49.9	37.3
	✓	✓	27.2	**55.6**	**48.2**

Mluti-modal Prompts with Feature Decoupling. Our experimental results are presented in Table 2. The first row demonstrates the results of utilizing text prompts only, which are inferior to the original results due to the limitations of our experimental conditions. The second row presents the results of multi-modal prompts without feature decoupling. We refer to the ViLD [5] prompts construction method to average the region embedding with the text prompts embedding of the category to which they belong. Since the region contains only the base category and the region embedding directly acts on the text prompts without decoupling, the result of the novel category drops significantly and the promotion of the base category is limited. The last row presents the results of multi-modal prompts with feature decoupling. We apply the decoupled region embedding to different positions of the text prompts, which enhances the discrimination of prompts among base categories, increasing the mAP_B by 4.9%. Meanwhile, we control the influence of the decoupled region embedding by the intensity parameters, which reduces the number of novel categories that are misclassified into base categories, thus alleviating the sharp decline in model performance on novel classes. Multi-modal prompts with feature decoupling endow the model with stronger discrimination ability and can effectively distinguish novel categories from base categories.

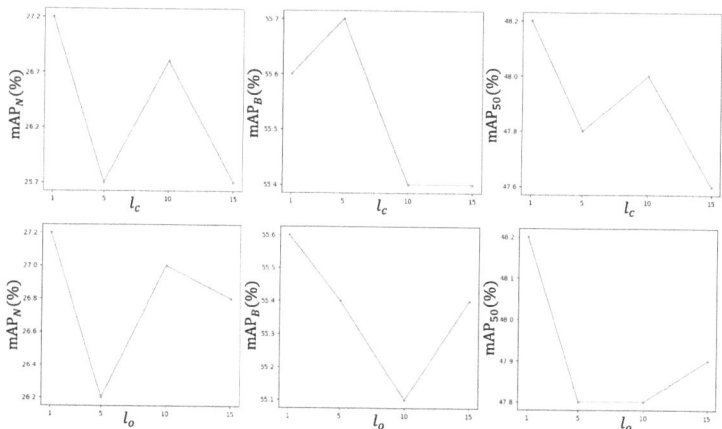

Fig. 3. Ablation study of the hyperparameters l_c and l_o.

We have further studied the impact of two intensity parameters l_c and l_o in multi-modal prompts on the model performance. The results are presented in Fig. 3.

Region Expansion. The experimental results are presented in Table 3. The first row demonstrates the results of not employing the region expansion. The lack of visual context information in the multi-modal prompts leads to poor performance on base categories. The second row exhibits the results of only applying the long-edge expansion strategy. Although contextual information is supplemented, the small-encompassed area fails to efficiently enhance the performance. The third row presents the results of utilizing both the long edge and multiple expansion strategies. The results indicate that supplementing additional context regions can effectively enrich the contextual information of the multimodal prompts, leading to better performance. The last row indicates that offset can effectively reduce the impact of meaningless regions beyond the boundary on multi-modal prompts, thereby further improving the performance.

Table 3. Ablation study of region expansion on OV-COCO dataset.

Expansion Form	mAP_N	mAP_B	mAP_{50}
No Expansion	27.1	50.5	44.4
Long Edge	27.1	52.7	46.0
Long Edge + Multiple	27.1	53.9	46.9
Long Edge + Multiple + Offset	**27.2**	**55.6**	**48.2**

5 Visualization

We visualize the projection of multi-modal prompts in the feature space. As shown in Fig. 4(a), although there are some cases where the prompts of novel categories and base categories are close to each other, there is no overlap between them. The distance between the prompts of base categories is large enough, allowing for effective discrimination. Figure 4(b) illustrates the superclasses corresponding to all the categories, revealing that most of the closely situated categories belong to the same superclass.

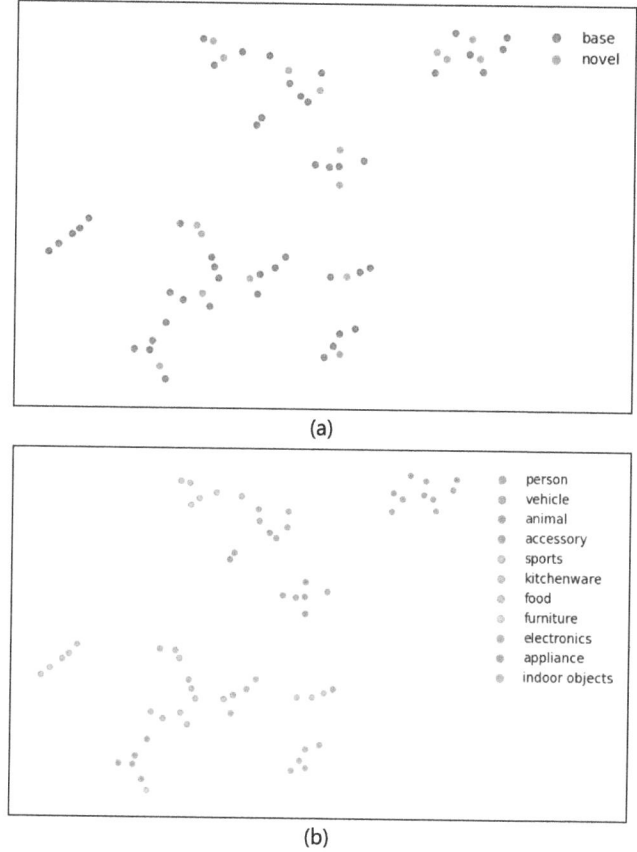

Fig. 4. Visualization of the projection of multi-modal prompts in the feature space. (a) Categories of multi-modal prompts. (b) Superclasses of multi-modal prompts.

6   Conclusion

This paper proposes a novel multi-modal prompts construction approach based on feature decoupling to enhance the predictive capability of open-vocabulary object detection models. Specifically, we decouple the visual region and text description into context and target components respectively. Then, we align and fuse these two parts and encode them uniformly to form multi-modal prompts. To further improve the discriminative ability of multi-modal prompts, we introduce a region expansion strategy to incorporate additional context information. Finally, the effectiveness of our proposed method is fully demonstrated through the results obtained on the OV-COCO dataset.

Acknowledgments. This work is supported by grant No. KZ46009501.

Disclosure of Interests. The authors have no competing interests to declare that are relevant to the content of this article.

References

1. Bravo, M.A., Mittal, S., Brox, T.: Localized vision-language matching for open-vocabulary object detection. In: Andres, B., Bernard, F., Cremers, D., Frintrop, S., Goldlücke, B., Ihrke, I. (eds.) DAGM GCPR 2022. LNCS, vol. 13485, pp. 393–408. Springer, Cham (2022). https://doi.org/10.1007/978-3-031-16788-1_24

2. Du, Y., Wei, F., Zhang, Z., Shi, M., Gao, Y., Li, G.: Learning to prompt for open-vocabulary object detection with vision-language model. In: Proceedings of the IEEE/CVF Conference on Computer Vision and Pattern Recognition, pp. 14084–14093 (2022)

3. Feng, C., et al.: PromptDet: towards open-vocabulary detection using uncurated images. In: Avidan, S., Brostow, G., Cissé, M., Farinella, G.M., Hassner, T. (eds.) ECCV 2022. LNCS, vol. 13669, pp. 701–717. Springer, Cham (2022). https://doi.org/10.1007/978-3-031-20077-9_41

4. Gao, M., et al.: Open vocabulary object detection with pseudo bounding-box labels. In: Avidan, S., Brostow, G., Cissé, M., Farinella, G.M., Hassner, T. (eds.) ECCV 2022. LNCS, vol. 13670, pp. 266–282. Springer, Cham (2022). https://doi.org/10.1007/978-3-031-20080-9_16

5. Gu, X., Lin, T.Y., Kuo, W., Cui, Y.: Open-vocabulary object detection via vision and language knowledge distillation. In: The Tenth International Conference on Learning Representations, ICLR (2022)

6. He, K., Gkioxari, G., Dollár, P., Girshick, R.: Mask R-CNN. In: Proceedings of the IEEE International Conference on Computer Vision, pp. 2961–2969 (2017)

7. Huynh, D., Kuen, J., Lin, Z., Gu, J., Elhamifar, E.: Open-vocabulary instance segmentation via robust cross-modal pseudo-labeling. In: Proceedings of the IEEE/CVF Conference on Computer Vision and Pattern Recognition, pp. 7020–7031 (2022)

8. Jia, M., Tang, L., Chen, B.C., Cardie, C., Belongie, S., Hariharan, B., Lim, S.N.: Visual prompt tuning. In: Avidan, S., Brostow, G., Cissé, M., Farinella, G.M., Hassner, T. (eds.) ECCV 2022. LNCS, vol. 13693, pp. 709–727. Springer, Cham (2022). https://doi.org/10.1007/978-3-031-19827-4_41

9. Khattak, M.U., Rasheed, H., Maaz, M., Khan, S., Khan, F.S.: MaPLe: multimodal prompt learning. In: Proceedings of the IEEE/CVF Conference on Computer Vision and Pattern Recognition, pp. 19113–19122 (2023)

10. Kuo, W., Cui, Y., Gu, X., Piergiovanni, A., Angelova, A.: F-VLM: open-vocabulary object detection upon frozen vision and language models. In: The Eleventh International Conference on Learning Representations, ICLR (2023)

11. Li, S., et al.: Hierarchical perceptual noise injection for social media fingerprint privacy protection. IEEE Trans. Image Process. (2024)

12. Li, S., et al.: Towards benchmarking and assessing visual naturalness of physical world adversarial attacks. In: Proceedings of the IEEE/CVF Conference on Computer Vision and Pattern Recognition, pp. 12324–12333 (2023)

13. Lin, C., et al.: Learning object-language alignments for open-vocabulary object detection. In: The Eleventh International Conference on Learning Representations, ICLR (2023)

14. Lin, T.Y., Dollár, P., Girshick, R., He, K., Hariharan, B., Belongie, S.: Feature pyramid networks for object detection. In: Proceedings of the IEEE Conference on Computer Vision and Pattern Recognition, pp. 2117–2125 (2017)

15. Liu, X., Bai, S., An, S., Wang, S., Liu, W., Zhao, X., Ma, Y.: A meaningful learning method for zero-shot semantic segmentation. Sci. China Inf. Sci. **66**(11), 210103 (2023)

16. Ma, Y., et al.: Transductive relation-propagation network for few-shot learning. In: IJCAI, vol. 20, pp. 804–810 (2020)

17. Ma, Y., et al.: Transductive relation-propagation with decoupling training for few-shot learning. IEEE Trans. Neural Netw. Learn. Syst. **33**(11), 6652–6664 (2021)

18. Ma, Y., et al.: Few-shot visual learning with contextual memory and fine-grained calibration. In: IJCAI, pp. 811–817 (2020)

19. Ma, Y., et al.: SeeMore: a spatiotemporal predictive model with bidirectional distillation and level-specific meta-adaptation. Sci. China Inf. Sci. (2023)

20. Ma, Y., et al.: Regionwise generative adversarial image inpainting for large missing areas. IEEE Trans. Cybern. (2022)

21. Ma, Z., et al.: Open-vocabulary one-stage detection with hierarchical visual-language knowledge distillation. In: Proceedings of the IEEE/CVF Conference on Computer Vision and Pattern Recognition, pp. 14074–14083 (2022)

22. Radford, A., et al.: Learning transferable visual models from natural language supervision. In: International Conference on Machine Learning, pp. 8748–8763. PMLR (2021)

23. Ren, S., He, K., Girshick, R., Sun, J.: Faster R-CNN: towards real-time object detection with region proposal networks. In: Advances in Neural Information Processing Systems, pp. 91–99 (2015)

24. Wang, L., et al.: Object-aware distillation pyramid for open-vocabulary object detection. In: Proceedings of the IEEE/CVF Conference on Computer Vision and Pattern Recognition, pp. 11186–11196 (2023)

25. Wu, S., Zhang, W., Jin, S., Liu, W., Loy, C.C.: Aligning bag of regions for open-vocabulary object detection. In: Proceedings of the IEEE/CVF Conference on Computer Vision and Pattern Recognition, pp. 15254–15264 (2023)

26. Wu, X., Zhu, F., Zhao, R., Li, H.: CORA: adapting clip for open-vocabulary detection with region prompting and anchor pre-matching. In: Proceedings of the IEEE/CVF Conference on Computer Vision and Pattern Recognition, pp. 7031–7040 (2023)

27. Xie, J., Zheng, S.: Zero-shot object detection through vision-language embedding alignment. In: 2022 IEEE International Conference on Data Mining Workshops (ICDMW), pp. 1–15. IEEE (2022)

28. Zareian, A., Rosa, K.D., Hu, D.H., Chang, S.F.: Open-vocabulary object detection using captions. In: Proceedings of the IEEE/CVF Conference on Computer Vision and Pattern Recognition, pp. 14393–14402 (2021)

29. Zhang, S., Chi, C., Yao, Y., Lei, Z., Li, S.Z.: Bridging the gap between anchor-based and anchor-free detection via adaptive training sample selection. In: Proceedings of the IEEE/CVF Conference on Computer Vision and Pattern Recognition, pp. 9759–9768 (2020)

30. Zhao, X., et al.: Temporal speciation network for few-shot object detection. IEEE Trans. Multimed. (2023)

31. Zhao, X., Liu, X., Wang, D., Gao, Y., Liu, Z.: Scene-adaptive and region-aware multi-modal prompt for open vocabulary object detection. In: Proceedings of the IEEE/CVF Conference on Computer Vision and Pattern Recognition (2024)

32. Zhao, X., Ma, Y., Wang, D., Shen, Y., Qiao, Y., Liu, X.: Revisiting open world object detection. IEEE Trans. Circuits Syst. Video Technol. (2023)
33. Zhong, Y., et al.: RegionCLIP: region-based language-image pretraining. In: Proceedings of the IEEE/CVF Conference on Computer Vision and Pattern Recognition, pp. 16793–16803 (2022)
34. Zhou, K., Yang, J., Loy, C.C., Liu, Z.: Conditional prompt learning for vision-language models. In: Proceedings of the IEEE/CVF Conference on Computer Vision and Pattern Recognition, pp. 16816–16825 (2022)
35. Zhou, K., Yang, J., Loy, C.C., Liu, Z.: Learning to prompt for vision-language models. Int. J. Comput. Vision **130**(9), 2337–2348 (2022)
36. Zhou, X., Girdhar, R., Joulin, A., Krähenbühl, P., Misra, I.: Detecting twenty-thousand classes using image-level supervision. In: Avidan, S., Brostow, G., Cissé, M., Farinella, G.M., Hassner, T. (eds.) ECCV 2022. LNCS, vol. 13669, pp. 350–368. Springer, Cham (2022). https://doi.org/10.1007/978-3-031-20077-9_21

YOLO-FCNET: Enhancing SAR Ship Detection with Fourier Convolution in YOLOv8

Zihao Zhang and Ying Li[✉]

Navigation College, Dalian Maritime University, Dalian 116026, China
yldmu@dlmu.edu.cn

Abstract. Detecting ships in Synthetic Aperture Radar (SAR) images is crucial for maritime traffic surveillance and safety.Despite the extensive application of deep learning in SAR ship detection, accurately identifying ships, especially smaller ones, remains a significant challenge. The unique features of SAR images, including noise interference and resolution constraints, add complexity to the detection task. In this paper, we introduce YOLO-FCNET, a novel ship detection approach that leverages the frequency domain analysis based on YOLOv8, to enhance both the precision and efficiency of SAR ship detection.We begin by incorporating the FCSE Block, a module that enriches the model's feature representation by intelligently amplifying salient features through a channel squeeze-excitation mechanism, while muting less informative ones, thus sharpening the model's ability to identify critical ship attributes.Next, we introduce the Fourier Unit module, which empowers our model to discern periodic patterns and textures within the frequency domain via Fourier Convolution. This capability aids in filtering out noise and background clutter, thereby enhancing the extraction of meaningful signals.Finally, the Spectral Transform module is integrated to achieve a harmonious fusion of multi-scale and multi-feature representations. This module employs Spectral and Local Fourier Convolution to bolster the model's capacity to detect ships from various angles and sizes, and to adapt to diverse scale and shape variations.Experiments on a well-established SAR ship detection dataset (SSDD) have confirmed the efficacy of our proposed method. The results demonstrate that YOLO-FCNET significantly outperforms existing methods, particularly in the detection of smaller ships.

Keywords: Fourier Convolution · Spectral Transform · Deep Learning,SAR ship detection

1 Introduction

Synthetic Aperture Radar (SAR) is an advanced microwave remote sensing technology that can capture fine images of the Earth's surface around the clock, regardless of weather and lighting conditions. By applying advanced technologies such as virtual array technology and pulse compression, SAR can generate high-definition two-dimensional images that are of significant value in target detection and identification. SAR images have a wide range of applications, including military reconnaissance, environmental

© The Author(s), under exclusive license to Springer Nature Singapore Pte Ltd. 2024
J. Guo et al. (Eds.): IJCAI 2024, CCIS 2160, pp. 195–207, 2024.
https://doi.org/10.1007/978-981-97-6125-8_15

monitoring, natural disaster early warning, sea surface oil spill tracking, maritime traffic regulation, and sea surface ship monitoring. These applications benefit from the unique imaging principles and rich electromagnetic scattering information of the SAR system [1–3]. In particular, ship detection in SAR images with complex marine backgrounds has become a popular topic among researchers. With the development of SAR satellite technology, a large amount of SAR image data has been accumulated, and many institutions have successfully released SAR ship detection datasets for academic research.

Before deep learning gained attention in the field of SAR ship detection, researchers used traditional methods to perform SAR ship detection.The CFAR (Constant False Alarm Rate) detection algorithm [4] is one of the most widely used algorithms for SAR ship detection. It leverages the differences in grayscale between the background and targets to achieve detection functionality. In recent years, with the launch of PolSAR satellites, researchers have also taken advantage of the rich scattering information in PolSAR images compared to single-polarization SAR images. They have used the differences in scattering mechanisms between ship targets and sea clutter to distinguish targets from the background [5].

In recent years, deep learning has advanced object detection significantly. The main approaches are divided into two types: two-stage region proposal algorithms like R-CNN, and one-stage bounding box regression algorithms such as YOLO and SSD. The R-CNN algorithm, introduced by Girshick [6], generates multiple candidate bounding boxes using selective search and then employs a CNN for feature extraction and an SVM for classification. It refines results with non-maximum suppression (NMS). YOLO, proposed by Redmon et al. [7], is a one-stage detection algorithm that processes the image into a grid and uses a CNN to predict object classes directly, simplifying the detection process. To improve upon YOLO's shortcomings, Liu W et al. [8] introduced SSD, which enhances detection accuracy. After extracting features from the input image using a convolutional neural network, the SSD algorithm generates bounding boxes of various sizes and aspect ratios from feature maps at different depths. It then predicts the presence of various objects within each bounding box, thereby achieving the detection of targets and enhancing the model's accuracy in multi-object detection.

Despite these object detection algorithms being meticulously designed to enhance detection accuracy, they are primarily tailored for optical images. The imaging mechanism of SAR images is entirely different from that of optical images, they capture targets through the reflection of radar waves, which gives SAR images distinctive textures and structural characteristics. These features are markedly different from the color and shape-based features found in optical images. Consequently, deep learning models designed for optical images may not always be directly applicable to SAR images. Current methods face the following three main drawbacks: (1) In SAR images, small vessels often have low pixel coverage and inconspicuous spatial features. (2) SAR images generally suffer from pervasive noise and complex background clutter. (3) There are limitations to uniform scale feature extraction when dealing with the varied scales and diverse shapes of ships in SAR images.

To overcome these shortcomings, this paper proposes the YOLO-FCNET model, an improved version of the YOLOv8 network architecture.

Our main contributions can be summarized into three areas:

- We integrate the FCSE Block to address the detection of small maritime vessels in SAR imagery characterized by low pixel coverage and faint spatial features. This module leverages a channel squeeze-excitation mechanism to enhance key features and suppress irrelevant ones. This innovation overcomes prior models' limitations in detecting the nuanced details of small ships, significantly enhancing detection accuracy.

- To reduce pervasive noise and complex background clutter in SAR images, we have introduced the Fourier Unit module. This module uses Fourier Convolution to identify periodic patterns in the frequency domain, effectively filtering out noise and enhancing signals, thereby improving detection capabilities for small targets or those with low contrast.

- Addressing the limitations of uniform scale feature extraction when faced with the varied scales and diverse shapes of ships in SAR imagery, we incorporate the Spectral Transform module. This module employs Spectral and Local Fourier Transform to achieve a harmonious integration of features across multiple scales. This approach not only bolsters the model's capacity to detect ships from various perspectives and sizes but also enhances its flexibility to adapt to diverse scale and shape variations.

2 Related Work

2.1 SAR Ship Detection with Deep Learning

In recent years, the rapid development of deep learning technology has attracted widespread attention from researchers, who have begun to apply it to SAR ship detection. Unlike traditional methods that relied on manual feature extraction, deep learning has simplified the feature engineering process. The focus of research has now shifted to building robust and efficient network architectures that can accurately capture the features of targets in SAR images. As a result, convolutional neural networks (CNNs) have become the preferred choice for handling SAR image targets, especially in the field of ship detection, where various CNN techniques are widely used to enhance the performance and accuracy of detection technology. Gui et al. [9] developed an improved Faster R-CNN method called the Multilayer Fusion Light-head Detector (MFLHD) by utilizing low-level texture and high-level semantic features to enhance ship target detection performance. Lin et al. [10] proposed a channel attention-based Faster R-CNN method, which achieved better detection performance compared to existing Faster R-CNN methods by learning multi-scale features of targets and introducing a channel attention mechanism. In [11] and [12], attention mechanisms were also applied to Feature Pyramid Networks (FPN) to obtain more refined multi-scale feature representations. Li et al. [13] proposed a multi-domain deep learning network for SAR ship detection based on complementary features in the spatial and frequency domains to address the problem of ship rotation. For YOLO-based single-stage detectors, Mao et al. [14] proposed a simplified U-Net to achieve low-cost SAR ship detection. Long et al. [15] used DarkNet-53 to combine multi-scale features into an SSD network to improve multi-scale ship detection performance. Xu et al. [16] proposed a multi-level alignment network to learn SAR ship detectors from labeled optical images. Zheng et al. [17] proposed a dual-teacher framework to address the mutual interference between optical supervision and synthetic aperture radar supervision. Du et al. [18] proposed a novel semi-supervised synthetic aperture radar ship detection network through scene feature learning. Jiang et al.[19] established a Fast R-CNN for target detection and constructed an optimized Chan-Vese model for ship contour extraction. Zhou et al. [20] provided a side-aware small ship detection network for synthetic aperture radar images. Wang et al. [21] proposed a multi-feature fusion network (MFFN) for search and rescue ship detection. Zhou et al. [22] proposed a lightweight hybrid representation learning enhanced SAR target detection algorithm based on the unique features of SAR images, named HRLE-SARDet. Sun et al.[23] proposed a multi-level ship target detection algorithm based on superpixel segmentation. Liu et al. [24] proposed a hybrid-scale self-diffusion network (MSNet) for accurately detecting ships in synthetic aperture radar (SAR) images. Ju et al. [25] proposed a system called FPDDet for directional search and rescue ship detection. Wan et al. [26] proposed a synthetic aperture radar ship small target azimuth detector named FADet, based on semantic flow feature alignment and Gaussian labeling. Han et al. [27] proposed a knowledge-driven context-aware network (KCPNet) and constructed a public dataset called the Infrared Ship Detection Dataset (ISDD). Qin et al. [28] proposed a novel semi-soft label-guided network (S2LSDNet) based on self-distillation (SD) for SAR ship detection.

2.2 The Integration of Deep Learning with Fourier Convolution

At present, the combination of deep learning and Fourier Convolution is primarily used to address complex issues in the fields of signal processing, image analysis, and time series forecasting. Yi et al. [29] proposed a novel method applying frequency-domain Multilayer Perceptrons (MLPs) to time series forecasting. Yi et al. [30] proposed a novel method for multivariate time series forecasting, which constructs a hypervariate graph and applies the Fourier Graph Neural Network (FourierGNN) to handle spatiotemporal dynamics within a unified framework. L. Chi et al. [31] proposed a novel convolutional operator called FFC, which enhances non-local perception in deep learning models based on fourier spectral theory and supports cross-scale fusion. Wang, Kai-Ni et al. [32] propose a novel method to advance the classification of colon diseases in colonoscopy images from a frequency domain perspective. J. A. Stuchi et al. [33]proposed a novel method for feature extraction from the Fourier frequency domain.

Based on previous research, this study introduces an innovative approach that combines the frequency domain analysis capabilities of Fourier Convolution with the rapid target detection features of the YOLOv8 algorithm. The aim is to enhance the accuracy and speed of SAR ship detection, particularly in scenarios with small targets and complex backgrounds.

3   Method

3.1 Overall Architecture of YOLO-FCNET

We propose the YOLO-FCNET network structure for SAR ship detection. This structure, based on the Backbone class, integrates multi-scale feature extraction, residual connections, CSPNet, spatial pyramid pooling (SPPF), and custom frequency domain modules. It initially processes SAR images through a Stem layer, followed by Darknet residual blocks to enhance feature depth. CSPNet and SPPF contribute to computational efficiency and capturing a broader context, respectively. Frequency domain modules such as the FCSE Block and Fourier Unit enhance the model's robustness against SAR image noise and texture, while Spectral Transform improves the detection of small targets through Local Fourier Transform. The network also supports loading pre-trained weights to speed up convergence and improve accuracy, generating three enriched feature maps via forward propagation. YOLO-FCNET uses the FPN for cross-scale feature fusion, utilizing effective feature layers from the backbone for further extraction. It employs both upsampling and downsampling strategies to integrate features comprehensively. The Yolo Head acts as the network's classifier and regressor, operating on the three feature layers obtained after enhancement by the Backbone and FPN. It treats each feature point as a potential object, rather than a predefined box, assessing whether each has a corresponding object (Fig. 1).

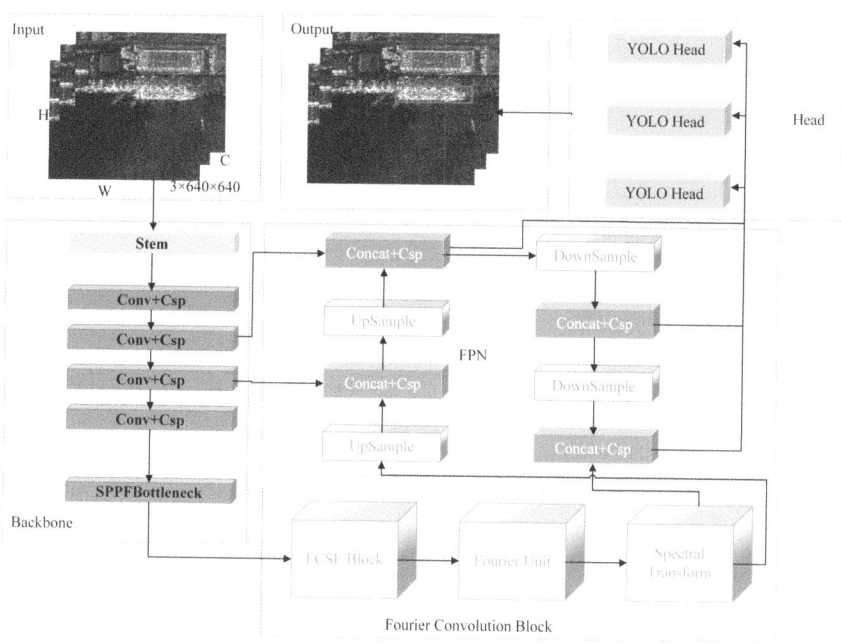

Fig. 1. Overall Architecture of YOLO-FCNET

3.2   FCSE Block

The FCSE Block enhances feature representation by employing an attention mechanism to focus on both global and local features. It integrates Adaptive Global Average Pooling to capture spatial information and 1x1 Convolutions to streamline feature channels, accompanied by a ReLU Activation Function for non-linearity. Separate convolutions

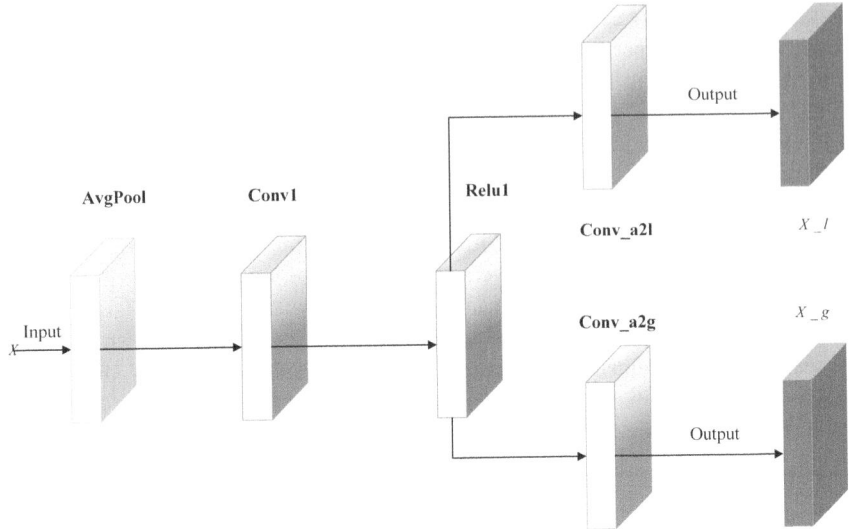

Fig. 2. Architecture of FCSE Block

are applied for local and global feature transformation, and a Sigmoid function assigns importance to these features. The FCSE Block processes the input to produce weighted local and global features (X_l and X_g), enhancing the model's ability to discern critical ship attributes (Fig. 2).

3.3 Fourier Unit

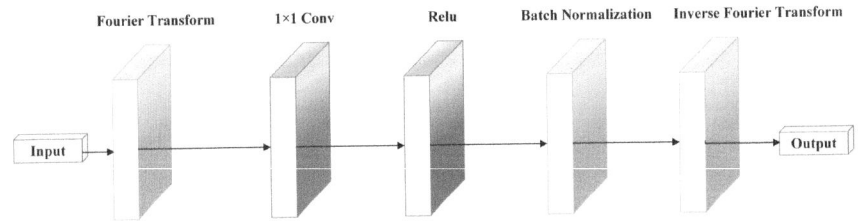

Fig. 3. Architecture of Fourier Unit

The Fourier Unit class acts as a frequency domain transformation module, enhancing the model's capacity to detect multi-scale and multi-frequency features via Fourier Transform. Firstly, by applying the Fourier Transform, we convert the SAR image $I(t, s)$ from the spatial domain to the frequency domain $I(u, v)$ with the following formula (Fig. 3):

$$I(u, v) = \iint I(t, s)e^{-j2\pi(ut+vs)}dtds \tag{1}$$

In the frequency domain, we apply a 1x1 convolutional layer, which efficiently processes the features of SAR images in the frequency domain by reweighting and mixing different frequency components, enhancing advanced abstract features that are useful for ship detection tasks. This type of convolution not only reduces the number of model parameters and prevents overfitting through parameter sharing but also enhances the expressiveness of features by introducing non-linearity through batch normalization and ReLU activation. This allows the network to automatically learn and recognize periodic patterns and key frequency features caused by ship structures in SAR images, even if these features are not obvious in the spatial domain.Fianlly the Inverse Fourier Transform converts theprocessed imageback to the spatial domain:

$$I'(t, s) = F^{-1}\{H(u, v) \cdot I(u, v)\} \tag{2}$$

3.4 Spectral Transform

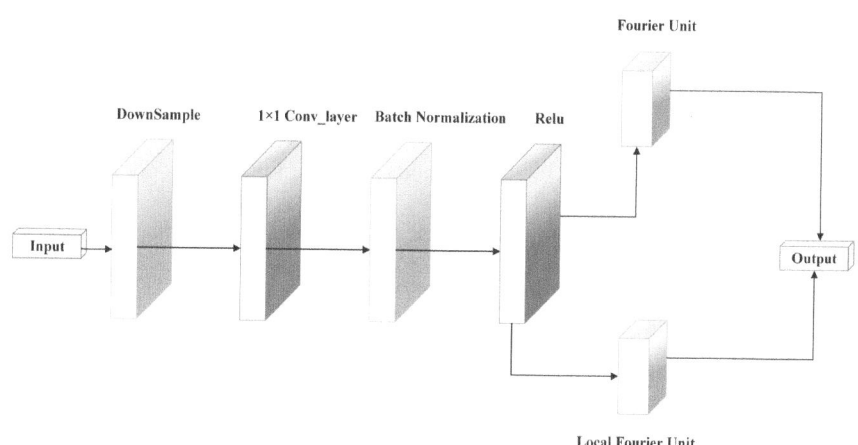

Fig. 4. Architecture of Spectral Transform

The Spectral Transform class is an advanced module for feature enhancement through Fourier Transform, consisting of a downsampling mechanism, a preprocessing sequence with 1x1 convolution, batch normalization, and ReLU activation, a Fourier Unit for global transform, and an optional Local Fourier Unit for local transform. It processes input through these components during forward propagation, optionally integrating global and local features, to produce an enriched feature set that captures comprehensive spatial and frequency domain information (Fig. 4).

4 Experiment and Analysis

4.1 Dataset Introduction and Experimental Settings

This paper employs the SSDD dataset to train and test the ship detection model. The SSDD dataset is based on the PASCAL Visual Object Classes annotation format, hence the code that uses the PASCAL VOC annotation format dataset can be directly employed to train SSDD. The ships in SSDD can be categorized into large, medium, and small targets based on the size of the targets, with small targets making up the majority of the SSDD dataset. SSDD includes imaging results from various satellite sensors such as TerraSAR-X, RadarSat-2, and Sentinel-1, featuring four different polarization modes (HH, VV, HV, and VH), and resolutions ranging from 1 to 15 m. The richness of the data allows for more robust training of detectors, but it also complicates detection, potentially reducing detection performance. The SSDD dataset comprises 1160 images containing 2456 ships, averaging 2.12 ships per image.This paper divides the dataset into training, validation, and test sets in a 9:1 ratio.

This experiment was conducted with a NVIDIA GeForce RTX 3060, Windows 11 system,Python version 3.10.9, PyTorch version 1.13.0, and CUDA version 11.7.

4.2 Evaluation Metrics

Common performance evaluation metrics include the Intersection over Union (IoU) between the target box and the predicted box, Precision (P), Recall (R), Average Precision (AP), and Average Recall (AR), etc.

Precision indicates the ratio of positive samples among the images that are identified as such, while recall indicates the proportion of all positive samples in the test set that are correctly identified. The calculation methods for these two metrics are as follows:

$$
\begin{aligned}
P &= \frac{TP}{TP + FP} \\
R &= \frac{TP}{TP + FN}
\end{aligned}
\tag{3}
$$

True Positive (TP) refers to the positive samples that the model correctly identifies as positive.False Positive (FP) refers to the negative samples that the model incorrectly predicts as positive.False Negative (FN) refers to the positive samples that the model incorrectly predicts as negative.True Negative (TN) refers to the negative samples that the model correctly predicts as negative.

AP (Average Precision) indicates the area under the Precision-Recall (P-R) curve for a specific class within all images. The higher the AP value, the better the performance of the model.

$$
AP = \int_0^1 x\,dx
\tag{4}
$$

AR, which stands for Average Recall, measures the average performance of the model's recall across all possible classification thresholds. The specific formula is as follows:

$$
AR = \frac{1}{N} \sum_i^N Recall_i
\tag{5}
$$

4.3 Comparison with Classical SAR Ship Detection Algorithms

This paper compares YOLO-FCNET with various SAR ship detection algorithms. Specifically, it selects one-stage algorithms (such as the YOLO series), two-stage algorithms (such as the R-CNN series), and compares them with the algorithm presented in this paper using data from the SSDD dataset.

The evaluation metrics used are AP-0.5:0.95, AP-75, AP-S, and AR-S (since the majority of targets in the SSDD dataset are small, AP-S and AR-S are adopted).

Table 1. Comparison results of the training.

Methods	AP-0.5:0.95(%)	AP-75(%)	AP-S(%)	AR-S(%)
FasteRCNN [10]	48.6	48.2	36.9	51.1
SSD [8]	47.8	44.9	37.8	51.9
Retinanet [34]	53.8	65.3	47.7	49.3
Effcientnet [35]	48.0	55.9	36.9	40.8
YOLOv5 [36]	62.1	72.0	**59.1**	**64.5**
YOLOv8 [37]	63.2	73.9	56.4	61.1
YOLO-FCNET	**64.6**	**77.2**	58.8	63.4

From the data in Table 1, it is evident that YOLOv5, YOLOv8, and YOLO-FCNET have the best performance among the contenders.It can be observed that compared to YOLOv8, YOLO-FCNET has improved by 1.4 percentage points on AP-0.5:0.95, 3.3 percentage points on AP-75, 2.2 percentage points on AP-S, 2.3 percentage points on AR-0.5:0.95 indicating that the incorporation of Fourier Convolution has significantly enhanced SAR image recognition. However, YOLOv5 demonstrates better performance in AP-S and AR-S, suggesting that YOLOv5 may have some advantages in handling small targets. The visualization comparison results of each algorithm are shown in Fig. 5. Compared to other algorithms, the YOLO-FCNET algorithm has fewer missed and false detections.

4.4 Ablation Experiments

From the results of the ablation experiments, it is clear that the following conditions hold (Table 2):

1. After adding the FCSE Block alone, the model performance declined compared to the baseline. This may be due to the increased complexity of the model by the FCSE Block, without a corresponding enhancement in feature representation, leading to reduced performance.
2. Following Ablation 1, we continued to add the Fourier Unit, the model performance still did not return to the baseline level. This indicates that while the Fourier Unit provides frequency domain features to the model, it may not be sufficient to overcome the performance loss caused by the FCSE Block.

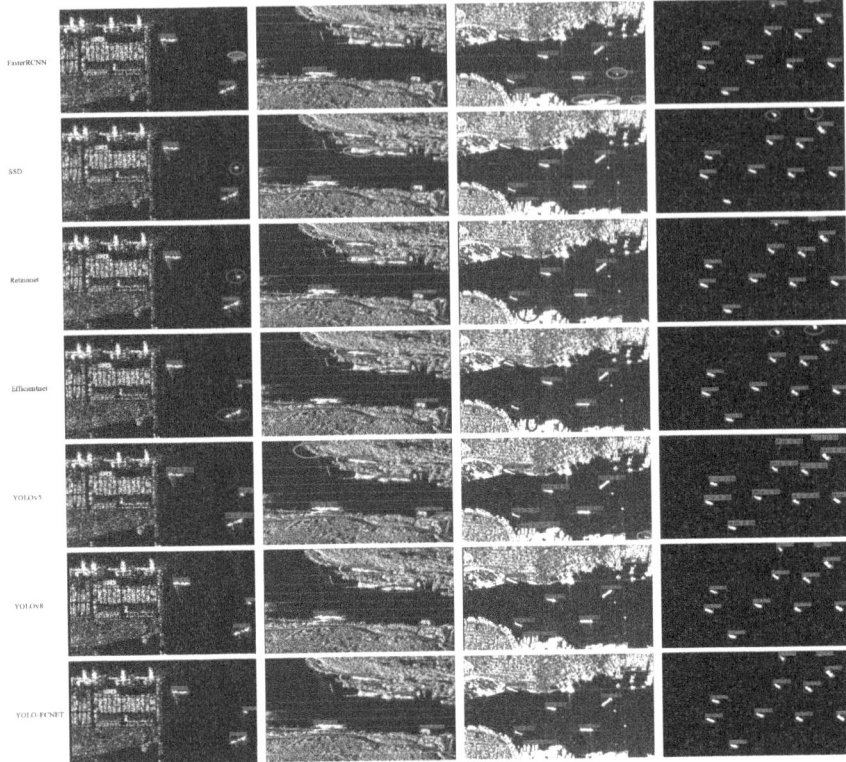

Fig. 5. Comparison results of algorithms. The blue circle indicates the missed target and the green circle indicates the target of misdetection.

Table 2. Comparison results of the Ablation Experiments.

FCSE	FourierUnit	SpectralTransform	AP-0.5:0.95	AP-75	AP-S	AR-S
✗	✗	✗	63.2	73.9	56.4	61.1
✔	✗	✗	62.3	70.6	55.8	61.0
✔	✔	✗	63.2	72.1	56.3	61.2
✔	✔	✔	**64.6**	**77.2**	**58.8**	**63.4**

3. Following Ablation 2, we finally added the Spectral Transform. We observed a significant improvement in performance. This indicates that the addition of Spectral Transform, by integrating local and global features, has enhanced the model's ability to detect ships from multiple scales and perspectives, thereby achieving an overall improvement in performance.

Overall, the FCSE block, when not integrated with other components, may fail to exert its full potential, resulting in a performance decline. The Fourier Unit, despite

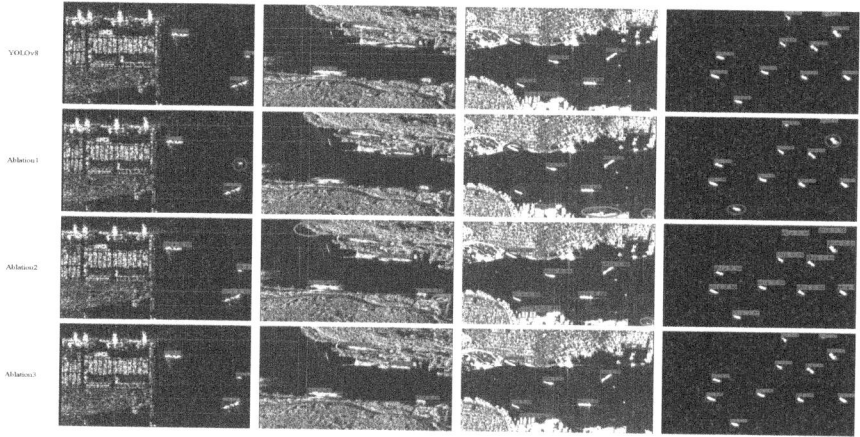

Fig. 6. Comparison results of ablation experiment. The blue circle indicates the missed target and the green circle indicates the target of misdetection.

supplying frequency domain features, might need to work in conjunction with Spectral Transform to realize its best efficacy. Spectral Transform appears to be crucial for boosting performance, as it not only enriches feature representation but also improves the model's sensitivity to small targets via local Fourier Transform. The visualization comparison results of ablation experiment are shown in Fig. 6.

5 Conclusion

This paper introduced an enhanced YOLO-FCNET model that significantly improved the detection of small target ships in SAR images by integrating an FCSE Block, Fourier Unit, and Spectral Transform. Ablation studies showed that each component enhances performance, with the greatest improvements achieved when they work together. The FCSE Block initially caused a slight performance drop but has potential when combined with other components. The Fourier Unit provided frequency domain feature expression, which was essential for subsequent transformations. The Spectral Transform, crucial for performance enhancement, integrates local and global features to improve detection of ships at various scales and perspectives. Despite YOLO-FCNET's better adaptability and accuracy compared to YOLOv5 and YOLOv8, especially for small targets, YOLOv5's precision and recall for small targets indicate there is room for further optimization. Future work will focus on optimizing the model structure, reducing computational complexity, and developing efficient feature fusion strategies to improve small target detection in SAR images. The YOLO-FCNET model is expected to offer new insights for SAR image processing and provide valuable references for related research.

Acknowledgments. This study was funded by National Key R&D Program of China(grant number 2023YFB4302300), Fundamental Research Funds for the Central Universities (grant number 3132023507), Dalian High-Level Talent Innovation Program (grant number 2022RG02).

Disclosure of Interests. The authors declare no conflict of interest.

References

1. Shahzad, M., Maurer, M., Fraundorfer, F., Wang, Y., Zhu, X.X.: Buildings detection in VHR SAR images using fully convolution neural networks. IEEE Trans. Geosci. Remote Sens. **57**(2), 1100–1116 (2019)
2. Du, L., Dai, H., Wang, Y., Xie, W., Wang, Z.: Target discrimination based on weakly supervised learning for high-resolution SAR images in complex scenes. IEEE Trans. Geosci. Remote Sens. **58**(1), 461–472 (2020)
3. Yang, G., Li, H.-C., Yang, W., Fu, K., Sun, Y.-J., Emery, W.J.: Unsupervised change detection of SAR images based on variational multivariate Gaussian mixture model and Shannon entropy. IEEE Geosci. Remote Sens. Lett. **16**(5), 826–830 (2019)
4. Robey, F.C., Fuhrmann, D.R., Kelly, E.J., et al.: A CFAR adaptive matched filter detector. IEEE Trans. Aerosp. Electron. Syst. **28**(1), 208–216 (1992)
5. Atteia, G.E., Collins, M.J.: On the use of compact polarimetry SAR for ship detection. ISPRS J. Photogramm. Remote Sens. **80**, 1–9 (2013)
6. Girshick, R., Donahue, J., Darrell, T., Malik, J.: Rich feature hierarchies for accurate object detection and semantic segmentation. In: 2014 IEEE Conference on Computer Vision and Pattern Recognition, Columbus, OH, USA, pp. 580–587 (2014)
7. Redmon, J., Divvala, S., Girshick, R., Farhadi, A.: You only look once: unified, real-time object detection. In: 2016 IEEE Conference on Computer Vision and Pattern Recognition (CVPR), Las Vegas, NV, USA, pp. 779–788 (2016)
8. Liu, W., et al.: SSD: single shot multibox detector. In: Leibe, B., Matas, J., Sebe, N., Welling, M. (eds.) ECCV 2016. LNCS, vol. 9905, pp. 21–37. Springer, Cham (2016). https://doi.org/10.1007/978-3-319-46448-0_2
9. Gui, Y., Li, X., Xue, L.: A multilayer fusion light-head detector for SAR ship detection. Sensors **19**(5), 1124 (2019)
10. Lin, Z., Ji, K., Leng, X., et al.: Squeeze and excitation rank faster R-CNN for ship detection in SAR images. IEEE Geosci. Remote Sens. Lett. **16**(5), 751–755 (2019)
11. Cui, Z., Li, Q., Cao, Z., et al.: Dense attention pyramid networks for multi-scale ship detection in SAR images. IEEE Trans. Geosci. Remote Sens. **57**(11), 8983–8997 (2019)
12. Zhao, Y., Zhao, L., Xiong, B., et al.: Attention receptive pyramid network for ship detection in SAR images. IEEE J. Sel. Topics Appl. Earth Obs. Remote Sens. **13**, 2738–2756 (2020)
13. Li, D., Liang, Q., Liu, H., et al.: A novel multidimensional domain deep learning network for SAR ship detection. IEEE Trans. Geosci. Remote Sens. **60**, 1–13 (2021)
14. Mao, Y., Yang, Y., Ma, Z., et al.: Efficient low-cost ship detection for SAR imagery based on simplified U-net. IEEE Access **8**, 69742–69753 (2020)
15. Long, Y., Juan, S., Hua, H., et al.: SAR ship detection based on convolutional neural network with deep multiscale feature fusion. Acta Optica Sinica **40**(2), 0215002 (2020)
16. Xu, C., Zheng, X., Lu, X.: Multi-level alignment network for cross-domain ship detection. Remote Sens. **14**(10), 2389 (2022)
17. Zheng, X., Cui, H., Xu, C., Lu, X.: Dual teacher: a semisupervised cotraining framework for cross-domain ship detection. IEEE Trans. Geosci. Remote Sens. **61**, 1–12 (2023). Art no. 5613312
18. Du, Y., Du, L., Guo, Y., Shi, Y.: Semisupervised SAR ship detection network via scene characteristic learning. IEEE Trans. Geosci. Remote Sens. **61**, 1–17 (2023). Art no. 5201517
19. Jiang, M., Gu, L., Li, X., Gao, F., Jiang, T.: Ship contour extraction from SAR images based on faster R-CNN and chan–vese model. IEEE Trans. Geosci. Remote Sens. **61**, 1–14 (2023). Art no. 5203414

20. Zhou, Y., Liu, H., Ma, F., Pan, Z., Zhang, F.: A sidelobe-aware small ship detection network for synthetic aperture radar imagery. IEEE Trans. Geosci. Remote Sens. **61**, 1–16 (2023). Art no. 5205516

21. Wang, S., Cai, Z., Yuan, J.: Automatic SAR ship detection based on multifeature fusion network in spatial and frequency domains. IEEE Trans. Geosci. Remote Sens. **61**, 1–11 (2023). Art no. 4102111

22. Zhou, Z., et al.: HRLE-SARDet: a lightweight SAR target detection algorithm based on hybrid representation learning enhancement. IEEE Trans. Geosci. Remote Sens. **61**, 1–22 (2023). Art no. 5203922

23. Sun, Q., Liu, M., Chen, S., Lu, F., Xing, M.: Ship detection in SAR images based on multilevel superpixel segmentation and fuzzy fusion. IEEE Trans. Geosci. Remote Sens. **61**, 1–15 (2023). Art no. 5206215

24. Liu, S., et al.: A mixed-scale self-distillation network for accurate ship detection in SAR images. IEEE J. Sel. Topics Appl. Earth Obs. Remote Sens. **16**, 9843–9857 (2023)

25. Ju, M., Niu, B., Zhang, J.: FPDDet: an efficient rotated SAR ship detector based on simple polar encoding and decoding. IEEE Trans. Geosci. Remote Sens. **61**, 1–15 (2023). Art no. 5218915

26. Wan, H., et al.: Orientation detector for ship targets in SAR images based on semantic flow feature alignment and Gaussian label matching. IEEE Trans. Geosci. Remote Sens. **61**, 1–16 (2023). Art no. 5218616

27. Han, Y., Liao, J., Lu, T., Pu, T., Peng, Z.: KCPNet: knowledge-driven context perception networks for ship detection in infrared imagery. IEEE Trans. Geosci. Remote Sens. **61**, 1–19 (2023). Art no. 5000219

28. Qin, C., Wang, X., Li, G., He, Y.: A semi-soft label-guided network with self-distillation for SAR inshore ship detection. IEEE Trans. Geosci. Remote Sens. **61**, 1–14 (2023). Art no. 5211814

29. Yi, K., Zhang, Q., Fan, W., Niu, Z.: Frequency-domain MLPs are more effective learners in time series forecasting. In Proceedings of the Thirty-seventh Conference on Neural Information Processing Systems (2023)

30. Yi, K., Zhang, Q., Fan, W., Niu, Z.: FourierGNN: rethinking multivariate time series forecasting from a pure graph perspective. In: Proceedings of the Thirty-seventh Conference on Neural Information Processing Systems (2023)

31. Chi, L., Jiang, B., Mu, Y.: Fast Fourier convolution. In: Advances in Neural Information Processing Systems (2020)

32. Wang, K.N., et al.: FFCNET: Fourier transform-based frequency learning and complex convolutional network for colon disease classification. In: International Conference on Medical Image Computing and Computer-Assisted Intervention. Springer, Cham (2022). https://doi.org/10.1007/978-3-031-16437-8_8

33. Stuchi, J.A. et al.: Improving image classification with frequency domain layers for feature extraction. In: 2017 IEEE 27th International Workshop on Machine Learning for Signal Processing (MLSP), Tokyo, Japan, pp. 1–6 (2017)

34. Lin, T.-Y., Goyal, P., Girshick, R., He, K., Dollár, P.: Focal loss for dense object detection. In: 2017 IEEE International Conference on Computer Vision (ICCV), Venice, Italy, pp. 2999–3007 (2017)

35. Tan, M., Le, Q.V.: EfficientNet: rethinking model scaling for convolutional neural networks. In: Proceedings of International Conference on Machine Learning, pp. 6105–6114 (2019)

36. Ultralytics. YOLOv5 (2021. https://github.com/ultralytics/yolov5

37. Jocher, G., Chaurasia, A., Qiu, J.: Ultralytics YOLO (Version 8.0.0) [Computer software] (2023). https://github.com/ultralytics/ultralytics

Correction to: Integrating Text-to-Image and Vision Language Models for Synergistic Dataset Generation: The Creation of Synergy-General-Multimodal Pairs

Mao Xun Huang and Hen-Hsen Huang

Correction to:
Chapter 12 in: J. Guo et al. (Eds.): *Generalizing from Limited Resources in the Open World*, **CCIS 2160,**
https://doi.org/10.1007/978-981-97-6125-8_12

In the originally published version of the chapter, the author inadvertently updated wrong details in affiliation 1. The correct affiliation has been updated.

The updated version of this chapter can be found at
https://doi.org/10.1007/978-981-97-6125-8_12

Author Index

J. Guo et al. (Eds.): IJCAI 2024, CCIS 2160, pp. 209–210, 2024.
https://doi.org/10.1007/978-981-97-6125-8

SPRINGER NATURE

GPSR Compliance

The European Union's (EU) General Product Safety Regulation (GPSR) is a set of rules that requires consumer products to be safe and our obligations to ensure this.

If you have any concerns about our products, you can contact us on ProductSafety@springernature.com

In case Publisher is established outside the EU, the EU authorized representative is:

Springer Nature Customer Service Center GmbH
Europaplatz 3
69115 Heidelberg, Germany

The manufacturer's authorised representative in the EU is Springer
Nature Customer Service Centre GmbH, Europaplatz 3, 69115 Heidelberg,
Germany. If you have any concerns regarding our products, please
contact ProductSafety@springernature.com

Printed and bound by CPI Group (UK) Ltd, Croydon, CR0 4YY

29/04/2026

02099546-0002